RAIDERS PASSED

*Wartime recollections of
a Maltese youngster*

CHARLES B. GRECH

Translated by
JOSEPH GALEA DEBONO

Midsea Books
2002

Published by Midsea Books Ltd.
3a Strait Street, Valletta, Malta
www.midseabooks.com

Original Title: **Umbrelel Fuq Tas-Sliema**
© Charles B. Grech, 1979
Published by Klabb Kotba Maltin
Translated by Joseph Galea Debono B.A., Ll.D.

General Editor: Pawlu Mizzi, B.A., MQR

© Literary, the estate of Charles B. Grech, 2002
© Midsea Books Ltd, 2002

First published in 1998
This revised second edition 2002

ISBN: 99932-39-09-7 (Hardback)
ISBN: 99932-39-08-9 (Paperback)

Produced by Mizzi Design and Graphic Services Ltd.
Printed at Gutenberg Press Ltd, Malta

DEDICATION

To my brother Joe
and all other
Sliema war victims

To your memory, Charles
dear husband and father
thank you
we shall always love and remember you
Aida, Simone and Mark

INTRODUCTION

I chanced to be at the National War Museum in Valletta, watching a group of young men enthusiastically cleaning the main spar, of the wing, of a Junkers 87, Stuka. This aircraft had been recovered from the seabed in Grand Harbour, close to Senglea, by members of the Pioneer Corps. The young members of the War Museum Association were very energetically scraping away and chipping off barnacles which had grown on the aircraft during the thirty-two years it had lain submerged. One or two were using wire brushes. Others, with emery cloths, were very carefully polishing some of the parts which were beginning to look as new as when they had been manufactured.

One of these youths asked me whether I remembered anything about the Second World War. I started relating a couple of anecdotes which came to my mind on the spur of the moment. His friends gradually gathered around and listened with great attention. I soon found myself fielding an endless number of questions.

One of these young men then suggested that these stories be published in a book! I smiled back and replied that I was no writer.

However, my son Mark, who latched on to the idea, continued to encourage me to put these anecdotes in writing and my excuses that a long time had passed and that my memory was not that vivid to enable me to write a book, were to no avail. My wife Aida and my daughter Simone also joined Mark and encouraged me to take up the task and supported me throughout.

Finally, I decided that I would try my hand at it. I was at *Klabb Kotba Maltin*, talking to Pawlu Mizzi, when I brought up the subject. He promised me to give me all the help I needed. Later, when I happened to mention this to my colleague at Television House, Charles Abela Mizzi, he was also very enthusiastic about the idea and offered all his help, even though I told him that this might involve a greater effort than he thought.

As very little has been written about wartime Sliema, some may think that the war had hardly affected this town. This spurred me on to pen my remembrances and relate the principal events which took place in my home town Sliema, as well as other events which I have witnessed elsewhere.

After having researched exact figures, dates and times, I hesitantly put pen to paper and surprisingly, as soon as I started writing about these events, vivid pictures flashed to my mind in quick succession. Very often, I used to go back to the actual location where the event took place and this helped me even more to reconstruct what really happened in those dark days.

Every story in this book is authentic and I experienced each one at first hand. Most names, particularly those of my family, are real. This book is the result of my journey down memory lane. I would therefore like to apologise to the reader if there are some details or figures that are not accurate. This is because documents about the war in Sliema are very scarce.

I based this book mostly on the town of Sliema because that is where I spent most of the war years. But, I have also included other events that I witnessed outside Sliema. The narration of events which did not take place in Malta is based on historical documents.

I am sure that nobody will get the wrong impression and think that I am trying to portray myself as some sort of child hero. This is certainly not the case, because there are many who experienced far worse events; particularly those who were maimed for life or even perished. My main reason for writing this book is, so that today's generation will have an inkling of what we had to endure in those dark days and realise how hard we all have to strive for peace, to prevent a repetition of the ordeal we went through in the early forties.

This book is a translation of the original book in Maltese, *Umbrelel fuq Tas-Sliema*, published in 1979, by *Klabb Kotba Maltin*. It owes much to the encouragement and enthusiasm of my friend Dr. Joseph Galea Debono, who, on learning that the first edition of the Maltese version was out of print, urged me to publish an English version, which he generously offered to write in his all-too-limited free time. He also researched and collected further material for this second edition. To him go my gratitude and appreciation.

Charles B. Grech
January, 2002

CHAPTER I

JUNE 1940

T he war had already been raging for nine months. Hitler's Germany had occupied Poland. Britain and France had declared war on Germany. Hitler's armies were now picking on one country after another: Norway, Denmark, the Netherlands, Belgium and lastly France, which was swiftly being overrun by Nazi forces.

Benito Mussolini's Italy was also preparing for war and Malta was in danger of coming in the firing line. Everybody was expecting war to be declared. Many Maltese avidly followed these events through the local newspapers: 'The Malta Chronicle', 'The Times of Malta', 'Il-Berqa' and 'Il-Leħen is-Sewwa'; or listened to Rediffusion (Cable Radio) news bulletins.

Others, who were lucky enough to have a radio set, could listen to the news on the Italian State Radio which, because of its strong signal, was received in Malta loud and clear. Some tuned onto the B.B.C., if their set could receive on short wave. Radios, in those days, were usually large and enclosed in wooden cabinets. They were very different from today's small, powerful transistor radios

The civil authorities had already started setting up organisations like the Air Raid Precaution (A.R.P.), Air Raid Wardens (A.R.W.), the Special Constabulary (S.C.) and the Home Guard (HG). These were formed by volunteers and part-timers who later became full-timers. Even before war was declared, these units were being trained in first aid and anything connected with air raids, mostly gas attacks. Instructors came either from the police corps or from the three services.

Training against air raids started taking place mostly in Valletta. The sirens used to be sounded and everybody had to remain indoors. Shopkeepers had to close their shops and if any customers happened to be there, they had to remain inside for the duration of the exercise. Then, an aircraft, usually a naval Swordfish, would fly over Valletta and make dummy attacks, simulating the dropping of bombs or gas over the city. These dummy raids were usually announced before-hand in the newspapers and on Rediffusion and, very often, took place in the afternoon.

During these 'raids', which we used to watch from our rooftop in Sliema, soldiers would ignite some material to emit smoke, probably from a small smoke generator, to simulate a gas attack. Then members of the A.R.P. would act the part of injured persons, lying on the ground or in some damaged building.

On the 9th June, 1940, in the afternoon, my father and I were on our way to visit mother's relatives in Gzira. We came upon a training session of the Air Raid Precaution, Gzira Section. Air Raid Wardens were to be seen everywhere patrolling their sectors and Rovers and Boy Scouts were much in evidence performing duties of despatch riders and acting the part of "casualties". The A.R.P. ambulances and first aid squads were hard at work, all putting into practice what they had been instructed to do over the past months and testing out the system that had been put into place by their district committee, under Dr. F.C. Colombo, the Chief Air Raid Warden and Medical Officer in Charge, Msida Centre.

The mock air raid was timed to start at 3.00 pm and the "raiders passed" signal had to be given at 4.15 pm. The chief warden and wardens were at the centre, dealing with reports of casualties and damage received by telephone and despatch riders. The ambulances and first aid squads rushed out to various "scenes of disaster" and "casualties" were soon being loaded into ambulances. Some of these had been planted in various private houses in the most awkward of places, proving a thorough test in their handling and rescue. The enthusiasm of all those taking part in the exercise was boundless and it showed that the inhabitants of the neighbouring suburb of Gzira realised to the full their responsibilities and were determined to play their part if called upon. These exercises were mainly intended to deal with gas attacks. Ironically, no gas attacks were ever launched against these Islands.

What eventually happened had never been anticipated. Bomb attacks had been ignored, it seems. Even the shelters constructed were mostly intended against gas attacks and were called gas lofts. These were rooms which were supposed to be completely sealed off.

To enter them, one had to pass between two curtains, usually made of blankets. In case of a gas attack, these blankets were to be soaked with water. Rooms like these were situated in basements of Government schools and some private homes. This was because it was thought that gas, being lighter than air, would not go down into the basement but would rise.

At the onset of the war, these shelters strengthened with wooden beams, were opened to the public and served as "bomb-proof" refuges. In reality, the only air raid shelter that was truly bomb-proof was the old railway tunnel in Valletta. I remember that even before the war there was a small, yellow sign in black letters which read: AIR RAID SHELTER.

Once I asked my father: "What is an air raid?" and he, with great patience, explained what it was, as far as he could make out. Like most boys of my age, I could not help harking back to the subject and secretly wished that war would reach our shores too.

Gas masks were being issued to the population from police stations and from Government schools. They came in different sizes. Those worn by adults and children were of the same shape with a tin-like container in front and had to be carried at all times, according to law. Gas masks for babies were larger and the baby could actually be laid and enveloped in them. They came with a hand operated, concertina type bellows, pump fitted with an anti-gas filter and whoever was minding the baby, had to pump air into the container so that the baby could breathe the filtered air.

Instructors gave talks in schools and on Rediffusion on the use of gas masks and what one had to do in case of an air raid. In class, we were taught how to take cover if we were at home and had no time to reach a public shelter. They told us to go under the stairs or under some archway or under a solid table on which we were advised to put mattresses, in order to absorb the impact of falling debris.

We were also told to stick brown paper to window panes, in the shape of an **X**, in order to prevent broken glass from shattering inwards with the blast from bomb explosions and injuring us. Like most children, we tended to take these instructions rather lightly and we were quite excited at the thought of war approaching our shores, to experience at first-hand all that we were being told.

THE TEMPEST BREAKS

We did not have to wait long!

On the 10th June, 1940, at lunch time, my father told us that Mussolini would be making a speech on the Italian Radio, at about 6.00 pm. He told my brother Joe and me not to leave the house. My youngest brother, Victor, was not yet old enough to cause problems.

That day, we had planned to go to the beach for a swim and therefore we were rather disappointed but, once he had told us not to leave the house it was obvious that father was worried about something.

That afternoon, at about 5.30 pm, my mother, my brothers and I were in the back garden eating the typical Maltese bread with olive oil, tomatoes, capers, mint and pickled onions. My father had already switched on the radio set and from where we were sitting in the garden, we could already hear the crowd assembled in Rome's Piazza Venezia, shouting and singing fascist songs to the strains of the fascist hymn "Giovinezza, Giovinezza Primavera di Bellezza'. Then the Duce, with his usual oratory, came on the air:

13

"*Popolo d'Italia. . .*"

And the crowd exploded into shouts of: "*Duce, Duce, Duce. . .*"

"*Combattenti di terra, del mare e dell'aria,*" continued the Duce, "*l'Italia dichiara la guerra. La dichiarazione di guerra e` gia` stata consegnata agli ambasciatori della Francia e dell'Inghilterra.*" We were smitten. Father came out, looking very worried. "The balloon is up! Italy has declared war," he told us. "Perhaps it would be better to go up to the roof and bring down all the wood and anything that could catch fire."

Father changed into his working clothes. He put on a pair of shorts and an under vest and went up on the roof, while my brothers and I stayed in the garden.

I remember mother started crying at the news and went indoors. She then quietly prepared the space under the stairs for any eventuality. Father started throwing down the wood from the roof into the yard and my brothers and I carried it into the shed at the back of the garden

On hearing the noise of wood falling from the roof, our neighbour became curious and looked out of his veranda. "What are you up to Sur Anton?" he asked father. "We are preparing for whatever can happen, Sur Karm. Do you know that Italy has declared war?"

"I thought that it had already commenced." He was, of course, referring to the noise which we were making.

"If you have any flammable material on the roof, you had better do the same," said my father.

"Come on! Who would ever come anywhere near Malta, when we have such a large fleet?" Sur Karm smiled and left.

It was already dark when we finished the operation.

We had not gone swimming that afternoon but we were certainly wet with sweat. However, we handled all this with a spirit of adventure. When we went indoors, we found that mother had already tidied up the space under the stairs and moved our beds into the main bedroom, where mother and father slept. Father was very upset and asked mother why she had done all that work by herself without waiting for us to help her. She replied that we were already very busy and things had to get going.

Then mother suggested to father that we should go to Gzira and invite her uncle and aunts to come and stay with us. *H.M.S. Terror* was berthed at Gzira, in Lazzarret Creek between Manoel Island and Ta' Xbiex Point and people were rather apprehensive of this. My mother's uncle and aunts were rather old and as they were childless, they had brought her up. My mother had eight brothers and sisters.

Father promptly asked me to accompany him to Gzira, as he used to take me with him wherever he went. We went down to the Strand, near the Ferries at Sliema and boarded a route bus of the British Motor Company (B.M.C.). On the bus everybody was discussing the situation. At one point, a heated argument arose between two men who held different political views. One of them taunted the other: "As if the Italians would dare to come anywhere near Malta? They are cowards. They are the 'mamma mia' type. They are the 'cicci maccaroni' people."

"They will come and shower us with flowers and sweets because they like us," retorted the other, as if someone had insulted his parents. There were many others on the bus who seemed to share his views. The

15

argument became more heated and other passengers soon got involved, almost coming to blows. My father got very worried and rang the bell for the bus to stop. We alighted two stops before we were meant to get off!

Along the part of the road we still had to cover, I saw army lorries crammed with soldiers while other trucks were towing guns or large searchlights. Military police, or Red Caps, as we used to call them, were doing the round of pubs and calling out soldiers and sailors, some of whom were tipsy or dead drunk and needed to be helped out by their mates, to report to their units or ships. Some were picked up and carried off in army lorries, while those who were stationed nearby, in Fort Manoel or on some ship berthed in Marsamxett Harbour, walked groggily to their station. Civilians were talking and arguing and groups of women were chattering here and there. A shopkeeper, who was standing at the door of his shop, stopped father and solemnly exclaimed: "We are doomed, Mr Grech!"

We arrived at our aunts, who lived in front of the public garden, now called Council of Europe Gardens at Gzira. Uncle Zuz, whose real name was Umberto, was already at the door, taking in all that was happening outside. On seeing us, he walked anxiously towards us. "What do you make of all this Anton, eh? What do we do now?" Father quickly explained why we had gone there to see them. "Thank you, Anton," replied my uncle, "You have put my mind at rest. You know aunt Mary and aunt Carmela! They are shocked at the news."

By the time I went to fetch a *karrozzin*, or horse drawn cab, my uncle and aunts had packed some of their belongings to bring along with them. I had not walked more than a block, when I came across a *karrozzin* and

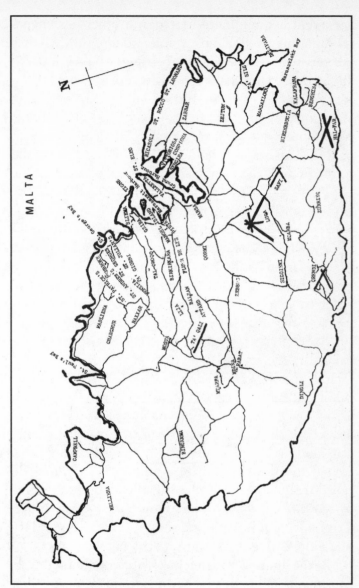

Map of Malta showing airfields and harbour areas.

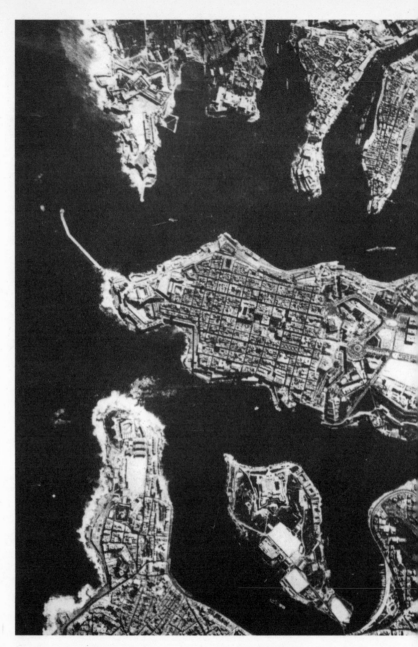

Aerial view of the harbour area. See overleaf for details.

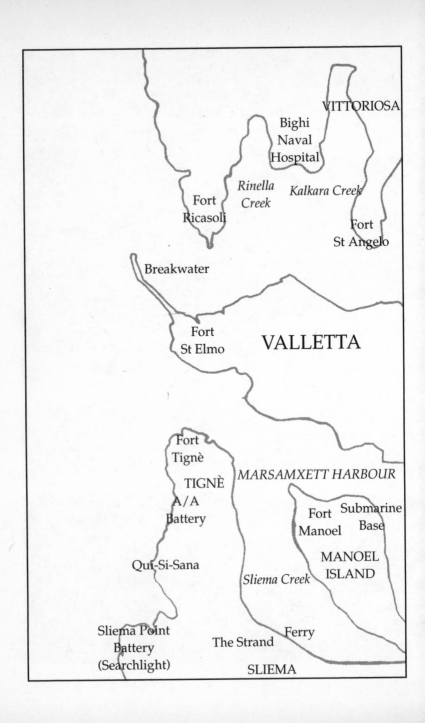

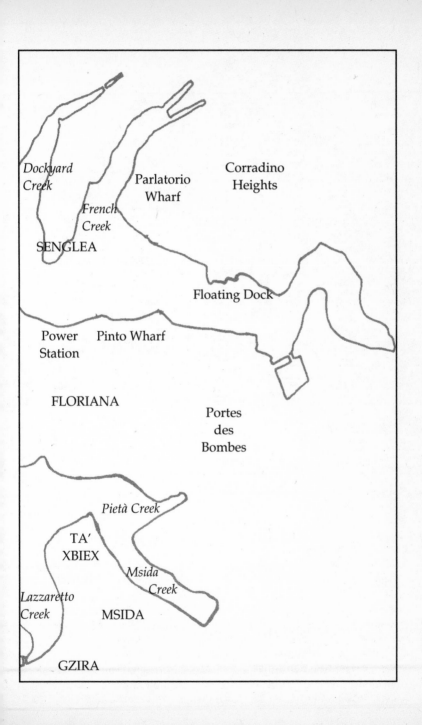

Map of Sliema showing the streets and locations referred to in this book:

1: Nazzarene Church; 2: Ferries Landing Stage; 3: Cab Stand; 4: Stella Maris Church; 5: Bofors Gun; 6: Pill-Box; 7: Sacro Cuor Church; 8: The Friary; 9: Author's house; 10. State School; 11: St Gregory's Church; 12: Salesian Oratory; 13: St Patrick's School; 14: Meadow Bank Hotel; 15: Modern Imperial Hotel; 16: Police Station; 17: Villa Portelli; 18: Balluta Buildings; 19: Carmelite Church; 20: The large shelter

Royal Engineers laying a barbed wire fence along the coast, spring, 1940.

Servicemen instructing children on the use of gas-masks, spring, 1940.

Civilian Home Guard volunteers during a parade at St. Julian's, summer, 1940.

St Julians's Home Guard Volunteers on parade, in their new uniforms.

Civilian volunteers of the Home Guard being given military training at the Empire Stadium in Gzira, summer, 1940.

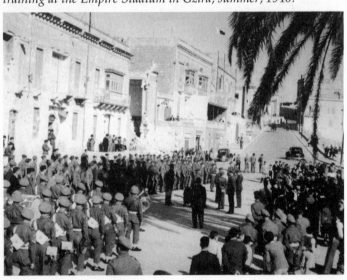

A parade by members of the Home Guard outside of the Police Station at St. Julian's.

(Top) The last
photograph taken
in 1939, showing
the children who
used to attend
the Church of
Sacro Cuor, many
of whom lost
their lives on the
1st April 1942. In
the centre is Fr.
Alessandro
Azzopardi. The
author is fifth from
the right in the top
row.

Casa Depiro,
Mdina.

Casa Depiro: Entrance hall (top left), first floor corridor (top right), and rear veranda (bottom).

Aerial view of Hal Far Airfield.

Aerial view of Ta' Qali Airfield during the blitz.

Aerial view of Safi strip.

Aerial view of Luqa Airfield.

stopped it. The coachman agreed to take us from Gzira to Sliema for about sixpence – taxis were still very rare in those days. Very soon, all of us were on the *karrozzin* with the few belongings we had brought along with us.

I rode near the coachman. When we arrived at the Sliema Strand, father asked him to stop. He alighted and went over to speak to a man who owned a removals truck and the latter followed us home. Mother was waiting at the door behind a small iron gate and a great deal of hugs, kisses and invocations of Our Lady were exchanged between the women.

Father called my brothers and told us to go on the removals truck and guide the driver to Gzira, where Uncle Zuz was waiting to bring over the beds and mattresses from his house.

After supper, we recited the Holy Rosary. There were frequent interruptions between one prayer and another as Mussolini's name came up again and again. On hearing a noise, someone would stop and ask, "What is that? Is that gunfire?" Again, on hearing another noise they would stop and ask, "Is that the sound of an aircraft?" Already signs of fear and tension could be seen on everybody's face.

The Governor General Sir William Dobbie, in a broadcast over the Rediffusion system to the people of Malta and Gozo, expressed his absolute trust in the people, maintaining the utmost calm and trust in God, which was the greatest contribution civilians could make to the common good and towards the defence of their Island home. He added: "We have prayed for justice and peace. Mussolini, against the wishes of the Holy Father and the people of divided Italy, has decided upon war. Malta is ready for it both in the matter of military defence and passive defence needs of the Island, provided the people, under the guidance of their passive defence organisations and their own common sense, maintain the disciplined action which their leaders in this grim struggle expect of them." General Dobbie concluded his broadcast by saying: "We need all persons of goodwill to play their part and I know, full well, that the people of Malta will show themselves worthy of the trust reposed in them by our Empire. May God help each one of us to do our duty unstintingly and may He give us His help."

BAPTISM OF FIRE

The following morning, 11th June, 1940, we were not to sleep late! At 6.30 am Malta's radar detected incoming enemy aircraft and at 6.50 am, the first air-raid warning of the 3,340 which followed during the next three years was sounded and we heard three large bangs of petards that were fired from the rooftop of the Sliema Police Station, in the junction between Rudolphe Street and Prince of Wales Road (now Manwel Dimech Street). This was a warning that the enemy was near. Mother and father darted out of bed and started shouting, "Wake up, wake up. It's an air raid!" There was total panic. Some hurriedly donned their clothes while others were milling around in a daze. Everybody rushed down the stairs and took cover underneath the stairway. This was what we had been told to do and this is what we did. The first to go down were our two aunts. Aunt Carmela, who was quite fat, grabbed the railing and descended as fast as she could, kissing all the holy pictures on the walls on her way down. I do not know whether, in the general confusion, she also kissed a picture that included Satan, because I heard her sister, Aunt Mary, telling her. "No! Not that one, Carm!"

My elder brother Joe and I went out on the balcony to see what was happening outside. Many people were running hither and thither. We heard a bicycle bell and a police whistle and, looking in the direction of Prince of Wales Road, we saw a man wearing a steel helmet and a white band on his arm, with black letters: S.C. He was blowing his whistle, shouting and waving his hand in our direction.

"Everybody inside. . . Everybody indoors. . ." he bawled. He saw us in the balcony and shouted at us, "Get away from those glass panes and get in from that balcony. Do you think you're going to see angels? Close that door!" It was against the law to stay outside during air raids.

For a moment we started laughing but we did not laugh for long! My brother Joe and I agreed to go on the roof, so up we ran. From the highest point on the roof we could see the wide panorama that stretches from Għar id-Dud to Marsamxett Harbour, Luqa Airfield and then on to the west of the Island, up to Rabat. We could see all that was going on and how the air raid was developing.

At the first salvo fired from the four 3.7 inch anti-aircraft guns of Fort Manoel, we were frightened. We saw white puffs of smoke very high up, looking very much like pieces of cotton wads. Higher up, approaching from the south-east, we could see four white aircraft; tiny specks in the blue sky.

Joe went downstairs to fetch the binoculars but these were not very powerful, as they were only meant for the theatre. In fact, we used to take them to the Royal Opera

House during the opera season. But at least they were better than nothing. Joe identified the aircraft as Savoia Marchetti SM79s. I heard father calling me to go downstairs and take cover under the staircase but I pretended not to hear him.

Suddenly, there was a big blast which made us duck behind the wall. It was *H.M.S. Terror*, firing her ten anti-aircraft guns simultaneously, against the raiding aircraft.

The guns of Fort Tigne' now also joined those of *H.M.S. Terror* and Fort Manoel and the first blast of the guns seemed like the first lines of the Sequence from the Mass of the Dead, 'Dies Irae' (Days of Wrath).

It was not long before we heard the sound of explosions from enemy bombs. Turning towards Fort St. Elmo, we saw a pall of black smoke rising from the bastions of the old fort, built by the Knights of St. John. This was unlike the smoke of the guns which was light brown. We could see other palls of smoke beyond Valletta, in the direction of Grand Harbour. Another rose near Porte Des Bombes and another from Pieta'. In the distance, we could also see smoke from explosions, in the direction of Hal Far Airfield. These were the first bombs that fell on Malta and they had already claimed their victims.

We heard a purring noise and then the noise of metal hitting the roof. It was shrapnel from a shell fired by one of our guns falling at great speed. This quickly persuaded us to seek shelter down below. I was about to pick it up when other pieces of shrapnel of all shapes and sizes started raining down on us. Some were up to five inches long and were as sharp as blades and, on touching them, one could still feel the heat from the explosion.

We went under the stairs to find mother hugging my brother Victor to her. Uncle Zuz and aunts Mary and

Carmen were terrified and praying. They were reciting the Rosary and had already started the Litany. On seeing us, they stopped and scolded us for staying out on the roof during the raid. I wonder what they imagined was happening, with all the noise that was going on. From their refuge under the stairs, they could not distinguish the explosion of a bomb from gunfire. Nobody had any experience of war, as yet.

Today, I realise that they had every reason to be terrified and that we were in real danger on the roof, if not from the bombs, from the shrapnel that rained down from the sky. About an hour later, we heard the siren sounding the "raiders passed" signal. There was silence. We crept out from under the stairs. The adults were under shock and frightened. Father helped mother out and tried to calm her down. Uncle Zuz assisted his wife, aunt Mary and her sister and took them out in the garden for some fresh air.

Joe and I rushed up to the roof again, to gather more pieces of shrapnel. There was a smell that I had never smelt before. It was the acrid smell of cordite from the guns and bomb explosions which the wind blew in our direction. I went down again with the trophies that we had found on the roof and proudly showed them to those present. On that first day, we thought and acted as if it was our first and last opportunity to gather pieces of shrapnel. Little did we know that we would have three full years ahead of us to do so. Father warned me to be careful as to what I picked up or touched as there could have been some unexploded object.

After the "all clear" was sounded, I went out in the street. There were many people running around in total panic. The hawker, who had been selling vegetables in front of our house, jumped on her donkey and cart and left in a hurry to her home town, Qormi. The bread seller quickly distributed his goods and scurried off. Many people who were in congregation at the Sacro Cuor Church, left hurriedly for their homes. They were all shouting, "Good Heavens. What are we in for?" Others were angrily complaining: "The enemy never gave us a chance. They came right away." Everybody was shocked. Housewives finished their shopping very quickly, in case there would be another raid.

Mother sent me to Grandma, who lived in St. Lawrence Street, close to the Strand in Sliema, to see whether she was all right. My mother's brothers and sisters lived with her and I asked them to come over to our house so that we would all be together under one roof. We thought that the war would probably last four or five days!

Grandma accompanied me to our house and my six uncles and aunts stayed behind to pack their belongings and load them in Uncle Charles' car, prior to moving in with us. Now, in our house there were fourteen of us. All of us were still under the effects of the first shock, particularly Grandma who was quite advanced in age. The siren sounded eight times that day. However, on five occasions the enemy did not appear over the Island.

At about 7.30 pm there was another air raid warning. This time we did not go on the roof so as not to worry the adults. Everything was quiet. The older people were under the stairs again and more crowded together than in the first air raid. Father and my uncles were in the hallway discussing the situation. Joe and I were sitting on the stairs and my younger brother, Victor, was with mother and the other women under the staircase, reciting the Rosary.

We heard gunfire from some distant anti-aircraft batteries. Joe and I went into the garden to see if we could spot any aeroplanes. We searched the sky but we saw nothing. Gradually we could hear the gunfire increasing and then Fort Manoel opened fire with her 3.7s, followed by Fort Tignè and *H.M.S. Terror*. Everybody rushed underneath the stairs for cover. We heard explosions and strong blasts following them. One of the men exclaimed, "These are bombs falling close by!"

He hardly uttered these words, when I heard a rustle followed by a terrible explosion and an enormous blast that made the house shake. The garden door burst open. There was dust everywhere as we had just begun whitewashing and redecorating the house. Some glass panes shattered. The women were beside themselves. My youngest brother started crying and, in the panic that gripped us, one or two even thought that the bomb exploded in the garden.

When the gunfire subsided and we heard the "raiders passed" signal, we thanked God for keeping us safe and sound. We then opened the doors to let some fresh air in and to see for ourselves what damage had been done. Everything looked normal. There was no damage in the garden; no destroyed walls or bomb craters. Everything was as we left it, except for a lot of fine, grey dust that covered the leaves of the fruit trees in the garden. I went out in the street as it was now all clear. I was keeping my fingers crossed that everything would still be standing. However, on looking in the direction of the upper part of St. Mary Street, I saw a small crowd of people. Then I heard Toni, the grocer, say that a bomb had landed on the Modern Imperial Hotel. I rushed up to see what had happened because I was very curious to see the effects of a bomb explosion. There were already some policemen, special constables and members of the A.R.P. as well as many curious onlookers, on the scene.

"Another dozen of those and Malta will be pulverised!" one woman cried. Little did she know what was in store for us! A roof had collapsed and two walls were damaged by the blast. The bomb was a very small one, weighing only 50kg. It fell in the hotel's garden. But who had had any experience of bombing and air raids on that first day?!

Other bombs had fallen in Parallel Street, now Sir Luigi Camilleri Street, in St. Charles Street, in Sliema, and on buildings in Ponsomby Street, Gzira, killed seven persons and injured many others. One of the first bombs dropped by the Italians on Malta in the early morning raid had exploded on Fort St. Elmo and killed six Maltese soldiers of the Royal Malta Artillery, including a boy soldier of sixteen. They were Bombardier Joseph Galea and gunners Michael Angelo Saliba, Richard Micallef, Paul Debono, Carmel Cordina and boy soldier Philip Busuttil.

To this day, visitors to the cavalier of Fort St. Elmo can still see a small memorial plinth marking the spot where these soldiers were stricken down. The inscription reads:

THESE SIX MEN WERE THE FIRST SOLDIERS WHO
DIED IN MALTA IN THE SECOND GREAT WAR
THEY WERE KILLED IN ACTION WHILST ON
DUTY
EXACTLY ON THIS SPOT
AT 7.45 AM ON THE 11 JUNE, 1940

On that first day, we had seven alerts but only two bombing raids and a reconnaissance sortie materialised. In the first raid, ten Savoia Marchetti SM79s had dropped bombs on Hal Far Airfield, Tarxien, Zabbar, Fort St. Elmo, Grand Harbour, Marsa, Porte Des Bombes, Pieta', Gwardamangia and Msida. In the evening raid, twenty-five Savoia Marchetti SM79s dropped bombs on Hal Far and Luqa airfields, the Grand Harbour, Sliema and Gzira. During this first day of the war, eleven civilians were killed and one hundred and thirty were injured.

Father suggested that Uncle Charles should go to his fiancée's family who lived close to Fort Tigne', and ask her father whether he wanted to come and lodge at our house as well, provided they brought their own bedding. We had ample space in our house and by 9.00 pm, there were twenty-one of us in there. My brothers and I were very excited because now we had friends of our age and, when it was bedtime, we could hardly go to sleep. The adults were still shocked and terrified.

We were even tenser than we had been that morning because, in the last raid, the bombs fell very close. The women were again recounting the adventures of the day and the men were in deep thought, pondering whether, on the morrow, they would have to find some other accommodation far away from Sliema.

CHAPTER II

REFUGEES

The following day, 12th June, we all got up very early. Mother and some of my aunts made coffee. We queued to the bathroom. We children found this quite amusing. First it was the boys who went in together and then the girls. After coffee, father, Uncle Zuz and Uncle Charles agreed that they should make up a 'delegation' and go and seek a residence in the country-side. I begged father to go with him. He looked at Uncle Charles as if to ask him, "Do you have space for him?" Uncle Charles nodded, "Of course he'll come. Children should be represented as well." Father was pleased because he always took me with him, wherever he went.

We got into the car and drove away. "Where are we going Anton?" asked Uncle Charles. "I don't know. Perhaps we should go to Mdina. I know a friend of mine there. I haven't seen him for the last twenty-five years. We'll ask for him and if we find him, I'm sure he will oblige," said my father. I was very excited because I had only been to Mdina once in my short lifetime.

Up in Mdina, we did not have to look for long, for the man my father wanted to see. Father spotted him standing in a corner, near the square, in front of the Cathedral.

I remember that they were very pleased to see each other, not having met for such a long time. They immediately started reminding each other of their youthful pranks. I was struck by the smart way in which this gentleman was dressed, so much so, that for a moment, I thought that he was one of the nobles who lived at Mdina.

I can still visualise his appearance today. He had a slim figure with, whitish hair and a goatee beard. He was wearing a dark jacket over a white, starched shirt, a grey tie with a jewelled tie-pin, a grey waist coat and pin striped trousers. He held two white gloves in his left hand and a walking stick with a silver handle. He was also wearing a bowler hat. I asked father who he was. "This is Wistin Gatt," he replied, "the tailor who used to live in front of our house and who I always mention to you when I relate to you the stories of my youth."

Father explained why we had gone up there to see him. After giving the matter some thought, Wistin told us to follow him to a house. We walked through a street that was very narrow, compared to the wide roads of Sliema. When we came to the building, which from the outside seemed like an ordinary old house but was very impressive indoors, a maid opened the door and on seeing Wistin, she let us in. Shortly after, a middle-aged man appeared and came up to Wistin. We were introduced to the Noble Alexander Apap Bologna. My father quickly explained the purpose of our visit.

Sur Sander, as the landlord was affectionately called, told us that he had an empty house that had been closed up for many years. He was prepared to let us move in without paying any rent. "What generosity and what a noble heart!" I remember having muttered to myself. How times have changed! How different things are now!

Sur Sander motioned us to follow him in the direction of the house. We crossed the square towards the Cathedral and turned left in the direction of St. Dorothy's Girls' School. We stopped in front of a palace with a big dusty door, over which protruded a beautiful balcony, flanked by large windows. "This is the house." We looked at each other thinking: "Does he really mean this?"

Sur Sander opened the main door with a rusty key which had probably not been used for ages and the screeching proved that it had not been opened for a long time. "Come in . . . Come in, this is what I can offer you. All I can tell you is, clean it up and try to take good care of it." My father and uncles thanked him, looking rather astonished while he handed us the keys and left.

We started exploring the palace and I thought it was quite scary. It was so large! Every room was enormous, with high ceilings and beautiful mahogany doors. Our feet were actually sinking into the fine dust that had gathered throughout the ages, we also walked into some large cobwebs. A big rat scurried off like a rabbit. The rooms were not furnished. However, there were paintings on the walls. We went out into the spacious courtyard which had a large Oleander tree on either side and onto a balcony emerging from the bastion wall. The panorama stretched from Mtarfa to Mosta, to Naxxar and beyond, to Sliema, Valletta and the Three Cities, the town of Pawla and in the distance Zejtun, Ghaxaq, Gudja, Mqabba, Zurrieq, Qrendi and all the way round to Siggiewi.

We went up a wide marble staircase that led to a landing and a spacious corridor with wide arches. It was a veranda, where indoor plants were usually kept. On the right of the stairs, there was a gilt gate with an altar behind it. Apparently, when the palace was inhabited, Mass used to be said there, because there was a consecrated marble plaque on the altar. The congregation stood in the corridor.

On the left-hand side of the corridor, there was a large dining room in which many dinner parties must have been held in the past. It had a parquet floor. On one side stood a large mahogany sideboard, in which cutlery and other items were kept. There was also a service lift, descending to the large kitchen which occupied half of the entire basement under the palace. We explored many other rooms until we finally came out onto a terrace from where we could once more view one of the most beautiful sights I have ever seen.

I could now also see Ta' Qali Airfield in the foreground and, to the right, Luqa Airfield with Hal Far in the distance. I said to myself, "I will be able to see all the aeroplanes I want from here." Engrossed in my thoughts, I was oblivious of what father and my uncles were saying. We closed up the place, thanked and said goodbye to Wistin and drove down to Sliema again. This was Casa Depiro, the former residence of Monsignor Giuseppe Depiro, founder of the Missionary Society of St. Paul.

Back home, we immediately started the evacuation operation. We packed sheets, blankets, clothes and towels in suitcases or bags. Glasses, plates and other utensils were packed in boxes. At about one o'clock in the afternoon, I happened to be at Tony's Grocery, buying some groceries to take with us to Mdina, when there was commotion in the street. I heard drivers tooting their car horns and people rejoicing. A very excited woman entered the shop and shouted, "Italy has surrendered . . . Italy has surrendered . . .!" Although I was still a young lad, I couldn't really accept this. "How is it possible?" I asked myself, "As far as I know, not one single aircraft or anything else has approached Italy and dropped a single bomb." I also pondered, "Is this the way wars go?" Later on, I even saw people drinking in a bar, at the top of St. Mary Street, to celebrate. I went home to tell father, to be sure of the situation before we moved to Mdina. It was not long before we heard the siren go. However, the enemy did not approach the Island and a quarter of an hour later we heard the "raiders passed" signal.

It was a rumour that had spread around Malta like wildfire. However, it was a false hope and, probably, the alarm signal was given to calm the situation down.

The first trip which Uncle Charles made to Mdina was to take my aunts, fully equipped with buckets, brooms, floor cloths and all the necessary paraphernalia for "Operation Clean-Up" of Casa Depiro, before the main party arrived. I am sure that Uncle Charles' car had never covered so many miles in one day. On that day alone he made seven trips between Sliema and Mdina. The beds, tables, chairs, and other pieces of furniture were transported by a removals truck. The whole operation took two days until we settled in and we were very lucky that the driver co-operated because it was very difficult to find a lorry.

For the young ones, it was just like going on a summer holiday. This was a great adventure, loading and unloading furniture, boxes and other items and jumping on to lorries. Father and mother were the last to leave our house at number 19, St. Mary Street, Sliema and on closing the main door, they looked up and down the street and at the house that my grandparents had built and lived in since 1895, wondering whether they would ever return.

CASA DEPIRO

Many other families like ours, who wanted to find refuge far from the areas which were vulnerable to air attacks, had to leave their houses and moved to the outlying towns and villages

On arriving at Mdina, we found our uncles and aunts, their fiancée's and their families there. They had already cleaned up the lower floor rooms and posted some beds and mattresses on the floor. The women were preparing a light supper because it was already 7.30 pm by that time. Father and I started fixing some electric bulbs to have some light in the rooms.

At 8.00 pm we went indoors because of the curfew which, for security reasons, barred everybody from staying outside at that hour. During blackout it was pitch-dark and people were in serious trouble if they allowed a chink of light to appear from within. If they did, they would soon hear a knock on the door and face an irate policeman or a special constable, wearing his tin hat, telling them that a light was visible from outside. He would also take down their particulars and have them prosecuted in court. These people were full of self importance.

After having supped and recited the Rosary, the children and older folk went to bed. However, the adults

stayed up talking and planning the next day's programme. We, teenagers, stayed up playing games which
we had brought along with us. All of a sudden we heard
women screaming and there was a lot of running around
and a whole hullabaloo. They had seen a rat! What else
could one expect in such a large house that had been built
during the time of the Grand Masters and had been
uninhabited for such a long time? The few beds which
we had taken to Mdina had been allocated to the older
people; the rest were all sleeping on mattresses, on the
floor. After the appearance of the rat, the women did not
want to sleep on the floor, so they slept together on the
grand beds.

All was silent for a while but not for long. My mother
came along and whispered to father that in the room
where the children were sleeping they could hear groaning. I felt a shiver run down my spine and we all looked
at each other, sharing the same thought. "This old house,
who knows whether this is some...?!" Father and two of
my uncles went to investigate. I remember them opening
the door, little by little, and peering inside the room
apprehensively. All of them were trying hard to pretend
that they were not afraid. Then the unexpected happened. Uncle Charles dropped a large biscuit tin on the
floor and everybody jumped in terror. They reluctantly
entered the children's room and heard the groaning. I
saw one of my uncles withdraw very discreetly. "It's
true, I can hear something groaning," he whispered. We
were petrified. Shortly after, my father and my other
uncles came out of the room and told us that they
discovered where the groaning was coming from.

It was emanating from a chimney of a fireplace which
had formerly been used to heat the room. When the wind

blew down the chimney from the roof, it caused that strange noise. We all breathed a sigh of relief and went to sleep, the children in one room, the women in another and the men and the older boys in yet another room.

The following morning we started cleaning and tidying up the upper floor to be able to go and sleep upstairs. Some of my uncles went back to Sliema to try and bring up some other pieces of furniture, particularly more beds. They came back with a load of furniture on a horse-drawn cart as no mechanical transport was available.

During the day, many people turned up at the door asking whether we could spare a room. There were all types from different social classes. When father saw this he went to ask Sur Sander if it were possible to let them into Casa Depiro and Sur Sander replied right away, "Yes. Let as many people as you can."

In just two days Casa Depiro became the residence of some 180 people, one family to each room, with the exception of our family. The large hall was the women's and young children's dormitory as they were the largest number. A small part of it also served as kitchen and refectory. The men and the older boys slept in another room that was also large but not quite as spacious as that occupied by the women. From its veranda, we males could enjoy the beautiful panorama.

Although now there were many families from different backgrounds in this house, we lived there as one family. Everybody co-operated. Surprisingly even the children got along well and played together without quarrelling. We teenagers, girls and boys, found each other's company very interesting and although there was very little we could do, we managed to pass the time enjoyably. Some of the men and young women set up a school because proper schools had already closed down. In the morning we had secondary school for the teenagers and in the afternoon, it was time for the primary school, for the younger children.

On Sunday afternoons, we teenagers used to go for a hike, exploring the countryside and during the week we used to go down on the Despuig Bastion which had by now, become for us very much a meeting place, just like Għar id-Dud promenade in Sliema. Instead of having the sea as a backdrop we had a unique and very beautiful view of the whole countryside. I remember Archbishop Maurus Caruana sitting in an open balcony, at the back of his palace, reading and watching us and telling us to be quiet whenever we became a bit noisy.

In the evening, a bell tolled in Casa Depiro and we all gathered in the corridors and on the staircase of the large house to recite the Holy Rosary. Afterwards we used to organise some sort of entertainment as everybody had to remain indoors because of the curfew. Sometimes we played tombola, with a three pound prize for a house and ten shillings for a line which in those days, were good prizes. Sometimes we had musical entertainment from a refugee by the name of Prato, a well known guitarist who also lived in the palace. He used to accompany some singer from amongst us. The men played cards while women talked about household chores and cookery. The teenagers used to spend time on the terrace, unseen from outside, talking under the watchful eyes of the adults. The men amused themselves in a manner that, really and truly, I should not be mentioning here. They went out onto a corner of the terrace and competed in producing the loudest "noise". This kind of competition, of course, had to be held out in the open air because indoors it would have had very obnoxious effects, probably even necessitating the wearing of gas masks!

Once, some government officials came along and inspected the palace and ordered us to paint all the window panes of the corridor facing the veranda blue, so that no light would show through at night-time. We also had to stick strips of brown paper in the shape of an X on all window panes.

Come October, when the bird-trapping season starts, I acquired a small trap and to kill time, I used to go bird trapping with some of my new friends. We never went home with a single bird in the trap but we always made it a point to take back some fruit, kindly given to us by the farmers. They used to pity us, seeing us wasting time looking at the trap and hoping to catch the bird which never came.

The fruit we ate helped to assuage our hunger because the pinch of the scarcity of food had already started to be felt. However, on eating some unwashed fruit I was confined to bed with a tummy ache and high temperature. I had come down with Colitis. Mother and father became very worried because even medicines had become scarce and the little medicine that father had managed to lay hands on from a doctor friend of his were samples made in Italy, which if I remember correctly, were called "Fermenti Lattici". When the medicine was exhausted, I had to live on water from boiled rice.

Meanwhile, my brother Victor was sent to the quarantine hospital, which had been transferred from Manoel Island to St. Vincent de Paule Hospital situated very close to Luqa airfield. He was diagnosed ill with scabies, a contagious skin disease which causes itching. At that time, there was an epidemic of scabies in Malta. One day, while my brother was in hospital there was an air raid. I heard some gunfire in the distance. Father and mother looked out of the door overlooking the terrace from where we could see most of the Island. At one point my mother shouted; "Maria Santissima, the bombs are falling on the hospital where Victor is." She started yelling and crying and very soon she passed out and fainted, luckily falling on a bed nearby instead of on the floor.

Father quickly rushed to wet a handkerchief with water from a jug which was lying near my bed. I wanted to help but I could not force myself up from the bed with the high temperature I was running. Soon after, my mother's sisters came to help. When she recovered she insisted on going to the hospital at Mgieret. As soon as the "all clear" sounded, she donned an overcoat and hurried out. She and dad took a *karrozzin* from Saqqajja Square to the Hospital.

On arriving there, they found a scene of devastation. The ward where my brother was being kept had been hit and part of it was demolished. Father asked somebody whether any patients had been injured and they told him that luckily nobody had been hurt because the part that had been hit was empty. On speaking to a doctor about my brother's condition my parents were told they could take him back home as he was only suffering from a minor allergy. Poor Victor! What a useless fright and ordeal he had had to go through! He even had his hair shaved.

Apart from this episode of my brother's and my own illness, we were simply living it up in a holiday atmosphere. The war was distant. Sometimes we would hear the sirens wailing far away. Some aircraft would appear flying at a very high altitude. We would hear anti-aircraft fire in the distance as there were no anti-aircraft batteries in the vicinity and bombs would be dropped on Hal Far and Luqa Airfields or on Grand Harbour area.

The airfield at Ta' Qali was not yet in use for operational duties. It was obstructed with old buses, wrecked cars, lorries and hundreds of fifty gallon, oil drums filled with earth. They were dispersed all over the airfield in order to prevent gliders or transport aircraft from landing there, in case of an airborne invasion.

Although the airfield had not yet been put to operational use by the Royal Air Force, we once noticed there was a biplane looking very much like a Gladiator or a Swordfish parked on the grass, on one side of the airfield, very near the Chateau Bertrand or "The Madhouse" as it was nicknamed by the R.A.F. pilots who used it as a mess and a control tower. It was extensively damaged by bombing (later in the war) and subsequently demolished as it was a hazard to flying. On one of our first hikes we decided to go near the airfield, to have a closer look at this aircraft. On getting there we found out, to our disappointment, that this was not a real aircraft. It was a dummy made of wood and sack-cloth and it was set up as a decoy to give the enemy the impression that the airfield was operational, in order to divert attacks from other targets, thereby giving Luqa and Hal Far airfields a respite. This is in fact what happened. The fish soon swallowed the bait.

On Saturday, 23rd November 1940, there was an air raid on Luqa Airfield. The residents of Casa Depiro, as usual, went down to the basement. However, I had devised a way to watch the air raids and keep track of all that was happening outside. I had discovered a room, far inside the huge basement which, back in time, when the palace was in its hey-day, was probably used as a stable as there were traces of animal excrement. This room had a small window hewn through the bastion wall and I used to stay there, exactly as if I was on the veranda, looking down at the view of the Island. All the others were in the main room of the basement which used to be the kitchen of the palace. It was the strongest room because the ceiling was vaulted and had big wide arches. The bombs which were dropped by Italian bombers in the early days of the war, weighing between one hundred and fifty and two hundred and fifty pounds, would not have threatened our safety.

I could hear gunfire in the distance. On Luqa airfield, I could see smoke from exploding bombs. Looking through a pair of theatre binoculars, which I secretly used to take down with me to the basement, I could identify them as Savoia Marchetti SM79s. These were three-engine bombers which could fly at a speed of two hundred and sixty miles per hour and could carry a bomb load of 2,205 pounds.

Shortly afterwards, I heard a whistling sound, followed by a tremendous explosion and a very strong blast. I was thrown inwards and found myself sprawled on the floor. I got up quickly and terrified, rushed to where the others were. They were in a state of panic. Some were crying and one or two were unconscious. Others were asking whether their relatives were unharmed.

Considering the confusion there was in there, one would have thought that there had been a direct hit on the palace. When the air raid was over, I quickly ran to the veranda to spot where the bombs had fallen. As I was rushing up, father asked me where the devil I had been, as he had been looking everywhere and mother was very worried when she had not seen me in the confusion. I had to tell him a lie as I did not want to give away my secret 'hideout' from where I could observe the air raids.

The bombs had fallen in a field about four hundred yards away from the Despuig Bastion and had only caused three craters in the soil. Nonetheless, everybody was dazed. Nobody had any experience of war. We were in for far worse things. Other bombs fell in the fields between Saqqajja and Tal-Virtu'.

As usual, everyone had his own different views about the matter. Some said that the bombs were meant for that dummy aircraft at Ta' Qali and that it was not right for the authorities to put it there. Others blamed the old cannons, from the time of the Knights, lying in front of the Cathedral. These guns and another small one, which was on Despuig Bastion, were removed shortly afterwards.

In fact, two days after these three antique cannons were removed, the Italian radio had commented; "We do not know why the two ornamental bronze cannons which were lying in front of the Mdina Cathedral have been removed. We are aware that these cannons were only ornamental and date back from the times of the Knights of Malta. These cannons cannot shoot down aircraft of the Regia Aeronautica."

Although it was prohibited to listen in to enemy radio stations, those of us who had a radio set used to tune in to listen to what the other side had to say. We used to get only two newspapers, the English daily "The Times of Malta" and the Maltese daily "Il-Berqa". But these gave only one sided version as did Rediffusion, which relayed the B.B.C. news in English and Maltese. Radio sets were not as efficient as today's, particularly the one owned by my father, which only received medium wave broadcasts and which had been bought in 1936 during the Abyssinian war.

The propaganda and barefaced lies which came over the radio, particularly the Italian station, had to be heard to be believed, so much so, that even small children took such news with a pinch of salt. I remember that once, the Italian Radio had announced that the Regia Aeronautica had bombed and destroyed Malta's railway system! Malta's railway had stopped running in 1932. On another occasion, they had said that they had destroyed our coal mines!

Foodstuffs, matches and kerosene became even scarcer. We had started to eat bread and butter which tasted very strange. Protection Offices were being set up and they were put in charge of food control. The Office at Mdina was situated in the small Church of St. Roque, opposite the Church of Our Lady of Mount Carmel. Father was offered a post in this office and we were very happy to learn this, as he had not had a gainful occupation since the onset of war with Germany in September 1939, almost a year before. When the war started, my father was an importer and had built most of his business with German firms. When the war was declared his business had to stop. In fact, some remittances which had not yet been paid had to be paid to the Maltese Government, under the Enemy Property Act. There were many other businessmen who were likewise affected.

The Protection Office, besides organising the distribution and supply of food, provided accommodation to the refugees and to those who were bombed out of their houses. Even petrol grew scarce and private cars could not take to the road. The only exemptions were those vehicles driven by doctors and high government officials. Public transport was running to a very limited timetable. If one had to transport something heavy, he could do it only by horse-drawn carts because lorries were no longer available.

Christmas 1940 was fast approaching so we decided to lay something special to celebrate this first wartime Christmas. The women took it upon themselves to prepare the food and the young men and small children took care of the decorations. This was exactly what my father had been waiting for, as he enjoyed putting up decorations. He told me, "You know what we should do! We'll go down to Sliema and fetch the Christmas decorations, festoon and lights and put them up over here." He used to import these himself, we had loads of them at home.

Next morning, we woke up early and after hearing Mass at the Cathedral, we went down to Sliema. It was like a ghost town. Not a soul could be seen in the streets except for the odd, emaciated dog or cat. The shops were all boarded up and, the streets which had always been full of life were now deserted. Even our footsteps echoed in the silence. One could hear a pin drop.

On entering the house, there was a musty smell. We opened the doors and windows to let some fresh air in. When we looked out of the balcony, from where I used to look out onto a lot of activity before we left Sliema, I saw an empty street. Houses were all closed and there was no sign of traffic or life. I felt sad at this. I told father that we had better take our things and get back to Mdina as soon as we could, lest something should happen, otherwise mother would worry her head off. Father did not seem keen to leave the house. He had inherited it from his parents shortly before Italy declared war and loved the place. He was born and raised there and lived in the house even after he got married.

While we were tying up the cardboard boxes containing the Christmas decorations, there was an air raid warning signal. Soon we heard gunfire, probably coming from Fort Spinola, followed shortly afterwards by the anti-aircraft guns of Fort Tigne' and those of Fort Manoel. As the house was quite bare, the noise echoed through the empty rooms. But when *H.M.S. Terror*, which was still berthed at Lazzarett Creek, opened fire, Sliema trembled. *H.M.S. Terror* and her large anti-aircraft 4.5 inch guns was indeed a terrifying spectacle to the inhabitants of Sliema and Gzira because her guns were fired simultaneously, unlike the guns in anti-aircraft batteries which fired separately.

Father looked anxious and we took cover under the staircase. The gunfire lasted about ten minutes and gradually faded in the distance until it stopped. This was followed by perfect silence, so much so that we could hear the officers bawling their orders to the gun crews at Fort Manoel. When the "all clear" was sounded, we hurriedly left the place and returned to Mdina.

We were quite happy to have brought the Christmas decorations to Mdina, where other preparations were also underway. My father was very excited because it was his hobby to prepare and decorate for any party that came his way, more so, when he had such a big palace to decorate.

On Christmas Eve, after reciting the Rosary, we heard Mass at the Chapel of Casa Depiro. It was said by Canon Martinelli, who himself was a refugee from

Vittoriosa and resided with us. On Christmas Day, we threw a party, which was good by the standards of those days and everybody enjoyed every minute, particularly the teenagers. For a few hours, everybody seemed to have forgotten the war and was joking and laughing.

The Christmas lunch was not a bad one for those times, for father managed to get hold of a turkey from a farmer, who lived in the region of Wied il-Qlejja and who owed my father a favour. We had made many friends among the farmers and they used to furnish us with greens. They seemed to feel honoured when we visited them because we came from the more sophisticated part of the Island. We also had cakes, biscuits, custard and non alcoholic drinks. Alcoholic drinks had vanished and whoever had some in stock used to hide them away, valuing them as much as gold.

The situation on the war front seemed to have calmed down somewhat and air raids were on the decrease. When the air raid warning signal was given, very often, it was a false alarm and most times it would be a reconnaissance sortie. Sometimes, after reconnaissance raids, bombing attacks would follow. Most of the bombs were dropped on Hal Far and Luqa Airfields, far away from the main towns and villages.

Many families gradually started to return to their homes because they thought that the war would follow this pattern and that the danger had passed. Although my parents wanted to return to Sliema, they were hesitant as to what they ought to do, because of us children.

But, as things turned out, they did not have to think about it too long because we suddenly had to leave Casa Depiro as it had been requisitioned to serve as an alternative school for St. Edward's College. So, on Monday,

43

5th January 1941, we returned to Sliema. Those who lived in the Cottonera district and who were still afraid to return to their houses also had to leave and unfortunately, some eventually fell victims to bombing attacks on their return to their home towns. Shortly afterwards, we learnt that Casa Depiro had not been turned into a college after all but was again full of refugees. However, we also heard that the atmosphere that had prevailed when we lived there had changed completely.

Reconnaissance sorties by enemy aircraft were now becoming more frequent. Some of us were optimistic and started to say that the Italians had run out of bombs. Others suggested that they were afraid to renew their attacks. At that point in the war, the Italians were suffering one defeat after another in North Africa and perhaps this was the reason why they were leaving us in peace.

Many, now, very often remained outside during air raids, carrying on with their business as usual. Those who were at work would continue until gunfire started and only then would they seek shelter. Everybody had got used to this routine and life had almost returned to normal.

Many families now had returned to Sliema. Some shops had reopened and there were people moving about in the streets again. Old friends met again and our 'club' was at the Franciscan Friary. Schools reopened as well, although for half days. I remember that my class was in the Salesians Oratory. The senior classes were held in the theatre hall, four at a time. Students could not pay much attention during classes because all the time, they were being distracted by what was going on in the other classes. Our proper school, which was large and comfortable, was in Blanche Huber Street. However, this had been taken over by the A.R.P., as an emergency station for casualties and to give temporary refuge to those who lost their homes.

School books also became somewhat scarce, especially mathematics ones. Sometimes, three of us had to make use of the same text books and to do our homework, we had to go to each others houses and study together.

Copybooks, likewise, were not available and we used lined foolscaps until even these became scarce. Later, we had to make use of any paper that came our way and used to stitch them to form copybooks. My father used to make me copybooks out of papers he used for correspondence when he was still in business, until these too ran out.

We could only find ink at school and whoever had a fountain pen could fill it up there. At home, we only used pencils but these later became scarce as well. Then we even used slates for our rough work to economise on paper and pencils.

Our education took a downturn. Nevertheless, our teachers deserve to be praised, because they were so dedicated and did their best to educate us in the circumstances. Lessons, during the half-day period, were very often interrupted by some air raid and we had to go down into the wooden shelter which was set up in the basement of the theatre. During the gunfire barrage, the teachers cracked jokes to distract us and tried to make us forget our fear. This was something new for us because, before, our teachers had been very straight-faced.

Chapter III

MAELSTROM

T owards the end of 1940, rumours were spreading around that squadrons of the German Luftwaffe had been stationed in Sicily. Some believed these rumours, others did not. However, there is no smoke without a fire.

On 29th December 1940, a train, code-named "Adler" (Eagle), laden with ground crews of the Luftwaffe and war material arriving from Germany, was unloaded at the railway station of Comiso in Sicily. Four hundred and fifty German aircraft started to land on the Sicilian airfields of Catania, Gela, Gerbini, Comiso and Palermo.

These were made up as follows:

102 Messerschmitt Me 109	Fighters
36 Messerschmitt Me 110	Twin-engine fighters
72 Junkers Ju88	Bombers
12 Junkers Ju88	Photo Reconnaissance Bombers
144 Junkers Ju87	"Stuka" Dive Bombers
36 Junkers Ju52	Transport aircraft

| 36 Heinkel He111 | Torpedo Bombers |
| 12 Heinkel He111 | Mine layers |

On Friday, 10th January 1941, at about 10.00 pm, the aircraft carrier *H.M.S. Illustrious*, listing to one side, entered Grand Harbour. She was one of the most modern aircraft carriers (23,000 tons) of the Royal Navy at that time. On her way to Malta, she had been attacked repeatedly by German and Italian aircraft, had suffered considerable damage and many of her crew had been killed or wounded. *Illustrious* berthed alongside the quay known as Parlatorio Wharf, under Carrodino Hill, where No. 6 Dock of Malta Dry Docks lies today. Repairs got under way but first the casualties were taken ashore and after them, the dead were carried on board *H.M.S. Fermoy* and buried at sea, about two miles outside Grand Harbour.

The following day, an aircraft flew in very low from the direction of the sea, over Sliema towards Grand Harbour and Marsaxlokk Bay. All those who saw it thought it was one of our aircraft, but when it passed overhead, those who perceived the black crosses on its wings, realised at once it was German. Some thought it was an ambulance aircraft but in fact it was a reconnaissance Dornier Do17S. We had never seen an enemy aircraft flying so low. It confirmed the rumour regarding the arrival of the Germans in Sicily. The appearance of this Dornier Do17S was an ominous portent of what was in store for us, over the next few months.

There was not a single underground rock shelter in Sliema then. The only ones available were made of wood. These were, very often, rooms in basements propped up with wooden beams from the ground and reinforced by wooden planks, under the roof.

Obviously, this type of shelter was not bombproof. Nonetheless, there were a number of cases where people taking refuge in them survived when bombs fell nearby, without taking a direct hit on the house. Most of these shelters consisted of one compartment and certainly were not very spacious.

I remember it was Thursday, 16th January 1941. At school, we had just finished classes for the day and were reciting prayers. At about 1.45 pm, the sirens sounded. Mr Debono, our school teacher, who was also a special constable, told us to hurry home. However, two of my schoolmates and I decided to go near St. Julian's Tower, where some Irish Fusiliers were posted to guard the coast. We walked down Sir Adrian Dingli Street and on arriving at the bottom, near the tower, four shots from the 4.5 inch anti-aircraft guns of Fort Spinola frightened us out of our wits. We had not heard such gunfire for some time. Spinola Battery was armed with larger calibre guns than other batteries.

On looking at the sky in the direction where the guns were pointing, we heard someone shouting. We looked back and saw Manuel, the school janitor, wearing his air raid warden's steel helmet, yelling at us to get home as quickly as we could because there were many German aeroplanes coming in very low.

The gunfire increased in intensity. My friends and I rapidly dispersed and hurried home. I did not even spare a look to see what was in the skies above us. It was one big run for home and I think I never ran so fast in my life; not even on school sports day. I could not find anywhere to take cover. There was not one house that was open, nor any shelters nearby; everybody had gone indoors.

When I arrived near the Modern Imperial Hotel, at the upper end of St. Mary Street, the tempo of the gunfire increased. For the first time, I heard a new sound coming from the guns. This had a different rhythm; it was faster than that of the other guns I was familiar with. These were the Bofors, smaller guns with a higher rate of fire. They weighed two and a half tons, had a calibre of 40 mm and fired a shell weighing two pounds. Their rate of fire was one hundred and twenty rounds per minute with an effective range of 12,000 feet. Each gun had a crew of six.

This type of anti-aircraft gun was designed to engage low-flying aircraft. As they were smaller, they were not deployed in batteries, like the bigger guns, but were dispersed everywhere and were very mobile. We could see their shells rise to the sky because they had a tracer which illuminated the trajectory of the shell on being fired.

Tracer shells had various uses. The principal one was to enable the gunners to follow the fall of shot and correct their aim. The shell was an incendiary projectile and was meant to deter and confuse the pilot of an attacking aircraft, on seeing tracers rising towards him.

I was the only one of my family who was still out during that raid. I found mother waiting for me behind a small, iron gate at the front door of our house. I asked her whether my father and brothers were at home. She replied that my brother Victor was under the stairs with our aunts and father had gone up on the roof to tell my brother Joe to come down.

No sooner had mother turned to leave for the staircase refuge, then I immediately ran up to the roof to watch the spectacle. I was more afraid when I could not see what was happening and could only hear gunfire and explosions. Father told me to go back down at once as many splinters were raining down from the skies. Nonetheless, I managed to persuade him to allow me to remain in the washroom, on the roof and see what was going on in the sky.

For the first time ever, I saw Junkers Ju88s and the Junkers Ju87 Stukas.

The Junkers Ju88 was a twin-engine aircraft with a crew of four and could carry a bomb load of 1,550lbs. It could fly at a top speed of two hundred and eighty-six miles per hour and was the most versatile aircraft in the Luftwaffe.

The Junkers Ju87, better known as the Stuka, was a single-engine dive bomber, with a crew of two, a top speed of two hundred and thirty-two miles per hour and a maximum bomb load of 1,540lbs. This aircraft had already become the terror of many European countries.

I saw the Stukas approaching in Vic formations of three. Then, one after the other, they dipped their noses and dived straight down on their prey, very much like hawks.

As I have never witnessed such an attack before, at first I thought that these aircraft were being hit. The density of the anti-aircraft fire was terrific. We ventured out on to the roof to see what part of the Island was being raided and as the gunfire was not over us and no splinters were coming down at the time, we could emerge from cover. It was obvious that the target was Grand Harbour. Father said, "They are bombing the *Illustrious*."

It was a spectacle the likes of which we had never seen. We were astonished at the courage shown by the Germans when we saw them flying in so low through the intense anti-aircraft fire thrown up at them from the ground. The sky was clouded in smoke from the anti-aircraft fire and from enemy bombs. My brother Joe exclaimed: "They've hit one. I can see smoke coming out of it." Then we saw an aircraft flying very low, dodging from side to side, as if the pilot was drunk. It was emitting a lot of smoke from one side. I saw something fall out of the aircraft and shouted, "One must have bailed out". I expected to see a parachute open but instead, the object I saw came straight down onto some houses in Valletta and immediately, a pall of smoke rose. It was a bomb which, I later discovered, had fallen in Old Mint Street and demolished some buildings and killed one person.

There was a short interval which enabled everybody to catch his breath and in that hush, we could hear the orders being called out to the gunners on Manoel Island. The smoke from the bombs and the guns was abating and only came from the bombed buildings.

The guns opened fire again. The second wave was coming in and this time, the aircraft were Ju88s, which launched their attacks in a different way from the Stukas. Whereas the latter dived almost perpendicularly, the 88s had a shallow dive and jettisoned their bombs from a certain distance depending on their height and speed.

Many houses in Vittoriosa and Senglea were demolished and there were many casualties during this attack, which like the previous one, was concentrated on *H.M.S. Illustrious*. The greatest tragedy occurred in Vittoriosa, when a bomb hit the crypt at St. Lawrence Church and killed thirty-five people, who had taken cover there.

Despite these two heavy attacks, the Luftwaffe only succeeded in scoring one hit on the *Illustrious*, causing superficial damage to the flight deck. All other bombs dropped, ended up either in the sea in Grand Harbour, the dockyard or on the surrounding cities. The Germans lost many of their aircraft which crashed into the sea.

These raids lasted almost two hours and left everybody stunned. That evening, everybody was talking about them.

The Luftwaffe launched another heavy attack on Saturday, 18th January, this time on the airfields of Hal Far and Luqa with fifty-one Ju87s, escorted by a large number of Messerschmitt Me110s and Italian Macchi MC200s, causing considerable damage.

Another huge and even more ferocious raid than the previous ones, took place on Sunday, 19th January, by forty-eight Ju87s escorted by five Me110s, ten CR42s and eight MC 200s, when *Illustrious* was again the target. It was another failure for the Germans. This time, some bombs fell again on the dockyard, on Senglea and among buildings destroyed, there was the clock tower and the Basilica of Our Lady of Victories. Rescue workers were still searching for and rescuing victims from the previous Thursday's attack. Bombs also fell on Vittoriosa and demolished more buildings including the Church of the Annunciation. However, very few people died because after Thursday's raid, many people had sought refuge elsewhere.

This time, R.A.F. fighters went up in defence of the aircraft carrier and pilots of 261 Squadron, in their Hurricanes, were seen entering the heavy barrage of anti-aircraft fire with great courage and great risk of being hit themselves.

By this time, the R.A.F. had received its first batch of Hurricane fighters. They were a single-engine type with a speed of three hundred and twenty-eight miles per hour and armed with eight Browning .303 machine-guns in the wings. Although they were no match for the Messerschmitt 109f,s which had a maximum speed of three hundred and seventy-five miles per hour and were armed with two 7.9mm machine-guns and one 20mm cannon, the Hurricanes made short shrift of the German Ju88 and Ju87 bombers.

On that Sunday, I happened to be at The Strand in Sliema and took cover inside the Carlton Theatre, where Marks & Spencer Department Store stands today.

I did not have as good a view of what was happening as I had had of the attack on Thursday. However, I could see what was happening in the sky. The guns of Fort Manoel were firing incessantly and the sky was full of tracer and smoke.

The German Junkers were approaching from all di-rections. I saw an 88 coming from the direction of Floriana chased by a Hurricane. It emitted black smoke as it flew overhead, at a height of about 500 feet and flew on in the direction of Għar id-Dud. I am positive it never reached Sicily. After these three fierce attacks, the Germans licked their wounds for a while and prepared for the final attack to carry out the Fuhrer's order to General Geisler: "*Illustrious* Mussen Sinken!" (The Illustrious must be sunk!)

However, *H.M.S. Illustrious* left Grand Harbour dur-ing the night of Wednesday, 23rd January, en route for Alexandria. Next morning, enemy reconnaissance air-craft discovered that the bird had flown.

Once again, the population was overcome by panic and many began to leave Sliema and the towns around the harbours, to seek refuge in the outlying villages. Father decided that we should stay on, come what may, because he thought we could not be absolutely safe wherever we went. The friars of the Sacro Cuor Friary opened up the church as a shelter whenever there was an air-raid warning, day or night, and we started to go and take refuge under the spires. They had also emptied the storerooms in the friary, where *festa* decorations were kept and turned it into a shelter, by building two walls along the length of the rooms and laying a number of thick wooden beams on top of them, covering the lot with about twelve inches of concrete. It was meant for the monks but they opened it to the general public. This was the safest shelter in Sliema in those days and we had ample proof of this a year later.

Now, besides the larger and more powerful bombs of the Germans, we began to experience a new terrible ordeal – the all night raids. Fast asleep, tucked in bed, on hearing the siren's wail, mothers and fathers would wake up their children, wrap them up in a blanket or two and take them out into the cold, if not into the rain. It was indeed a cruel experience for children, babies, the sick and the aged.

We started taking shelter in the friary during night raids. My job was to take a folding chair and run to the shelter to reserve a good place for mother to sit on and keep my brother Victor on her lap so he could sleep comfortably. Father used to take care of a small box, containing some money and gold trinkets and my brother Joe carried a basket with a thermos flask with coffee and some bread with margarine. Butter had already disappeared from the market!

The shelter was not very spacious and, very often, men had to give up their places to women, children and old people. I used to take advantage of this, leaving the shelter to look for one of the friars, Fr. Diego who never came inside the shelter. Stealthily, lest the father guardian of the friary should notice, we climbed to the roof from where we could see everything. This was an even better view than the one I had from my home!!

During air raids, we stayed in a room at the top of the stairwell, leading to the roof. It had an open side and a window on each of the three walls. In this way, we were protected from falling splinters and other objects. We had to be very careful not to allow any low-flying enemy aircraft to see us, lest the pilot would think that we were observers and machine-gun us. The Germans used to shoot at anything that moved. They had a hawk's eyes.

Chapter IV

CONSCRIPTION

T he Governor of Malta and Commander in Chief of the Armed Forces was General Sir William G.S. Dobbie. When war was declared, he had found that the Islands were completely denuded of armaments, soldiers, munitions, food supplies and other necessary war material. Many of the British regiments that were stationed here had left, when war was declared on Germany. Others had left later to reinforce the army in North Africa.

The units stationed in Malta at the time came from: the Royal Artillery, the Royal Engineers, the Royal Ordinance Corps, the Buffs, The Royal West Kent and two Maltese Regiments: the Royal Malta Artillery and the King's Own Malta Regiment.

The first raids caught the defenders completely unprepared for war. In 1940 there were only thirty-four Heavy anti-aircraft guns and eight Light Bofors, 40 mm anti-aircraft guns, deployed mostly for harbour defence. A small radar station, known officially as No. 241 A.M.E.S. (Air Ministry Experimental Station), had been erected on top of Dingli Cliffs, in March 1939. In June 1940, the second Radar Station: No. 242 A.M.E.S. was brought into operation. It was proposed that the defence of Malta should include: one hundred and seventy anti-aircraft guns, searchlights and four squadrons of fighters but Britain failed to produce the required number of guns and aircraft deemed vital for Malta's defence.

Ironically, on 11th June 1940, The Governor, Sir William Dobbie had received a message from the Chief of Staff:

"Wish you and all under your command
every good luck in whatever lies ahead."

General Dobbie replied:

"Many thanks for your telegram which is much appreciated. All here are in good heart and ready for all eventualities."

There was hardly any air defence to speak of. The total R.A.F. strength was five target-towing Swordfish aircraft, one Queen Bee pilot-less target drone aircraft and four Gloster Sea Gladiators assembled from eight crated ones, earmarked for embarkation on H.M.S. *Glorious* and left ashore when she sailed hurriedly for Norway. These later became known as the legendary "Faith", "Hope" and "Charity", which became immortalised in the story of the Battle of Malta. The Gladiator Flight was flown by seven officers without any battle experience. They were:

C.O. Flight: Squadron Leader Alan "Jock" C. Martin from Staff Hal Far

Flight Lieutenant George Burgess, Personal Assistant to the Air Officer Commanding
Flight Lieutenant Peter Keeble, from the original Hal Far Flight
Flying Officer Peter Hartley, Staff Pilot No. 3 A/A Co-operation Unit
Flying Officer John Waters, Staff Pilot No. 3 A/A Co-operation Unit
Flying Officer William Woods, ex-Station Flight pilot; and
Pilot Officer Peter Alexander, from the Radio-Controlled Queen Bee experimental flight.

Shortage of pilots dictated the use of a shift system using two flights of three pilots:

A Flight	on standby from	dawn	to	08.00
B Flight	on standby from	08.00	to	12.00
A Flight	on standby from	12.00	to	16.00
B Flight	on standby from	16.00	to	dusk

Later, on 7th August 1940, they were reinforced by Hawker Hurricanes which were 'requisitioned' by the Air Officer Commanding Malta, Air Commodore F.H.M. Maynard. These Hurricanes were on their way to Egypt and had stopped in Malta to refuel. Eventually, the first R.A.F. fighter squadron, No. 261 was formed from these elements.

The first problem which General Dobbie had to face was that of showing and explaining to the Maltese population, the situation that the Island was in. He explained that it was not enough to remain passive and that as we are in a state of total war, we could not survive without making an effort. We had to fight or perish and if total war required total service he would have to impose conscription on the Maltese population. For a people who, as yet, never been at war, the news that conscription was being introduced came like a bolt from the blue. There were many objections and protests, even from some members of the Council of Government, but the Governor held firm.

The forces which he had at his disposal in Malta were not enough for the requirements of the defence of the Island and he knew that he could not expect any reinforcements from Britain because Britain itself was expecting an invasion from the Germans. He knew, as well, that the Island had to survive the onslaught that was being prepared for it and that it had to prepare itself, in the shortest possible time, to defend itself.

On 20th February 1941, the daily newspapers, 'The Times of Malta' and 'Il-Berqa' carried an extract from the Compulsory Service Regulations. This provided for compulsory service, either in the military or in the civil sector. Those who were over twenty-one years old but not over twenty-five, on 3rd March 1941, had to register for military service. Those so conscripted did not have to serve outside Maltese territory, unless they were serving in the Royal Navy.

This announcement caused great tension. Mothers cried because their sons were being recruited as soldiers. Wives worried for their husbands. Many were those who tried to avoid military service but this had become a law and those who failed to register were imprisoned. The only men who were exempt were those who did not pass a medical test or those who were the only or the eldest sons of the family. Uncle Charles was the first to be recruited from members of our family. Grandma shed many tears and so did my mother and her sisters. It was just as if he were going to the front and when he returned home on leave, after fifteen days of service training, everybody came down to grandma's house to greet him.

Mother, on seeing her younger brother in uniform, started crying and hugging him. I took his forage cap and put it on, hung the anti gas-respirator on my shoulder, took his Lee Enfield rifle, which he had brought along with him and started parading up and down the hall and performing the drill that I had learnt when I formed part of the Salesian Boys Brigade. Men in military service had orders to carry their small arms with them, wherever they went.

Uncle Charles told me, "It's a pity that you are still under age because you could have joined my regiment and you would have managed to take over from our instructor. There are many who cannot understand what he is telling us, as they do not speak English. Mother looked daggers at him as if to say: "Thank God for that!" She knew that I was mad about life in uniform.

The introduction of conscription proceeded apace and in the following months, officers and non-commissioned officers from British regiments stationed here, worked incessantly to train men, who never knew what military discipline was like, to become effective soldiers.

One of the three difficulties they encountered was to introduce some form of obedience, by teaching the conscripts to give orders with conviction and to obey and execute orders without any arguments.

The Maltese recruits learned fast. Very soon, they became part of the adventure of military life, although they were not used to do things in a hurry and to living with others under the same roof. At the beginning they would think twice before giving an order because they considered their fellow soldiers as brothers or friends. However, they soon got used to the idea and many ended up as non-commissioned officers and even as commissioned officers.

The second difficulty was with those who did not know how to dress properly. There were some who had never worn shoes in their life. There were others who were never properly dressed. Now they had to get used to the idea of appearing smartly turned out. According to a British military saying: "A dirty soldier means a dirty rifle. A dirty rifle means a dead soldier."

The conscripts not only got used to wearing shoes but also wearing the heaviest type of boots, with studded soles and steel heels, even at the cost of getting blisters on their feet. In those days, there were still a number of people who went around barefoot, especially in the villages. Luckily, with the advent of war, this habit came to an end. Others learnt to wear a tie for the first time and the new recruits found out how it felt to have a cold shower in the morning after an hour's physical training or after a route march. Those who had never brushed their teeth now had to do so daily. They were now driving lorries, tractors, a small tank or Bren Gun Carrier instead of a horse-drawn cart. Instead of a shotgun, they now carried a rifle, machine-gun or even larger weapons.

The Maltese soldier very soon learnt how to dismantle the mechanism of his weapon and reassemble it, blind folded, so that in cases of emergency, he would be able to do it even in darkness. He learnt how to walk smartly and not slovenly, with his hands in his pocket. Those

61

who had servants at home and had never done any housework, now had to learn how to make their beds every morning, to sweep the floor of their barrack room and wash it and to eat wherever they happened to be, even under a tree or a wall. They had to find out where they could wash their mess tins and repair socks, which often got torn after a route march. They now had to wash their clothes and iron them. They learnt how to "blanco" their webbing and to polish the brass of their uniform buttons and badges until they shone like gold. Although initially, military life was somewhat tough, the Maltese soldier got used to it very quickly.

The new recruits learnt map reading, the use of certain instruments which they had never seen before, like wireless and walkie-talkie sets and how to send messages in Morse code or in Semaphore. It was a very difficult task for the instructors to teach conscripts all these things in such a short time, when normally it took two or three months. Turning somebody into a soldier is not that easy. However, the new Maltese soldiers learned quickly and became as efficient as professional soldiers. The British instructors were full of praise for the way these conscripts got the hang of things, so quickly.

The third difficulty was the language. Although there were many who could speak some English, there were others who could not understand a word of it. However, the English professional soldier had his own way of solving this particular problem. He would rely on a certain jargon, of 'Pidgin English' and through it and a good deal of gesticulation and shouting, he got his message through. Very shortly, the King's Own Malta Regiment had four Battalions: the 1st, the 2nd, the 3rd and the 10th. The Royal Malta Artillery had five Regiments and a Searchlight Battery, these being the 1st Coast Regiment, the 3rd Light Anti-Aircraft Regiment, the 5th Coast Regiment, the 2nd Heavy Anti-Aircraft Regiment, the 11th Heavy Anti-Aircraft Regiment (Territorial) and the 8th Searchlight Battery. These units became an integral part of the British Army, together with the 16th Fortress Corps Royal Engineers. Many other Maltese joined the Royal Navy and others enlisted in the Royal Air Force.

By that time, three Hurricane Squadrons were formed in Malta. These were: No. 185 Squadron, at Hal Far under the command of Squadron Leader P.W. Mould. This was formed from Hurricanes and crews of C Flight of No. 261 Squadron, which had been disbanded; No. 249 Squadron at Ta' Qali, with Hurricanes Mk. IIa, commanded by Squadron Leader R.A. Barton and No. 126 Squadron at Luqa under the command of Squadron Leader A.C. Rabagliati. There was also No. 148 Squadron, flying Wellingtons, stationed at Luqa. The strength of the Air Force in Malta was subsequently further reinforced by fifty Hurricanes Mk.IIa and IIb, which flew to Malta on 12th April, 1941.

Chapter V

A WORSE MENACE

I became somewhat disorganised with my home-work. I did it in fits and starts, whenever I found some time. In the afternoon, I had to go and queue to buy the pint of milk that we were entitled to and usually, this meant that I had to stay there for over an hour. If, while I was in the queue, there happened to be an air raid, I moved up the queue as, very often, people were afraid and fled to seek cover.

There was a great deal of quarrelling, especially when somebody tried to jump the queue. Once I was summoned as a witness when, as it happened, I was not even present to witness an argument. To give evidence, I had to go to the temporary Court House at the Magistrates' Court which was situated at the Lija Government Girls School and just for stating that I was not there during the fight, I was paid the handsome sum of one shilling three pence. However, I quickly spent the shilling on transport to go to Balzan and return to Sliema. As it was the first time that I had been to court, albeit only to give evidence, I was more scared of this event than I was of the German bombs.

Once, while I was studying, at about 9.00 pm, the siren sounded. It was Friday, 14th March, 1941. I left everything and, as usual, grabbed the folding chair and ran to the shelter at the friary. When mother arrived, I gave her my chair and went out to meet Fr. Diego, with the intention of going on the roof. I found him running up the stairs to the roof and he warned me, "We won't stay in the room outside because it is very cold and I don't want to catch a cold and spend four days in bed." So we remained in the room at the top of the stairway.

The drone of the aircraft was getting louder all the time. We could hear some men talking downstairs and passing information on what they were seeing, to those inside. There was no gunfire and the silence was suddenly broken by a shout, "Put out that cigarette! Can't you hear they are flying over us?" I recognised that voice. It was that of Special Constable, Swetu, who used to perform his duties very efficiently. He did his rounds in the streets in the vicinity during air raids, telling people to take cover, controlling them in the queue or helping old people to seek cover. He was always around on his bicycle and would never remove his steel helmet. Poor man he was bald of course!

The searchlights were turned on and their glow, especially when the sky was overcast, lit up the darkness. They were like the tentacles of an octopus, probing the sky seeking their prey. They started following the droning of the aircraft, in the direction of Valletta.

From the convergence of the searchlights, I could see that the aircraft was circling over Grand Harbour. Suddenly, the searchlights caught the aircraft in their beams and the anti-aircraft guns opened fire. We saw something drop from the aircraft which was flying at about 3,000 feet. "He's hit . . . He's hit! The crew are taking to their parachutes!" Fr. Diego excitedly exclaimed.

It appeared to me that the parachute was larger than usual and that what was dangling from it was not a human being. I could see machine-gun tracer bullets being aimed at this parachute. One searchlight followed it down, while the others kept tracking the aircraft. The object under the parachute continued drifting down until it landed on some building on the lower end of Valletta. Then a huge ball of fire rose up to the sky and we heard a terrific explosion, the likes of which we had never heard and felt before. This was accompanied by a very strong blast. The aircraft changed course to return to its base in Sicily, followed by anti-aircraft fire from the ack-ack batteries. The following day we learnt that the strange object we had seen was a parachute mine which had fallen in the lower part of Merchants Street, near the Camarata Barracks.

As Uncle Charles, who had been recently conscripted, was stationed at Camarata, mother asked father to go to Valletta and check if anything had happened to him. I begged father to go with him. At first he refused but then he gave in. Due to lack of petrol, the buses worked to a limited timetable. However, the people of Sliema and those of Cottonera were lucky because they could cross over to Valletta by ferry which ran at all times of the day. These ferries had coal fired steam engines and were painted black. They belonged to The National Steam Ferry Boat Company. It was a very pleasant means of transport and it's a pity that this service had been discontinued for many years. These ferries had a funnel amidships and a cabin on the stern. The steam engine was visible below deck, in the centre and it was operated by an engineer, who also performed the role of stoker. The helm was right in front and, immediately behind it, there was a high chair for the skipper.

When it was time for the ferry to leave the pier, the skipper came along in a white and black peaked cap and a badge sporting a blue pennant with an orange ball, the logo of the company. He used to board the ferry and walk straight to the helm. Then he would shout, "Cast off Gus," and the sailor in charge of the moorings would cast off the rope. "Astern!" would be the second order and immediately the engineer would turn a small wheel, pull a lever on the side of the engine and this would be followed by a hissing sound, the sound of steam entering the engine. "Chlukk, chlukk, chlukk…" the engine came to life and the pistons would start moving up and down, slow at first and then quicker and quicker. The ferry turned on its aft moorings until it headed towards Valletta. Then the skipper would give the order, "Go ahead" and the ferry would set out on the short crossing to Valletta, under the orders of the skipper, who never forsook his pipe.

Occasionally, a group of musicians would board the ferry. They were two elderly men playing guitars, accompanying a boy playing the violin. One of the guitarists, I remember, was blind. They played popular melodies and then the boy would go round with a violin in one hand and a small plate in the other, collecting some money from the passengers. It was in those days that the following popular song was composed:

"One ferry is arriving,
the other departing
from Sliema to Marsamxett,
the captain, pipe in mouth,
conning the boat.

In mid-stream,
I heard the strains
of a lone violin.
I was feeling sea sick
with the rolling of the boat
and the strumming of the violin."

Besides the ferries and the buses, one could also get to Valletta by *dgħajsa*, the Maltese oared boat, that carried up to ten passengers, besides the two oarsmen.

Father and I took a ferry to Valletta and walked to the centre, up the steps through Marsamxett tunnel. This had two blast-proof walls on each entrance because it was also used as a shelter for people arriving from or going to the ferries, who happened to be caught in an air raid. We walked up St. Lucia Street and when we came to the corner with Old Mint Street, it was blocked with rubble from houses that had been destroyed during the first German attack of 16th January. I remarked to father, "These are not like the Italians. They get their job done!"

When we got to the Camarata there was utter devastation. Many houses and a state school had been destroyed. I could not believe that all that destruction had been caused by just one explosion. I had only seen one bomb dangling under the parachute. But of course, I could not tell my father this!

We found Uncle Charles safe and sound, although

visibly shaken. He had been detailed as a spotter on the roof of Camarata Barracks when the mine fell. When he saw it, he took cover under the stairs leading to the roof and managed to escape unscathed. He asked us not to tell anything about this to grandma, as it would worry her no end.

When we came out of the barracks and looked around the devastation from the bomb damage, we saw men and women foraging amongst the ruins, trying to save some of their belongings. Most of them had lost all they possessed and were now homeless. I saw a woman with four little children wailing at her plight. Her husband was hugging her, trying to console her.

There was a group of dirty children, covered with bomb dust, eating a scrap of bread which was given to them by their neighbours. Two men were shouting at each other. Initially, I thought they were quarrelling but in actual fact, one of them was simply trying to invite the other to take his wife and children to his house, until they could find alternative accommodation. Sitting on a stone, was a mother breast-feeding her baby. She was in tears and looking at what, up to a few hours earlier, had been their humble home.

Back in Sliema, we stopped at grandma's house and told her that Uncle Charles was safe and sound, naturally without mentioning what had actually happened to him. We then went up to our house and father related everything to my mother. He did not dwell on the destructive power and devastation caused by these mines, so as not to alarm her. He only told her that some houses had been demolished and that gone were the days when it was safe enough to take cover under the stairs.

Some days later, I had the opportunity to go over to

Cottonera with one of my uncles, to inspect some buildings which he had in that area and which had been bombed out. I did not want to miss this opportunity because I had never managed to go that far on my own, as it was very vulnerable to air attacks. I took up this invitation right away. At about 7.00 am we took the ferry to Marsamxett and on arriving in Valletta, we went into a café, called Café San Paolo Naufrago, by the steps at St. Lucy Street. The owner could serve neither coffee nor tea, as these were rationed and any person who was caught selling them on the black market, was prosecuted.

Food rationing had been introduced in February 1941 as certain items like sugar, soap, coffee, tea, matches, edible oil, margarine and kerosene were already in short supply. Other items like butter, lard, cheese, tomato paste, flour and petrol were absolutely unavailable. You could only obtain tinned milk for babies and cigarettes on ration basis, when available. Later on, shoes and clothes could only be bought against the exchange of coupons.

In July 1941, the Governor authorised the mixing of wheat with potatoes up to a ratio of thirty per cent, for the production of bread. Whoever infringed this order could, on being found guilty, be fined between ten and one hundred pounds or even be sent to jail for a period of one to three months.

Some shops had special authorisation to sell a cup of tea or coffee. However, only its colour was that of tea or coffee. It was only hot water vaguely reminiscent of coffee or tea, but certainly not tasting like either.

The shop we entered was not authorised to sell tea or coffee, but my uncle wanted to stop there because, before the war, the shopkeeper used to send coffee to his office in St. Paul Street. I remember we had cocoa, as this was the only thing he had which was not rationed. We provided our own sugar and milk which we had brought with us from home.

My uncle discussed at length the situation of the Islands with the shop owner and two or three others who were present. They started reminiscing about the pre-war days and drawing comparisons with what they were going through now. They spoke about how many people perished in air raids and speculated when the next convoy was due. They went on to discuss the North African campaign and the names of Rommel and the 8th Army were banded about. I was getting very impatient. At long last, when they seemed to have exhausted all they had to say, we left to get the ferry to Vittoriosa.

There was not a single vessel in Grand Harbour. The ferry made a brief stop in Senglea and then we left for Vittoriosa. The skipper pointed out a block of building which had been destroyed by bombing and told us: "That was bombed last night." My uncle replied: "Up to now, we have been left in peace in Sliema. Compared to here, we don't even know what bombing is like."

We alighted on the quay at Vittoriosa and made our way through the rubble of the demolished crypt of St. Lawrence Conventual Church, where thirty-five people had lost their lives during the January 16th attack. We trudged up to Victory Square, where we saw the ruins of the old historical Clock Tower, then turned to the right, towards the Inquisitor's Palace. There was not a soul in sight, a deadly hush! The only noises to be heard were coming from the direction of the dockyard. We had to go up and down mounds of debris which were blocking the roads. On the right-hand side, the Church of the Annunciation and the Dominican Friary had been completely destroyed.

My uncle muttered: "I don't think we shall be finding anything standing here." "It doesn't look as though there are any more buildings still standing," was my reply. We stopped by a bombed site and my uncle sadly acknowledged that that house was one of his properties. Nothing was left, except for debris and twisted beams. My attention was attracted by the mewing of a cat. It was on top of the debris, as thin as they come. The smell of dead animals and rotting food buried underneath the debris was something out of this world.

We then went to another street, if it could still be called so! Occasionally, we were startled by the noise of falling masonry from walls which seemed suspended in mid-air and which were collapsing at the slightest gust of wind. We were getting edgy at the slightest noise, in this dead silence. Again, suddenly, some dust and stones fell from a partly ruined building and we heard moaning. I moved closer to my uncle and asked him whether he had heard it too. He said that he had. Shortly afterwards, we saw a big, skinny dog, digging amongst the rubble, perhaps in search of some rat, as they were not rare in those days. They certainly did not go hungry with the happy hunting grounds in demolished buildings.

We did not find what we had crossed over to see, as everything had been demolished. That day, my uncle, who usually was an extrovert and a big talker, fell silent, when it dawned on him that all his property had been reduced to rubble.

Chapter VI

TRAGEDY IN ST. RITA STREET

Since the outbreak of hostilities, we had seen very few vessels berthed in Marsamxett Harbour. The last vessel to be berthed there was *H.M.S. Terror* which had later sailed for Tobruk, where it had gone to the bottom as a result of enemy action. Sometimes, a small minesweeper would sail into the harbour and then sail out again quickly. As Sliema Creek was empty of warships, the Germans were not wasting their bombs on this side of Valletta, but were concentrating their bombing on Grand Harbour and the aerodromes.

This situation lulled the people of Sliema into a false sense of security. During air raids, we now remained at home and, sometimes, some of us even ventured to walk out in the streets. Those who were working would carry on, ignoring the danger. Even at night-time, many remained asleep in their houses or else took to the streets and chatted with neighbours on their front door, as if they expected the bombs would give them time to take cover before exploding. It was also becoming very common to see groups of people outside the entrances of the shelters, thereby blocking the entrances and exits. Then, on hearing the slightest noise, they would rush to get inside. Some people died as a result of this over-confidence.

On 10th March, 1941 an old tanker that had been berthed at Ta' Xbiex Point before the war, was towed to Sliema Creek. It was a ship from the First World War that had never moved from Ta' Xbiex except occasionally, when towed to the dockyard, to be scraped from rust and barnacles. It formed part of the reserve fleet. This tanker, *Plumleaf*, had secured between two buoys, in front of the Nazzarene Church, near Tigne' sea front. On seeing this, the inhabitants of Sliema became quite perturbed as they feared that the Germans, who had left that side of the Island alone, would now attack this ship. The Germans were determined not to leave anything afloat. In our house, the orders of the day were: "Upon hearing the first sign of an air attack, everybody should rush to the friary without delay." Sure enough, the morning after the arrival of *Plumleaf*, we had a visit from the Luftwaffe. A Ju88, escorted by four Me109s, flew over Sliema at about 15,000 feet and then flew back out to sea. The guns of Fort Manoel and other anti-aircraft batteries engaged it for about ten minutes. I could see it clearly from the roof as the visibility was very good and I shouted down to my mother that she need not go to the shelter as this was merely a reconnaissance aircraft which had already turned tail and was heading for Sicily. When father came back from work, for lunch, we talked about this incursion and its probable consequences. I half expected the enemy to pay us a visit late in the afternoon, but they never did. I told father, "They will leave it until tomorrow once they have not come during the daylight hours."

At about 9.15 pm, the air raid signal sounded. In a jiffy, we were at the friary. There were more people than usual. Probably, nobody wanted to take any risks, now that the *Plumleaf* was berthed close by. Then there was the usual lull. Outside the friary, there were many adults and young men, some of whom were my friends. I joined them for a chat. We complained about the scarcity of shelters in Sliema, particularly rock shelters. Soon after Fr. Diego joined us. After much discussion and debate as to whether we should dig a rock shelter in the friary, he asked us to give him time to think about it and he would then come up with some idea of his own. Fr. Diego was very good with his hands and he could reproduce or copy whatever he saw. The walls of his cell, in the friary, were covered with all sorts of tools.

When Fr. Diego left us, I could hear the droning of aircraft approaching and I whispered to one of my friends; "I think Fr. Diego left us to go on the roof." One from the crowd around us shouted: "I can hear them approaching!"

The searchlights were tuned on and I could guess the likely course of the aircraft, even though they had not yet beamed on it. Soon after, the aircraft was illuminated in the searchlights' beams and I exclaimed: "There it is! They've got it!" This was the cry which we always uttered when we spotted an enemy aircraft in the sky.

I had barely uttered these words when we heard a terrible screech. "Falling bombs!" Somebody shouted! There was a general rush to the friary door and down the shelter which was already full of people. Somebody had tripped on the top of the steps and fallen down and this added to the confusion. When the explosion came, somebody panicked and tried to close the front door of the friary. I found myself face down on the ground with the crowd treading over me. The coat I was wearing was torn.

A man came running from the direction of Carmel Street and shouted that the bomb had probably fallen somewhere near Annunciation Square. More people, who had remained at home, started arriving when they heard the explosion but they could not enter the friary, as it was full up.

When the confusion had somewhat subsided, I managed to wriggle in and spotted Fr. Diego speaking to my father and other friends. I heard him say that the bomb had probably fallen at The Strand, as he was watching the aircraft that dropped it.

As it was not permitted to wander around outside during an air raid, I had to wait for the "raiders passed" signal before I could go and see where the bombs had fallen. When the signal was finally given, I asked father if I could go. He angrily replied, "Where do you want to go? There could be some other unexploded bomb around!"

But kind Fr. Diego intervened and told my father that he himself was going to take a look and that I could go along with him. Reluctantly, father joined us and we all hurried down to The Strand. In the darkness, we could hardly see anything coming down Prince of Wales Road but, on arriving at The Strand, we saw a crowd of people. I asked a man in the crowd what had happened and he sadly replied: "The bomb fell in St. Rita Street and there are many dead and wounded."

I tried to go into St. Rita Street but was promptly held back by a policeman who told me not to proceed any further as there are live electricity cables, dangling down or lying in the street. Few were the rescue workers who actually ventured into St. Rita Street. The first thing they had to do was to find out where these wires were. All one could see at the top of the street were the lights of electric torches and hurricane lamps which the rescuers were using. In the darkness, I could not see the demolished buildings or any other damage. I could only hear women crying hysterically, up the street.

Some men then tried to get through the police cordon and enter St. Rita Street, to find out what had happened to their relatives or their houses. The police had a hard task to keep them back and calm them down because all of them were beside themselves. A man, who was going up the road, was calling out to his relatives, desperately wanting to find out what had happened to them. After a while, we could not hear him anymore. He had trodden over or got entwined with one of the electricity cables lying on the ground and had been immediately electrocuted in the darkness and died on the spot. Poor man! He escaped the enemy bomb, only to die from electric shock!

I heard someone calling from where they were unearthing the victims: "We need a stretcher up here." This attracted the attention of onlookers. Some of the people awaiting news of their relatives who were missing moved in that direction. A woman, who was missing her son, started shouting and stamping her feet on the ground because she wanted to find out whether her son had been found or not. A few men tried to calm her down and keep her back.

An eight year old girl was crying and calling out to her missing father. After a while some rescue workers came down with a stretcher, carrying a casualty covered with a blanket. He appeared seriously injured. A man, who, up to that time, had appeared quite calm, suddenly shot off towards the casualty. He spoke to one of the stretcher bearers and the latter shone his torch on the face of the casualty. He tried desperately to make the casualty talk. Later I discovered that the casualty had been his brother but I cannot understand how he had recognised him as, from the little that I had seen, the casualty's face was covered in blood and caked dust and was unrecognisable.

I remained there for about an hour and a half looking on and, in the general confusion and in that darkness, I got separated from dad and Fr. Diego. When I returned home, I found father waiting at the door. He was quite angry because I had stayed out so late and also because, had there been another air-raid, I would have been caught outside the house. That would have worried them no end. Then father told me to go to the friary and spend the rest of the night there so that, if anything else happened, we would be ready for it. Mother stayed in the wooden shelter with my younger brother Victor, caressing his head, resting on her lap. My brother Joe and I lay down on the steps of the friary, nodding off, sleeping now and then. The only thing that I still remember well is that the following morning my back was aching terribly because of the cold I had felt throughout that night.

That morning, the majority of people who had spent the night together in the friary went down to the Sacro Cuor Church, for the early morning Mass, at 5.00 am. In those times, the friary was connected to the church by a tunnel that ran under the street. I do not remember how many Masses I served before daybreak. At first light, everybody started going back home. I had already had a bowl of coffee and a slice of bread from the friary because it was a custom that, after serving Mass, we would go up to the friary with the priest and share a small breakfast with him. Although foodstuffs had become pretty scarce by then and were rationed, the friars always gave us some of theirs.

As my parents were still in a panic on that day, they did not send us to school. So, after carrying the shelter stool back home, I went down to The Strand to see the damage caused by the bombing during the night. I could see that they were still looking for casualties buried under the debris in St. Rita Street. Of course, in daylight, the rescue workers could work better and with greater efficiency. The houses in the upper part of the street, particularly the right side, were completely demolished and there were many piles of rubble blocking it.

I could see some corpses on the pavement. These were covered with blankets awaiting transportation to the morgue in Floriana. Nobody was allowed to walk up the street except those who resided there and had had their houses bombed down, to be able to identify some trinkets or personal belongings which had been found. Whenever a victim was unearthed from below the debris, there was the inevitable anxious rush by members of his family, who happened to be close by.

Some of my young friends had died in that tragedy. When I asked about them at school, I was told that some of them had been buried under the demolished houses of St. Rita Street. I remember that I had made a resolution not to remain outside anymore during air raids. However, I never kept it, mainly because of the claustrophobic atmosphere of the shelter. I used to get a choking feeling and was terrified at hearing the least explosion when I was below ground.

A collection for those who had lost their houses and belongings was held in the Sacro Cuor Church and the parishioners responded generously. In all, twenty-five people had been killed and another thirty were wounded during that raid. The bomb in St. Rita Street remains etched in our memory as one of the biggest tragedies of the war in Sliema. Many blamed all this upon the *Plumleaf* and they clamoured that the authorities should never have moored the vessel in Sliema Creek.

PARACHUTE MINES

Sliema had not seen the last of its aerial mine attacks.

On the 31st May 1941, at about 8.30 pm, there was another air raid warning. As usual, we went up to seek shelter in the wooden refuge of the friary. Mother, my brothers and aunts entered the shelter and I remained at the entrance with father. He was talking to some of his friends about parish matters. Had everything been normal, at about that time, they would already have started to prepare for the *festa*, setting up decorations in the streets and organising the band marches and all the pomp and ceremony that went into the celebration of the feast of Our Lady of the Sacred Heart of Jesus.

For father, the church, the Sliema Band and the *festa* were everything. He was one of the founders of the Sliema Philharmonic Society. In normal circumstances, it would have been difficult to find my father at home, after working hours, on days preceding the feast. When mother needed him and sent me looking for him, I did not have to search far to find him. He would either be at the club, where he acted as secretary and at times, even as Vice President of its committee, or at the friary, where he was also the secretary of the committee responsible for the organisation of external festivities. Sometimes, I would find him on the church parvis, speaking to some of the monks and planning the organisation of the *festa*.

These, however, were now things of the past. Now the 'bangers' in the sky, came from anti-aircraft guns. We also had Chinese crackers but these came from machine-guns. The bigger bangers came from steel bombs which rained down from the sky, smashing and blowing up everything, burying and killing people under debris and tearing others up with splinters.

Before hostilities started, even young people took part in the setting-up of the street decorations. This was quite an exciting adventure, as our parents let us stay out late, sometimes even up to 2.00 am. We put up paper or wooden decorations, climbing on a mobile ladder with four wheels which we enjoyed pushing around the streets. We always had a crate of beer and one of lemonade handy as we joked and played pranks until somebody came out on a balcony and told us off because the fracas was not letting him sleep. Others used to welcome us, joked with us and gave us a glass of beer or lemonade and perhaps even a slice of cake. All these happy memories kept flashing before my mind's eye, while I was listening to father and his friends talking about past *festas*.

Through the main door of the friary, I overheard some men saying that they were hearing the sound of aircraft in the distance and that the searchlights had been turned on. I was about to go out and see for myself, when

81

Fr. Diego mischievously suggested that we should go on the roof, to get a better view. Downstairs, under the spiral staircase leading to the roof, we saw Fr. Felic, a rather old monk, who did not have the strength to go up and down the stairs to take cover in the shelter. He only took refuge under the staircase. Fr. Diego never went down into the shelter and I would always stick by him to keep him company, during air raids that happened to be in the vicinity of Sliema.

Before racing up to the roof, Fr. Diego told Fr. Felic that we were going up to see from which direction the aircraft were approaching and that then we would go down and tell him whether they appeared to be attacking our area. Fr. Felic mumbled something to himself and told us that we were risking our lives and that we were asking for trouble.

From the roof, we could see searchlights fingering the heavens, probing the sky above the entrance to Marsamxett Harbour. There was a slight breeze blowing from the East. The rumble of approaching aircraft could be heard very well, in the deadly silence. From the sound, we could tell that there was more then one aircraft and that they were flying in formation. Up to now, the guns had held their fire. The drone of these aircraft varied as if the aircraft engines were not properly synchronised or not revolving with the same power. This was an indication that there was more than one aircraft. The searchlights gradually converged over Tigne' Point.

Suddenly, in one of the searchlight cones, I could see a large parachute with a long object, looking very much like an oil drum, dangling underneath it. At once, the light anti-aircraft guns and machine guns opened fire at the parachute. I told Fr. Diego, "That's a mine and unless they hit it, the wind will blow it in this direction!"

Red balls of tracers from Bofors shells and other small calibre guns were now also going up towards the mine, which was slowly descending upon us, swinging from side to side. The rhythm of gunfire now reached a crescendo.

Another parachute appeared in the searchlight beams and then another. Now we had three mines above us, stacked on top of each other. I could see flashes of gunfire from the Fort Manoel battery which was frantically pumping up shells towards the mines. The first one was by now on top of us. A rain of shrapnel from exploding shells started coming down and Fr. Diego told me to take cover because it was obviously becoming too dangerous. Besides, he wanted to go down and give an account of what was happening to Fr. Felic. We flew down the steps. Downstairs, where Fr. Felic was taking cover, there was a little window. While Fr. Diego was describing to Fr. Felic what we had just seen, I remained glued to it, looking at the menacingly, approaching mine.

Initially, I could not see it well because the church dome was blocking my view. All I could see were the searchlights' beams and the Bofors' shells and machine-gun bullets racing up towards it. Then it appeared fleetingly between the church spires and the dome. I could not tell how high it was but, from what I could make out, it could not have been higher than 1,000 feet.

I pulled Fr. Diego to have a look at it himself. When he saw it, he warned Fr. Felic; "This is it Felic! It is coming down, right on the church!" Fr. Felic immediately started invoking Our Lady of the Sacred Heart to spare us and protect us from the looming menace. His prayers appeared to have been heard because suddenly, there was a big ball of fire in the sky, accompanied by a heavy explosion and a hot, strong blast that made everything tremble. The guns had managed to explode the mine in mid-air, before it landed on the town. Fr. Diego exclaimed; "The Madonna has spared us from one. Let's hope it will spare us from the others as well."

But the danger was not over yet. There were still two other mines dangling somewhere above us in the air, drifting down inexorably. Gradually, however, although we could not see the parachutes, from the direction of the tracers of Bofors' shells and machine-gun bullets and that of the searchlights' beams, we realised that the danger was over and that the mines had drifted past us. A sudden, huge explosion, like the previous one, but with a much weaker blast, that still made the ground shake, made Fr. Diego exclaim: "This must have landed on the ground and quite close too!"

We waited for the third explosion and braced ourselves, but it never came. We thought that the wind must have carried the mine towards St. Julian's Bay and that it had ended up in the sea.

After about twelve minutes of continuous, deafening gunfire and terrible tension, everything was ominously quiet. Except for the murmur of a few voices outside, in front of the friary, there was a deadly hush. Fr. Diego and I again went down into the shelter. There we found many terrified women with children clinging to them, while the men were doing their best to calm them down.

Father told us that when the first mine, that is the one that was hit in mid-air exploded, the main door of the friary had burst open and some glass panes had been shattered by the blast. At first, people thought that the mine had landed on the friary and there was great panic.

The second explosion had terrified everybody, especially old people, when they felt the ground tremble, so much so, that some had even passed out. Naturally, nobody inside the shelter knew what was happening outside. Had they seen the mine dangling down, heading towards the church, they would surely have panicked even more.

The distant sirens sounded the "raiders passed" but the one on the Sliema Police Station, at the top of Prince of Wales Road, remained strangely silent. More than twenty minutes had passed since gunfire had ceased, when Swetu, the special constable, wearing his steel helmet, came along and told us that the mine had landed on the new school of the Franciscan Nuns, St. Elizabeth School, in St. James Street. He also informed us that all the buildings in the block between St. James Street, Saviour Street, Prince of Wales Road and Rudolphe Street had been destroyed. However, as everybody had taken cover, there were no casualties. In fact, the mine had exploded, even before it landed on the ground and it was thought that it had been hit by rifle fire!

When we asked the special constable why the siren had not sounded the "raiders passed" signal, he told us that the electricity supply had been cut and that, for the moment, nobody could leave the shelter because in the garden of Villa Portelli, on top of Savoy Hill, there was still a huge, unexploded mine hanging from the trees. Until dawn, nobody was allowed to leave the shelter. The police gave instructions that all windows and doors should be left open, until the Bomb Disposal Squad defused the mine. People were only allowed to leave the shelter at first light. The mine was neutralised at about 10.00 am and the danger was finally over.

As the Protection Office, where my father worked, was opposite the Holy Trinity Anglican Church, I accompanied him there to take a closer look at the mine which had fallen in the garden of nearby Villa Portelli. With the help of a friendly police officer, I managed to get close enough to see it. It was about twelve feet long; aluminium grey in colour and it had a fuse half way between the head and the tail, where I could see the parachute lines attached to it. The parachute was of a bluish-green colour and it was still entangled in the boughs of the trees around the villa. There was a large hole where the mine had bounced in the driveway. I thought that the mine must have been a faulty one because, on hitting the ground with such force that it caused a dent on the mine's head, it was bound to explode. We knew all too well how sensitive the fuses of such mines were. Had it exploded, nothing would have been left of Villa Portelli, the Savoy Hotel and the surrounding buildings.

This type of magnetic mine weighed 1,800 lbs, of which 1,500 lbs were T.N.T explosive. Other mines had fallen in the sea off Għar id-Dud and on Fort Manoel. Sliema had had a stroke of good luck that day because, had the three mines landed and exploded on the ground, there would have been total destruction and also many deaths, particularly as there were not enough rock shelters and the wooden shelters were certainly not strong enough to take the blast from such mines. The damage would have been enormous because, if the first mine had not been exploded in mid-air, it would have certainly landed on the Church of Our Lady of the Sacred Heart. Together with the one that fell on St. Elizabeth School and that on Villa Portelli, which were eight hundred yards apart, the cumulative blast would have been even more devastating, because most buildings would already have been damaged by previous explosions.

The 31st May, is the day dedicated to Our Lady of the Sacred Heart.

Chapter VII

A SEABORNE ATTACK

On Saturday, 26th July 1941, at about four in the morning, we were in the shelter in Prince of Wales Road. Although the air raid warning signal had been given earlier, everything was quiet and there was no gunfire. It was one of those alerts where nothing seemed to happen. These were laid on simply for nuisance value - they tired out people and lowered their morale, creating physical and mental exhaustion. Sometimes, air raid warning signals were given at 7.00 pm and would remain in effect throughout the whole night, till 8.00 am the following morning. Women, children and older people took cover in the shelters and spent the entire night there. Some men, especially those who had a day's work ahead of them, would pluck up courage and sleep at home; they would only go down to the shelter when they heard gunfire. It was not unusual to see men racing for the shelter in their under-pants or pyjamas, like lost souls, and this scene would invariably be accompanied by wolf whistles, comments and other unpleasant noises, from those already inside the shelters. We had a good laugh whenever these men ran down into the shelter in various states of undress and only realised this when they got down there and stood there in front of a gaggle of wide-eyed women.

Sometimes, one or two women would also pluck up courage and leave the shelter and come back with some hot coffee and something to eat for their children or parents, or some warm milk for baby. Mother was quite organised for this eventuality and the first thing she did, in the evening, was to prepare a thermos flask full of coffee and to pack some food in her basket, in case of emergency.

That night, I left the shelter to go out for a breath of fresh air, after having slept for a while. I stopped near the entrance of the shelter for a chat and then a couple of friends of mine and I decided to go for a stroll down to The Strand. We walked down in pitch darkness and came to the bottom of St. Rita Street. Without wanting to, I looked up that street and sadly thought of what I had seen some weeks earlier, remembering the victims of the attack, particularly the ones I knew personally. We arrived at Villa Drago in Tower Road, where Vincent, one of my friends, murmured that he was hearing a noise similar to that of aircraft engines, a sound to which, by now, we had grown accustomed. Gradually, we became aware that the noise was coming from the direction of the sea. I surmised that one of our torpedo boats was probably cruising past. We walked towards Għar id-Dud. The siren sounded the "all clear" and we decided to walk back through Għar id-Dud Street.

It was now about 4.45 am. We had almost arrived near the Chalet pier, when there was what felt like a minor earthquake, followed by an explosion which seemed to come from the direction of the entrance to Grand Harbour. The searchlights of the coastal forts were lit. One of them shone from the old Sliema Point Battery close by and this was immediately followed by gunfire in a seaward direction. We glimpsed a small object racing on the surface of the water, illuminated by searchlights. At first, we thought this was some practice shoot because before the war, there had often been such shoots on small targets, towed by motor launches. However, that explosion soon caused us to think otherwise. Suddenly, a column of flame and smoke rose to the sky from the spot where we had last seen that object. Then, other larger objects were caught in the searchlights.

We were approached by two British soldiers who warned us to take cover because there was danger at hand but we did not want to miss out on such a big spectacle. Without questioning their advice, we went and hid in a veranda of a nearby building.

The guns of Fort St. Elmo, Fort Ricasoli and Fort Tigne' were firing incessantly on what appeared to be speed boats and larger vessels. We could trace the fall of shot from the tracer of the shells and, when these hit the water, they ricocheted into the air. When they hit one of the targets, a column of fire immediately went up into the air, followed by a huge explosion.

The objects we had seen were Italian Explosive Motor Boats (E.M.B.) or *"Barchini"* as they were known by the Italians and Motor Torpedo Boats (M.A.S.). The E.M.B.'s were like modern speed boats with a top speed of thirty knots, powered by an Alfa Romeo 2,500cc engine. The bow was laden with 300 kg of high explosive. The pilot sat on the stern and steered the E.M.B. The pilot's seat detached itself from the boat when it was close to the target. The pilot then climbed on to the buoyant seat, thereby cushioning his body from the shock-wave of the underwater explosion, which would be lethal to any person caught in the waters near the target. The Explosive Motor Boat could be used in two manners: either by exploding on hitting the target or else by breaking up in two, with the explosive sinking to the bottom, under the vessel and exploding beneath it. The latter was known as hydrostatic detonation. Each one of these E.M.B.'s caught in the searchlight beams, was being methodically blown up by the shells of the coastal guns. The Royal Malta Artillery gunners had, by that time, acquired a great reputation for their skill and precision in gunnery, both on coastal and anti-aircraft guns. The engagement lasted not more than six minutes in all.

Up to that night, there had been an iron bridge spanning the gap between St. Elmo Point and the break-water. Today, only one of the supporting columns remains in the centre of the gap where this bridge once stood. The harbours were blocked by a boom defence net. One of these booms sealed off the entrance to Grand Harbour, from Ricasoli Point to a place called "Taħt iż-Żiemel", near St. Elmo and another stretched between Fort St. Angelo and Senglea Point. Another boom sealed Marsamxett Harbour, between Tigne` Point and Valletta below St. Paul's Anglican Cathedral, with another between Lazzarett Creek and Ta' Xbiex Point, protecting the submarine base. Two other boom defence nets lay between Delimara and Benghajsa Points, protecting the R.A.F. Seaplane Base at Kalafrana and Marsaxlokk Bay and yet another one was at St. Paul's Bay.

These booms were intended to stop the enemy from penetrating into the harbours with surface or underwater craft. They were also meant to block any torpedo fired in the direction of the harbours from the open sea. Hanging from the spans of the breakwater bridge, were two nets, one from each span. They were unlike the others which were suspended from small buoys and could be opened to permit vessels to enter or leave the harbour. The nets were made from hoops of steel wire and extended to the bottom of the sea.

The plan for the E-Boats attack, which we had just witnessed, was that the sloop *Diana* would lead the E.M.B.'s to a point off Grand Harbour. M.A.S. 452 would then accompany them to five miles out and wait there for the results of the raid. M.A.S. 451 would tow two M.T.L.'s - electric powered boats - carrying two S.L.C. - human torpedoes - and their crewmen on board to five miles off the coast and from this launching point they would then proceed on their own power. It was planned that S.L.C. No. 1, piloted by Maggiore Teseo Tessei, had first to blow up part of the boom hanging from the breakwater bridge with explosives, in order to gain access into the harbour. The net was to be blown at 4.25 am. From there, they could speed in and attack ships that had arrived in harbour the previous day. The first explosion we had heard was that which was meant to give the attackers access into Grand Harbour and enable them to attack the ships with the E.M.B.'s. At the same time S.L.C. No. 2 would enter Marsamxett Harbour and attack the submarine base at Lazzaerett Creek.

The boats, from the Italian Navy's 10th Light Flotilla, arrived off Malta before midnight on 25th July and were sent off on their mission at 2.00 am the following morning, twenty miles north of Malta. Today, it is known that British Intelligence intercepted secret enemy messages about enemy shipping and aircraft movements, through the highly secret deciphering machine, called "Ultra", which was installed and kept closely guarded at the Lascaris War Rooms. One of these intercepted secret messages hinted at a possible seaborne attack on the Island. These messages were passed on to the Governor of Malta, the Vice-Admiral and the Air Officer Commanding Malta who had, in turn, ordered all coastal gunners to stand by and sleep by their guns. When Malta's radar, probably No. 502 A.M.E.S. at Fort Madliena, showed the flotilla on the screen, Malta's defence was brought to full alert.

The S.L.C. "Human Torpedoes", which the Italians called *"Maiali"*, were special torpedoes, guided by two frogmen sitting in tandem. These S.L.C.'s were carried on a larger vessel, generally a submarine. In this operation they were carried aboard M.T.L. electric-powered boats and then lowered into the sea, at a point, not far off from where the attack would take place. They would then be steered by the frogmen with their heads just above the water.

On approaching the target, the frogmen submerged the torpedo to the bottom to avoid detection. One of them would detach the explosive head of the weapon and either attach it to the vessel being attacked or place it on the seabed, where the sea was not too deep. After setting the fuse for the explosion, the pilot and his assistant would board the remaining part of the human torpedo and make off.

One of these S.L.C.'s was to blow up the boom hanging from the break-water bridge, so that the E.M.B.'s could enter Grand Harbour. The diverting air-raid came fifteen minutes late and when an explosion was heard at 4.25 am it was assumed that it was Major Tessei's S.L.C. In fact, it was caused by the bombing. When the E.M.B.'s approached the net, they found it intact, Sub Lieutenant Carlo Bosio charged the explosive and lept out, the boat hit the net and failed to explode. Another E.M.B. was aimed at the net but hit the wall of the breakwater and blew up, with the pilot still on board. This was to be the plan's undoing because the explosion was too strong and brought down half of the bridge which then completely blocked the entrance. It is thought that the explosion was premature. The commander of the operation, Major Teseo Tessei, lost his life in this first explosion.

Immediately after this first detonation, the searchlights were switched on and the order was given to the guns to open fire. An outright massacre ensued as the E.M.B.'s were blown out of the water, one by one. The M.A.S. boats and the larger ship, the *Diana*, which served as the headquarters ship of the operation, turned tail to escape from that inferno. However, they did not get too far before they were intercepted by R.A.F. Hurricanes of No.185 and 126 Squadrons, which strafed them on their way to Sicily and sank most of them. A 126 Squadron pilot reported that he attacked and sank M.A.S. 451. One M.A.S. boat was left badly damaged by 185 Squadron Hurricanes and could not return to her base. Only the *Diana*, which stayed out of range of the coastal guns, managed to reach her base to tell the tale of this shattering defeat. Two other E.M.B.'s were abandoned and captured intact. Seventeen Italian officers and men lost their lives in this operation and another fifteen were taken prisoners.

A unique and interesting incident in the history of the Royal Air Force happened when Pilot Officer W. Winton of No. 185 Squadron was flying a Hurricane in the counter-attack on the E-Boats. His aircraft's engine failed suddenly due to over heating as the coolant reservoir was damaged by return fire. Pilot Officer Winton had to bale out of his Hurricane and take to his parachute. He came down in the sea close by a M.A.S. Boat, No. 452. Winton paddled his rubber dinghy towards the M.A.S. boat and managed to board her. Everything was still and there was no sign of life. The eight members of her crew were dead. He tried to start the engines to no avail. As he could not tell whether he would be rescued by the Italians or the British or whether he would be finished off by his colleagues, he lowered the Italian ensign which was still flying on the yardarm, to half mast hoping that no side would fire at him. After about six hours, an R.A.F. Air Sea Rescue launch came alongside and towed him back to Malta, together with his prize. He thus became the first R.A.F. pilot to capture an enemy naval vessel single-handed.

By the time the spectacle was over, the first streaks of dawn could be seen in the East. Those who came up to Għar id-Dud, saw nothing except for wisps of smoke, rising from the water from some of the E.M.B. wrecks which were still burning. The attack had not lasted long and had my friends and I not decided to take that short stroll to Għar id-Dud, I would have missed witnessing one of the most dramatic local episodes of the war. There was a lot of praise for the gunners of the Royal Malta Artillery and for their accurate gunfire as well as for the courage shown by the Italians. In those days, it was not very common to praise the Italians, as they were disparagingly referred to as the "mamma mia" boys by most Maltese.

I overheard one of the soldiers, who had just come from Fort Spinola, telling a fellow soldier that they had spotted some unidentified objects on the water near Dragonara Point. These were probably survivors from the E.M.B.'s who were swimming towards St. George's Bay. On hearing this, as was to be expected, my friends and I dashed off to St. George's Bay, not to miss out on anything. There, we found a group of soldiers, armed with rifles, escorting two men in a very strange outfit, which was very tight and even covered their heads. When they removed the head-gear, we noticed that this outfit was made of an elastic material. They removed a kind of shoe in the shape of a frog's leg from their feet. They carried two large cylinders on their back connected to a face mask by a pipe. Of course, we had never seen anything like this before and it seemed, as though, we were looking at extra-terrestrials, from outer space. On asking one of the English corporals who these two men were, he confirmed that they were two Italian prisoners from the E.M.B.'s who had come ashore when their vessel had sunk. One was Tenente di Vascello Francesco Costa and the other Sergente Palombaro Luigi Barla. The two prisoners were taken away to the prisoner-of-war camp at St. Andrew's.

After this attack, which was quite innovative in its tactical approach, the authorities started taking stronger precautions against submarines and frogmen who might attempt some other similar attack.

The boom defence was doubled and another one was placed behind it. With the onset of darkness, roughly at fifteen minute intervals, depth charges would be set off

*3.7 inch anti-aircraft gun, covered with camouflage netting at Ta'
Giorni Battery.*

*3.7 inch anti-aircraft guns at Fort Tignè, engaging enemy
aircraft.*

Bagpipers of the Royal Irish Fusiliers near St Julian's Tower.

The attack on H.M.S. Illustrious on Thursday, 16 January, 1941.

An attack on Spinola Battery – the present site of Portomaso – St Gregory's Church in the foreground.

4.5 inch anti-aircraft gun destroyed by a direct hit on Spinola Battery.

Housewives queing for water.

Housewives crowding around a street hawker selling vegetables in Rudolphe Street, Sliema, 1941.

A pharmacy in Prince of Wales Road damaged by the mine that fell on St. Elizabeth School on 31 May, 1941.

The unexploded mine that fell in the garden of Villa Portelli in Savoy Hill during the same air raid.

St Elizabeth School demolished by a parachute mine on 31 May 1941.

Queing for bread in Valletta.

Bombs exploding on Fort Manoel and Tal-Qroqq A/A Battery in the background and in the sea on 1 November 1941, while the author was fishing on a dinghy in Sliema Creek.

People salvaging whatever they could recover out of their bombed houses in St. Rita Street, Sliema, after the air raid of 11 March 1941.

Bombed buildings at Qui-Si-Sana.

The Carlton Theatre at The Strand, Sliema.

Searchlights, tracer bullets and Bofors' shells illuminate the sky at dawn during an air raid on Sliema.

The pill-box situated at Qui-Si-Sana, which was demolished in the 1950's.

The boom defence vessel "Moor", which struck a mine and sank in Grand Harbour on 8 April 1941. From a crew of twenty only one survived.

The Submarine Base, HMS Talbot in Lazzarett Creek.

Service personnel and policemen building aircraft pens on an airfield, winter, 1942.

The Gaiety Theatre destroyed by a bomb on 7 February, 1942.

The destruction in Prince of Wales Road; between Prince of Wales Junction and Prince Albert Street, on the 7 March, 1942.

The devastation caused by the bomb that fell near Sliema Police Station on 17 March, 1942.

S.S. Talabot on fire in Grand Harbour, after the air raid of 26 March, 1942.

S.S. Pampas on fire in Grand Harbour, after the same raid of 26 March, 1942.

Amazon, Mary Ellul (known as Mary Man) member of the Sliema ARP, during rescue work in St. Trophimus Street, Sliema.

Damage left by German bombs which fell on Stella Maris Church, Sliema, 1942.

The passenger ferry sunk at The Strand in Sliema during the same raid.

underwater. These were weapons used against submarines. An explosion from one of these charges would be enough to crush the hull of a submarine, even if it was not a direct hit. One can only imagine what it would do to a swimmer under water!

As the entrances to the harbours were narrow, they were ideal for this sort of defensive precaution and these depth charges were fired from the shore. When they were dropped into the water, we could only hear a muffled explosion. If we happened to be at home, we could feel the ground tremble like in a mild earthquake. If we were underground, in a shelter, besides the trembling of the ground, we would also feel a gigantic thud, reverberating along the walls of the shelter. This tremor used to be felt, at intervals, all night long, until dawn. Those who slept lightly, like old people and children, were quite harassed by this new form of defence. However, one becomes accustomed to everything in this world. Gradually, as we got used to bombs, gunfire, life in the dampness of the shelters and lack of food, even these depth charges became part of everyday life.

Chapter VIII

SEARCHED FOR "SPYING"!

T he devil is always ready to stir up trouble! I have always been very keen on music, both contemporary and classical music. To this very day, in my leisure time, I still like to listen to a piece of good music.

On the 31st November 1941, in the afternoon, after a morning of air raids, one of which had concentrated on Fort Manoel, I had gone fishing with my friend Paul, who had a little dinghy. We moored to a buoy, baited our hooks and cast off our lines. We had caught a few fishes when, suddenly, we heard orders barked out from Fort Manoel and I saw the anti-aircraft guns being elevated towards the sky. This was unusual, because these guns were kept in a horizontal position so long as there was no air raid warning.

Without any warning from the siren, the guns opened fire and, on looking up, I spotted two Junkers 88s diving in our direction and releasing four bombs each. Paul grabbed the oars and as I was sitting in the bow of the boat, I turned to cut off the mooring rope of the dinghy with a penknife we used to cut up the bait. Paul started rowing away as strongly as he could before I could join him at the oars. We could not move fast enough! Two of the bombs fell into the sea about two hundred yards away and as they exploded, we felt the dinghy almost breaking up with the force of the shock waves in the water. Two columns of water mixed with black smoke shot up to the sky. Two other bombs fell on the rocks outside Fort Manoel and stones and splinters started raining down on us. A few stones also fell inside the dinghy.

We heard two other bombs exploding inside the Fort and one of the anti-aircraft guns was hit. It was a sight to remember. I was looking directly at the Fort whilst I was rowing away from it. The other two remaining bombs fell in the water on the Lazzarett side of the Fort, close to the submarine base.

Paul, who was terrified, turned quite pale and I thought he would faint any minute. From that day onwards, we never went fishing in the fairway again and always stayed close inshore.

That evening, after our dreadful experience on the water which I kept secret from my mother and father, I stayed at home. After finishing my homework, I turned on the radio and tuned in to a station which was playing music by Wagner and Beethoven. After about half an hour, the music programme came to an end and I heard a nasal voice say in English, "Germany calling.... Germany calling...." After a great deal of propaganda, which passed for news, the voice started reading out some messages. Among the information coming from the station, there was a part intended for the Maltese people. The voice said that it would be far better for us to surrender because, if we continued to fight, our small country would soon be reduced to rubble. It went on to say that, because of a handful of British soldiers stationed here, we were fast losing our relatives. The voice droned on saying that we had no hope of winning because the war was already lost as far as we were concerned and that we would starve because all the ships bound for Malta were being sunk and any supplies making it to port would be consumed by British soldiers. This useless chatter went on for ever, so much so that, after a while, I got fed up listening and tuned in to another station which was playing music. It was the first and last time that I had listened to 'Lord Haw Haw', whose real name was William Joyce.

The following morning, around 9.00 am, the doorbell rang and I went to see who it was. There were three men who asked after my father. I let them in, asked them to wait in the sitting room and went to call father. Some ten minutes later, father called me and asked me whether the previous evening I had been listening to the radio. I replied that I had. One of the men asked me what I had been listening to and I replied that I had tuned into a programme of classical music and that when this programme came to an end, there was an English announcer, to whom I continued to listen for a while, out of sheer curiosity. I also told him that this announcer had irked me with what he was saying, so much so, that soon after, I had tuned into another station.

After talking in whispers amongst themselves for a while, the man who had put questions to me, informed me that they were two police officers and that the other gentleman, an Englishman, was an Officer in the Intelligence Service

My father did not utter a word and on learning this, I froze. I thought to myself; "Surely I have done nothing wrong by listening to the radio, have I?" The British officer sternly warned me not to listen to that station ever again and then asked me to leave the room. I went straight into the garden and avoided my mother so that she would not ask me who those men were and bombard me with a series of questions. A short while later, I saw them leave the living room and enter into my father's study. I could see them turning over the contents of drawers, opening correspondence files and looking very closely at papers which were on my father's desk. From where I stood in the garden and through the study window, I could see that they were going with a tooth-comb through whatever was on the desk - the same desk on which I am now penning this account. I was tempted to again go down to my father's study, to see what exactly they were up to, but I decided not to. They searched other rooms and after about an hour, came down again. I was in the entrance hall and the officer who had spoken to me before and who seemed to be the senior one, tapped on my shoulders, warned me again not to listen to that station and apologised to my father. It appeared that, in the meantime, they had become quite chummy because they were on first-name terms, when bidding good-bye to my father.

Now I was in for it! Father called me and sternly asked, "What are you trying to do to us? Do you want to ruin us? Do you know that they have searched the whole house?" I asked him what they had been looking for. He replied, "A transmitter, because they thought that we were some sort of spies. See that you do not do anything of the sort again, because I do not want to find myself

101

locked up in Villa Portelli!" Villa Portelli which is situated at the top of Rue D'Argens, on Savoy Hill, was, in those days, used as a place for the detention of political internees. These internees had been kept in Tas-Salvatur Fort, in the Cottonera, when they had first been rounded up, in May 1940. On 7th July 1940, the Fort was bombed. Luckily, no one of the ninety internees was hurt. Because of the extensive damage, they were moved to the Corradino Civil Prisons at Paola on the same day. Following protests that the prison was crowded, conditions were bad and that they were not criminals but political internees; and that, if anything, they should be treated as prisoners of war, the Governor decided that they could choose either the Prison or Fort San Salvatore. They were also informed that all schools, convents and institutes were all occupied and there was nowhere else for them to be detained. Dr Herbert Ganado, one of the internees, suggested the newly built Monastery of St. Agatha at Rabat which was still empty. Dr. Ganado sent a letter through Major Orlino Briffa De Piro and this was delivered by hand to Monsignor Albert Pantalleresco, who was the director of St. Agatha. The latter petitioned Archbishop Dom. Maurus Caruana to give his consent for these internees to be transferred to St. Agatha's. The Archbishop agreed. Three days later, Mons. Pantalleresco himself was interned! Subsequently, they were again moved to Villa Portelli, in Sliema and from there, on 12th February 1942, forty-eight internees would eventually be deported to Uganda. I remember that amongst them, there was a lawyer, Dr. Giovanni Sammut, who had been a very close friend of my father. When, together with the others, he was deported, his wife died of grief. Among these internees there were also Dr. Enrico Mizzi, Malta's second post-war Prime Minister and Sir Arturo Mercieca, the Chief Justice.

Coming back to my story, father appeared greatly disturbed and mother even more so. When we all had somewhat calmed down again, I asked father how these officers had come to know that I had been listening to that radio station. Father replied that, according to what he had been told by the Inspector, somebody, probably a special constable, had overheard me listening to that station from the street, directly below the window and had gone to report that I had been listening to Lord Haw Haw.

These were difficult times and one had to be very careful what to say and what to listen to on the radio because there were always people ready to misinterpret what you had said. It was easy to land yourself in serious trouble over such matters. For example, if you saw a British aircraft being shot down and told somebody that a British aircraft had crashed, you could find some clever fellow who would think that you were spreading propaganda and he would go off to report it to the authorities. I know of cases where people were interned for the simple reason that they loved Italian literature. I know of other cases where someone wanted to take somebody else's job and would conveniently label him pro-Italian. In fact, father could have become a victim to one such rumour, had it not been for his Head of Department, who knew him well and who ignored what he had been told. Had this not been the case, father would probably, have lost the job which after a long interval of unemployment, he had finally managed to get. Who knows? Perhaps the house search we had been subjected to, had been inspired by similar motives?

Another somewhat similar incident occurred on the
25th July 1941. I happened to be at The Strand, in Sliema
with my Uncle Zuz in a crowd of people, watching a
dogfight between Italian and British fighters. No bombs
were falling close by, as the main attack was over Hal
Far, very far from where we were. The crowd was taken
up with watching the spectacle in the air above us. At
one point, we heard the whine of a crashing aircraft. It
was a Macchi MC 200, spinning down to earth. A moment later, the pilot baled out and took to his parachute.
Everybody started clapping, including a priest who was
standing nearby. The Macchi crashed down among ruined buildings, close by the Church of St. Francis in
Kingsway, Valletta, which had already been demolished
during an air raid. It seemed that everybody had been
concentrating on the enemy aeroplane and not on the
unfortunate pilot whose parachute had streamed and
failed to open. It was a horrible scene which I still
remember vividly to this day.

My uncle turned to the priest, who was still clapping,
at seeing the enemy aircraft crash and told him that, he
had better do his priestly duty with that pilot, rather than
go on clapping. That evening, we again had a visit by the
police, who warned my uncle to be careful about what to
say!

Chapter IX

UNDERGROUND

Complaints about the shortage of deep-rock shelters in Sliema were on the increase, particularly after the bombing of St. Rita Street and the parachute mines that had come down on the town.

The day the bombs fell in St. Rita Street, we had left Fr. Diego pondering what could be done to dig a shelter in the living rock. When we met him again in the friary, Fr. Diego suggested that a shelter should be dug in the rock under the friary itself. Miners for the digging of shelters were not to be found easily, because they had plenty of work with the Civil Government and the Military Authorities. Fr. Diego asked whether there were any volunteers among us and he promised to provide the tools himself.

The first part of the operation consisted in the emptying of water from a bell-shaped well. This well was at the site where the spiral staircase, leading down from the friary to the sacristy, is found today. Luckily, we found that there were not more than fifteen inches of water at the bottom of the well and in a day we managed to empty it completely, using buckets and a human chain.

The next step was to dredge the sediment at the bottom. Nenu, who was always the first volunteer for such jobs, was lowered down into the well, tied from the waist to a rope. We provided him with some light from an electricity bulb, to make it easy for him to see what he was doing. When he felt his feet touch the bottom, he shouted out: "OK! Let go.... let go..." We loosened the rope and at once heard Nenu yelling, "Pull me up...Pull me up. I am up to my knees in muck!" After leaving him down there for a few minutes, we hauled him up. I do not recollect Nenu ever using the colourful language that came up from the well, on that occasion.

We had set up a jib at the top of the well. It was made of three beams, a pulley, a rope and two baskets, one on each end, acting as counter weights. We had thrown some large stones inside the well and placed planks on top of them so that people going down would not share Nenu's fate and sink in the sediment. Most of the time, volunteers of all ages were working down this well or at the top. Those down the well loaded the sediment into the baskets and the others at the top, hauled it up. The material was then carted outside. After the first day's work, most of us, particularly those who were working on the ropes, woke up to find our hands full of blisters. For us youngsters, this was a new sport and we vied with each other in hauling up the baskets faster.

In two days, the well had been cleared of all the sediment and we were all set to start digging into the living rock. Fr. Diego had provided us with pickaxes, jemmies and a large, iron hammer, so we all got down to the work. We were so keen that very often we would quarrel about whose turn it was to have a go at the pickaxes. Little by little, the rock was being excavated. First, we would cut two trenches on either side and then another one on top, from one side to the other, about eight feet high and five feet apart. Then we would start cutting the rock in between and every bit that was chipped off would be hauled up the well and carted outside, right away. Another entrance was being dug in the tunnel which connected the friary with the church.

When a good part of the work had been completed and the shelter started taking shape, we even used small explosive charges, also provided by Fr. Diego, to speed up the work. After the blisters, we now had corns on our hands, made by the handles of the pickaxes. Some of us also got hurt in the process. Once, while digging a trench with a pickaxe, I crushed my middle right hand finger against the rocks and later I lost my finger nail.

Shortly after work had commenced on our shelter, another shelter started being excavated in Prince of Wales Road, at the corner with St. Joseph Street. There was a huge reservoir and the workers had spent whole days emptying it from the large volume of water inside it, using motor pumps. Then, they also had to take out the sediment that had gathered through the ages. Finally, this reservoir was roofed over with reinforced concrete and was divided by double walls into four compartments, measuring approximately twenty feet by fifteen feet. On top of these compartments, there was a concrete slab of about four feet in thickness. On top of that, a six - foot layer of debris, covered by another four feet of concrete and the latter was, in turn, covered with a large quantity of debris that lay under the road. This reservoir extended through the middle of Prince of

Wales Road between St. Joseph Street and St. Mary Street. Had it been hit by a bomb, it would have been strong enough to withstand it. In fact, this shelter was considered to be one of the safest. Eventually, more excavation into the rock was carried out, leading to another entrance in St. Mary Street. This shelter ended up having five entrances.

Until the friary shelter had been completed and as the shelter in Prince of Wales Road now had an entrance in the corner with St. Mary Street, our family started taking refuge there. Whoever had a well in his house and for some reason was not using it, they reinforced its roof and used it as a shelter for their family. Mr. Guze' Azzopardi had an empty reservoir and converted it into a shelter. He and his family used to sleep down there at night. Eventually they connected it to the large shelter in Prince of Wales Road.

Sur Guze' was a close friend of my father and he invited us to spend nights in his shelter. My father promptly accepted the offer and thanked him. We took some bedding which we could spare at home, down into this shelter. As this shelter was not strong enough against German bombs, we used to go and sleep there only to avoid the cold of winter. Whenever there was an air raid, we soon got to know because we heard people going down into the larger shelter. Some other families who were friends of Sur Guze' also started making use of this shelter. Looking back, it is amazing how war removed all inhibitions. Everybody slept in one room fully clothed; men, women, children, girls and boys. I remember there were four old women, who were not very prepossessing, sleeping down this shelter. Once, when gunfire could be heard outside, someone muttered: "It seems they are coming down for us." A man quipped, "If the Germans had to come down here, they would run out again, the moment they set eyes on them!" Whenever one of us appeared on the verge of panic, particularly the older folk, someone often cracked a joke or told some funny story, trying to boost their morale again.

I only went down into this shelter to sleep because as long as there was no gunfire, I used the bigger shelter. During these night-long raids, I stayed with my small group of friends, in a corner, near the entrance. One of us played the accordion and one of his sisters loved to sing. Sometimes we would form a chorus and hum some popular sing-along. There was also one fellow, who was very good in telling jokes and many adults used to stop by and encourage us. There were also some wet blankets, who would complain that they could not go to sleep and grumbled that it was not a time for jokes. They chided us, saying it would be better if we said our prayers instead.

Prayers were also said, of course, especially when bombs were raining down! Very often when there was a heavy air raid and when gunfire was very intense, imprecations, interspersed with comments, would echo through the shelter: "Hail Mary.... My God that was close!!! Full of Grace....these bombs are coming down on us!!!" The rest of the prayers would be punctuated by interjections, consisting of a running commentary on the intensity of the attack. When there was no gunfire, prayers were said with greater devotion and decorum, while everybody tried to concentrate on what he was saying. There were special prayers for those times and I remember that the Saints we sometimes invoked were complete strangers to my own Litany of Saints.

One or two people insisted on being the ones to lead the prayers when reciting the Rosary as though they had a God-given right to do so. Up to the recitation of the Holy Litany, everything ran smoothly. In those days, the Litany was said in Latin and more often than not, a massacre of this classical language followed. As I used to serve Mass and sing in the children's choir at church and as the monks were very particular on the pronunciation of Latin, I used to be the first to spot some howler and burst out laughing. Very often, I had to slip away not to be scolded by my parents. In some shelters, they taught young boys and girls religious doctrine, in preparation for their first Holy Communion. During Lent, spiritual exercises or sermons were also delivered to those gathered there.

The large shelter of Prince of Wales Road was unlike the other shelters, in that it was not excavated in the living rock, except for the part that connected it with the entrance at St. Mary Street. As I have already said, it was divided into four compartments and each compartment had wooden benches laid around the four walls. It was also well lit by electric bulbs. All those, who used it, had their own reserved seat. Older people had priority to sit on the benches so that they would not have to carry chairs or stools down to the shelter. The same applied to women with babies or very young children. These could leave their chairs in the shelter. Whenever one wanted to find somebody in the shelter, it was usually very easy to do so as everybody kept his place. We all got to know each other very well and we were like one family. I do not recollect that there ever was any friction. On the contrary, there was a courteous harmony. Women always helped each other with their children, especially if they had very young ones, particularly, at night. Even men and teenagers used to have little children sleeping on their laps during the night.

Although the shelter was well illuminated, everybody brought down a candle or a small oil lamp and the odd funeral-procession lamp. It was not unusual for the electricity supply to fail, especially when bombs fell close by and severed electric cables. When the shelter was full, it got rather stuffy and when the light failed and the people lit their candles or oil lamps, it became even stuffier, as oxygen was burned up at a quicker rate. Whenever we used to blow our noses, our handkerchiefs turned rather black. It was very damp down there and water always dripped down the walls. After spending a whole night in the shelter, the following morning our clothes were always very soggy. However, it was not too cold down there.

Once, early in the morning, there was panic and women were screaming and shouting. I happened to be in the small shelter. A huge explosion accompanied by a strong blast had blown the door in and a cloud of dust entered the shelter. Those inside ran to get out through the other door, while someone started shouting that we had received a direct hit. The lights went out and we lit our candles. The shelter was full of choking dust. On leaving the shelter, I realised that the four old women, who used to take refuge down there with us, had remained in their places stunned and unconscious. At first, I feared that they were dead and summoned some adults to their assistance. However they had only passed out.

Fortunately, nobody was injured, although the bomb, a small one of about two hundred and fifty pounds, had fallen right on top of the house next to our shelter and overlying one of the entrances. The roofs of the rooms close to the small shelter where we were, had collapsed and had the bomb fallen on the house overlying the shelter, I would probably not be here today to relate this tale.

Although we still had our fair share of air raid signals, bombing had decreased of late. Around November, we again started sleeping at home and whenever there was an air raid warning, we went down in the large shelter. I was always the last to leave the house with the excuse that I had to shut all doors and windows. However, very often, I would just go back to bed.

I did not do this for long however. Once, after having gone as far as the shelter entrance to reassure my parents that I was there as well, I turned tail and went back home to sleep. I do not remember how long I slept. Suddenly, there was a huge explosion, the window in my room was blown inwards and glass fragments flew all over the place. I darted out of bed and sped down the stairs in total darkness and, on coming out on the street, ducked into the shelter for cover in record time.

I went up to mother and father who at once realised that I had been in some kind of trouble and they gave me a piece of their mind. Then father asked me whether I knew where the bombs had fallen and I replied that, although they had fallen quite close, our house was still intact. I told him that I was going up again to check whether our front door was open and he offered to come with me.

When father and I came into the open, we saw many people gathered in the lower part of St. Mary Street. A bomb had fallen on Azzopardi's furniture shop. We could see nothing in the pitch darkness but we could feel many loose stones under our feet. We could not see any sign of damage on the outside as the bomb had fallen in the back gardens. We got back home and found the front door open and the glass of the inner door shattered. Father said that we were better off waiting for dawn before going back, lest we got injured in the darkness. He sent me off to tell mother to remain in the shelter with my brother Victor.

At the crack of dawn, we went back home and found a complete shambles: broken glass, dust and flaking whitewash all over the floor. We found two retaining walls in the back garden blown up and only then realised that another bomb had fallen even closer to us than the one that we had been told about. After we inspected all the ceilings for any broken slabs, we went up to the roof to have a look at the back of the house and saw a huge crater in the large yard of the Sliema Band Club, adjacent to our garden. The walls around this crater were all demolished. This bomb had fallen not more than one hundred and fifty yards from where I was sleeping. I was again lucky to get away unscathed.

CHRISTMAS 1941

Another Christmas was approaching but this one was going to be quite different from the ones before it, particularly from the one of the previous year, 1940, which we had spent in Casa Depiro at Mdina.

This time, our group of friends from the same shelter started planning well in advance how to spend Christmas Day. We knew that, very probably, we would have to spend the day underground. Someone suggested that we should organise some kind of event down in the shelter as this was always very full at night. People preferred to spend the whole night in the shelter, rather than go in and out of their house every time there was an air raid warning. One of the girls teasingly suggested: "Let's have a party with goodies and a bit of dancing." There were various other suggestions. At last, we decided to hold a procession with the Baby Jesus and sing Christmas Carols accompanied by two boys playing the piano accordion. We decided not to tell anyone and spring a surprise. There was one thing which we wished to have and which we knew would be rather difficult to obtain and that was some biscuits or cakes.

There was a bakery opposite where we lived but they only baked bread there. An idea crossed my mind. I visited Salvu, the baker and finally got round to asking him whether it was possible to procure some flour. Salvu asked: "How much?" "I want to make a somewhat large cake," I replied. He grimaced and said: "Do you want to send me to jail? Don't you know that flour is rationed and that I cannot dispose of it, except to produce bread?"

After explaining to him what we intended to do for Christmas, I told him that if I obtained some flour, my mother was sure to bake a cake. He smiled and told me that one could not bake a cake with just flour but one required sugar, margarine, eggs and other ingredients. Many of them were rationed. I replied that if he was prepared to procure some flour, then I was sure to get the other ingredients somehow or other.

Salvu did not reply and went on rolling the dough, thinking the matter over. He then went into the next room and reappeared with a little packet and handed it over to me saying, "This is simply out of the regard I have for your father. Go home and make sure that you are not seen by some policeman because otherwise, I will spend Christmas in jail." I was as happy as a lark and speechless, so much so, that I did not even thank him. I ran out, crossed the road like a thunderbolt and shot into my house. I went straight to mother who was in the kitchen. I laid the packet with the flour in it on the kitchen table and told her what I now wished her to do for me. She replied that she might just manage to scrounge some sugar perhaps and, if not, she would add syrup to it from her dwindling pre-war stocks.

She then sent me off to an old man and women who lived nearby. They were diabetics and when I explained what I had in mind, they handed over to me a whole tin of sugar. Usually they would sell it but when I offered them money, they refused.

Mother told me that I did not have to worry about eggs, because she would be able to use egg powder as she had some of this as well. She used lard instead of margarine but we had no sultanas. Instead she used mixed peel and vanilla. To try to kill the taste of lard, she had pressed orange and lemon peel which I had picked from our own garden, into it.

I do not know what mother had put into them but I remember we ended up with two sizeable cakes, which had a mouth-watering smell. Even this treat was kept secret so that it would be yet another surprise. At home, we were all like bees, buzzing round these two cakes and we could not wait for Christmas to come, to cut a slice and taste them.

Christmas Eve, 1941, was a Wednesday. I asked father to borrow the statue of the Baby Jesus which he usually set up in the dining room. I also asked him for the festoons and the electric bulbs with which we used to decorate the Christmas tree. Father carefully brought out the statue of Baby Jesus from the straw-lined box, where he kept it throughout the year. He offered: "Let me set it up for you myself." We went down into the shelter and father got down to putting up the Christmas decorations and hanging coloured festoons from the ceiling, in one of the four compartments of the shelter. There was a niche in one of the walls, with a figure of Our Lady of the Sacred Heart and we placed the Baby Jesus in it.

But the Luftwaffe squadrons on Comiso in Sicily had other plans for us that Christmas! These certainly did not include wrapping Christmas presents or some "Weihnachtman" (their equivalent of Father Christmas) into their Ju88s or Ju87 Stukas. That same evening, when it got dark, we had to go down to the shelter willy-nilly because there was an air raid warning.

Luckily, before taking cover, we already had had something to eat to avoid having to go up and down to the house later. We had also prepared the things we usually carried down to the shelter every evening, like blankets, pillows and a thermos flask laden with coffee and of course, the Baby Jesus, together with a basket containing the two precious Christmas cakes. I would not have carried the basket with greater care, had it been full of gold ingots.

Out in the dark streets, there was another kind of procession; not the Christmas procession of the Baby Jesus but one of people trooping off for cover in the shelter. It was a sombre procession in pitch darkness and in the cold of December. Women were pulling their children along, or carrying babies wrapped in mantles, shawls and blankets. Men were carrying small chairs, baskets and all sorts of cover, to keep their children warm and shield them from the cold and dampness of the shelter. My parents, my brother Victor and I headed for Sur Guze's shelter where, at least, we could lie down on a wooden bed. After putting everything down in there, I took the Baby Jesus and carried it down to the large shelter. There, I met my friends and put the finishing touches to our programme for the evening. Up to now there was dead silence outside.

When the neighbours went down the shelter that evening, they were pleasantly surprised on seeing the Christmas decorations in one of the compartments and the coloured electric lights, surrounding the niche. This was also lit up with coloured oil lamps, which, in olden times before the advent of electricity, were lit up on festive occasions. I could see many people whispering to each other in anticipation, wondering whether our group was about to spring further surprises. By then, we had become quite well known for our pranks. Their suspicions were further aroused when they saw us grouped together, whispering secretively in each other's ears. Then we went up, one or two at a time to the entrance of St. Joseph Street, from where we had planned to start with our little procession.

I do not remember whether the air raid warning was still on or whether the all-clear had sounded but everybody remained in the shelter. We could not hear any gunfire outside. When we thought that the time was right, we walked down the steps leading into the shelter, carrying the Baby Jesus in front, with two boys holding a candle each in their hands, on either side. They were

117

followed by the "musicians" and our small choir, chanting away. We sang the carols that we had been taught at the religious doctrine classes and in church. We placed the statue in the niche and one of the little boys started to deliver the Christmas Eve sermon. But he was not at it for long, when all the guns suddenly opened fire. There was great commotion with people shouting: "There go the guns!" "They are over us." Somebody was overheard saying sarcastically, "This must be Santa Claus! And I'm sure he is dropping Christmas presents!"

I could not take it any longer and made for the entrance to see what was happening but I was stopped by my friend William. Father realised what I was up to, as he was close by. He called me and asked me to go up to the smaller shelter and bring down the cakes. I obeyed and for a moment, I forgot about the gunfire and the war outside. I found mother still cutting up the cake into slices and I could now take these down into the shelter and, at last, have a small piece of cake myself. On going back down again, I proudly uncovered the basket, where I had the cake all sliced up and gave a slice each, to all present. I could not have derived greater pleasure from looking at the expressions on the faces of the little children, some of whom had never had a piece of cake in their life. As far as I remember, nobody said "No thank you!" and everyone munched away. Many were very thankful for this surprise which our group had sprung on the shelter inmates. But there are always those who see the negative side of things in life and somebody muttered: "No wonder they can afford to bake cakes. That boy's father works at the Protection Office!"

I was really hurt and disappointed on hearing this comment, especially when father had had absolutely nothing to do with these cakes. On the contrary, when earlier on I had asked him to see if he could procure some sugar, he had told me off in no uncertain terms, telling me that he was not prepared to do any such thing. This little incident had utterly upset me and, with the excuse that I needed to take the empty basket back home, I left the shelter through the entrance where there were only two men chatting and looking up at the skies.

It seemed that the raid had targeted Luqa airfield and the fingers of the searchlights were probing the sky above the airfield. I was wearing a very thick jacket, which often doubled as an overcoat as it was a few sizes too large. I had got this from one of my uncles. I wore a muffler wrapped around my neck and whoever looked at me, might have thought that it was snowing that night. But, in those hard days, nobody really bothered. If one were lucky enough to obtain some form of thick clothing, one would wear it, regardless of size and shape. I hurried down to The Strand to get a better view of what was happening over Luqa airfield.

Apart from the beams of the searchlights, I could see what appeared to be gigantic Roman candles, coming down from the sky, lighting up the night and turning it into day. These were parachute flares dropped from enemy aircraft to illuminate their target. In those days there were no sophisticated instruments to enable aircraft to radar bomb a target as they do with today's more advanced technology. These flares presented a very beautiful sight, when viewed from a considerable distance. But they were dangerous when they were dropped overhead because, besides illuminating the area as a target, molten aluminium rained down from them in flaming tongues and whoever was hit with these drops would be seriously injured.

119

Far off in the sky, I saw an enemy aircraft caught in the searchlights. I could see the glow of a fire on Luqa airfield. This was probably coming from some Wellington bomber that had been hit on the ground. Yellow flashes and thundering sounds were belching from the guns of Fort Manoel. The shells from the guns could be seen exploding around that tiny speck of an aircraft illuminated by the searchlights. The bursting shells looked like yellow flaming stars.

Then the speck, caught in the searchlights, became a ball of fire and started plummeting to earth like a meteorite. On hitting the ground, it transformed itself into a column of fire. The guns fell silent and I was about to return to the shelter, when the searchlights came on again and started probing the sky towards the seaward side of Ghar id-Dud. I could hear the drone of aircraft engines approaching. Then, for some unknown reason, the searchlights were turned off again. From the sound of the engines, I could tell that it was an enemy aircraft. By now I had become accustomed to the different sounds of aircraft engines.

I continued looking up in the direction of the noise, half expecting to spot the enemy aircraft in that darkness. The stars were very bright and looked like specks of silver. Suddenly, I saw two parallel lines of red balls chasing each other. I realised that one of our night fighters had probably tracked its prey on radar and was now attacking the enemy aircraft with cannon tracer shells.

I saw another long burst of red tracer piercing the sky. A few seconds later I heard the screech of falling bombs which made me freeze with terror. The ground leapt up underneath me and I heard a suppressed explosion. I crouched on the ground. Drenched with a heavy shower of salt water. I took cover in the doorway of a house nearby. The water had come from the sea as the bombs had exploded under water. These bombs had not fallen more than three hundred yards away from where I had been standing. As I could figure out, when the enemy aircraft had been attacked by the night fighter, it released its bombs at random to make a quick get-away.

After this "refreshing" incident, I returned to the large shelter. When I entered, William came up to me and asked: "You went off, didn't you? Where did the bombs fall this time?" I replied; "Look at my clothes and you'll know where!" William smiled and shook his head. When father, who was still unaware of my escapade, came along, he asked me to take the Baby Jesus away from the niche, lest it fell down and got broken with the blast. Had he lost that statue, he would not have come by another one very easily.

1942 was now fast approaching. Eighteen months had passed since the first bombs were dropped on Malta. During 1941, which was now on its way out, I had witnessed severe air attacks and air battles in the sky. We had suffered lack of sleep and food and long days and nights underground, in the humid and stuffy air of the shelters. I had seen the suffering of the older folk and the sick. Mothers often cried because their children were going hungry. Many were quietly mourning the loss of some relative. There were also those who became severely ill because of bomb fright or shell shock and other illnesses caused by the war.

The enemy kept visiting us up to the last second of the outgoing year and the New Year started like the old one had ended. On the stroke of midnight, we heard sirens sounding, not in a festive mood from the warships, as we used to have before the war, but in mournful air raid warnings. The worst one I remember, on the first day of the New Year, had come close to midnight. I had gone down to The Strand during an alert with my friends Joe and Edgar. We heard the drone of approaching aircraft; "They are coming in," said Joe. "We had better turn back."

We had walked as far as Tower Road and the sound of approaching aircraft seemed to be coming from the direction of Ta' Xbiex. The searchlights were switched on and started probing the skies, the guns were still silent however. The probing searchlights were gradually moving in our direction and this showed us that the aircraft were about to fly overhead.

We stared at the sky, expecting the enemy to be caught in the searchlights any moment now. This would make it necessary for us to take cover in the first shelter we came across, because, very frequently, when enemy aircraft were caught in the searchlight beams, they would jettison their bombs to be able to evade detection more easily. By the time we had got to Annunciation Street, we heard the bombs screeching down.

"Run! The bombs have been released!" shouted Edgar. We had not run far, when we were smitten by the blast of two explosions from the direction of Gzira. We raced each other up Prince of Wales Road and, in a jiffy, we were down the shelter. Those seeing us enter asked us where the bombs had fallen and we told them that they had fallen in Gzira, probably close to the Orpheum Theatre. There was a little commotion in one of the compartments because someone in there had relatives, who lived in that area.

News soon spread that the bombs had fallen in Stuart Street and that there were many demolished buildings and fatal casualties as well as a number of wounded. The following morning I went to see the damage with two of my friends. Twenty-seven houses were blasted out of existence and the road was completely blocked with rubble. There was dust, broken window panes and smashed balconies all over the place. Ambulance crews, policemen and A.R.P. personnel were running hither and thither. Priests, doctors and nurses accompanied survivors who were in tears or shell shocked. We were stopped a block away because of the danger of falling masonry and in order not to obstruct the rescue operations. We saw A.R.P. personnel emerging from between the mounds of debris, carrying a stretcher covered with a blanket and putting it inside an ambulance. Usually, if this drove off right away, it was a sign that the patient was still alive. If it remained lingering there for a while, it was a sign that the victim was dead. Twenty people had lost their lives and seventeen others had been wounded in that air raid.

WITHOUT WARNING

The suffering we were already undergoing was compounded by a higher incidence of sickness and disease. In March, 1942, I came down with a high fever and, as I could no longer take cover in the shelter during an air raid, mother and father would take me downstairs during the day and I would lie down on a couch, tucked under blankets. If there was an air raid over our town, I could at least, take cover under the staircase. This would have been of very little use in the case of a direct hit or if the whole roof caved in!

On 1st March 1941, I was running a very high temperature. The sky was overcast and it was raining. At about 4.30 in the afternoon, I heard the siren sounding the alert. At home, besides myself, there were mother, my brother Victor and Uncle Eddie, who had just come over after work to pay me a visit on his way home. He told mother to take Victor to the shelter and offered to stay with me at home. Mother refused and told him to go and take Victor with him. After much debate, he obliged. They had hardly gone out of the house, when we heard distant gunfire. Mother rushed to my bedside, wrapped me up in blankets and helped me under the staircase. I could hardly stand up, let alone take a single step, so I had to lean heavily on mother until I could flop down on an armchair. Then she took the rosary beads and began to recite the Holy Rosary. The gunfire increased in intensity and, very soon, the guns on Fort Manoel went into action. We could also hear the drone of approaching aircraft very clearly and, as the cloud base was low, the enemy could fly quite low themselves. Whenever the clouds were low, the guns used to fire in the direction of the sound of the aircraft and the fuses of the shells were set to explode at a lower altitude. In this way, the exploding shells made a louder sound and it was very dangerous to peep outside because there was a continuous rain of steel shrapnel falling from the sky. Mother hugged me close to her, to reassure me. We heard an explosion close by and this was immediately followed by another one, even closer than the first. A split second later, a strong blast made the house tremble and the ground shook. The fanlight above the door leading to the garden was dislodged by one of the bombs which exploded nearby and fell to the ground with an ear-shattering noise.

Mother was terrified and started praying to Our Lady of the Sacred Heart to spare us. The barrage from Bofors and machine-guns was uninterrupted and helped increase our fear. Although I was terrified, I tried to calm her down, as best as I could.

When the gunfire ceased, our neighbour, Mrs. Mizzi, who had to remain indoors during air raids as her disabled husband could not be carried down to the shelter, came over to see whether we were all safe and sound.

She was soon followed by Uncle Eddie, who immediately ran up to the roof to see where the bombs had fallen. When he came down again, he informed us that the dome of Stella Maris Church had been blown up and that a ferry was sunk at The Strand. He was holding in a handkerchief a piece of shrapnel which he had picked up from the roof. It was about five inches long and two inches wide with edges as sharp as blades. When he gave it to me to hold, it was still very hot. Father arrived about fifteen minutes later and was so anxious that he almost quarrelled with mother for remaining at home. When he had calmed down somewhat, he admitted that I had not been in a fit state to leave the house and go down into the shelter.

Father then left the house to see for himself the damage Stella Maris Church had sustained. When he came back, he confirmed that the dome had been completely demolished, that the church's interior was terribly devastated and that a woman, who was caught inside the church, had lost her life. I asked him whether there were any casualties when the ferry was hit. He replied that there were no passengers on board at the time and that the ferry had been moored to the pier.

After a few days, my fever gradually subsided and I started getting better. When I felt strong enough, I ventured outside and started going for short walks along the waterfront. Beyond the Nazzarene Church in Sliema, where the Hotel Fortina stands today, there was a field known as "Tal-Fatati", the ghosts' field. A Bofors gun was deployed in this field and on my way to the meetings of the Tigne Garrison Boy Scouts Group, I often stopped to watch the soldiers manning it. Very often, they gave me some spent, empty, brass cartridges, from the gun. Amongst these soldiers, there was an Irish sergeant, whom we called 'Paddy'. He was a Roman Catholic and he had a soft spot for the Maltese. Sometimes, between air raids, we often played football with the gun crew, in the clearing beside the Bofors gun.

Once, I was standing near this gun, while it was having its barrel changed. No sooner had they completed the job and put the new barrel in place, than the telephone near the gun rang. The soldier, who picked it up, shouted: "Alert". In a jiffy, the other members of the gun crew took to their stations: two on the sights; another standing by, laying clips of shells into the breach of the gun; the sergeant milling around, relaying orders he was receiving from the officer who had emerged from a nearby house; others feverishly handling the ammunition.

On receiving further orders on the phone, the officer asked me to leave and take cover. Shortly afterwards, the red flag was hoisted on the Palace Tower and the Police

Stations at Prince of Wales Road and The Strand, opposite Tower Road. This was the signal that the target was going to be the harbour area. A bugle call was sounded from the top of the roof of St. Patrick's Institute by a boy who, on seeing the red flag, sounded the alarm to the people in that area who were unable to see the flag. I hurried towards The Strand but, when the guns opened fire, I broke into a run, because it was dangerous to stick around the area, as Tigne' was a favourite enemy target.

When I arrived near the public toilets at The Strand, at the lower end of St. Vincent Street, I saw five Ju88s, at an altitude of some 10,000 feet. The guns of Fort Manoel quickly engaged them and the usual pandemonium broke out, with guns letting off from every quarter. It was about 11.30 am when the enemy aircraft approached from the seaward side and flew in our direction. The guns of Fort Manoel again belched yellow flashes. The enemy aircraft stuck to their course in a tight formation, surrounded by puffs of smoke from anti-aircraft fire, which looked like bits of cotton wool. Then, they rapidly started diving through the flak, only to be engaged at low level by the Bofors guns, as well.

There were two sheds besides the public toilets. The bigger one was a refuge for the *karrozzini*, the horse-drawn cabs; and the smaller one which was used by fishermen to sell their catch. The few coachmen, who happened to be under the shed, held fast to their horses which were unharnessed. They swiftly tied the horses to the iron supports of the shed and ran for cover inside the public toilets, to avoid being showered with shrapnel. One of these coachmen, who was quite advanced in age, seemed to be terrified and his friends were doing their best to calm him down. They kept urging him to go down into the shelter, assuring him that they will take care of his horse themselves. But he refused, wanting to keep an eye on his horse at all costs.

We heard somebody shout from across the road, where a few men were gathered, that one of the enemy aircraft had been hit. I looked up and saw a spiralling trail of smoke coming out of one of the Ju88s. The aircraft turned to the left, dipped one wing and left it to his mates to press on with the attack. Shortly afterwards, I saw a ball of fire and a big, black puff of smoke in the sky. The 88 had exploded in mid-air. I could see no parachutes but only pieces of flaming metal coming down into the sea.

By then, the other four aircraft were almost above Tigne' Point. I saw small black objects being released by one aircraft after the other. I followed these bombs down until the first stick of four bombs exploded on Tigne' Barracks, a short distance away from the Bofors gun. Smoke, dust and stones filled the air. Four tall columns of water rose up from the sea between Marsamxett and Tigne'. Another stick of bombs fell beyond Fort Manoel, between Lazzarett and Sa Maison, in Pieta Creek. The aircraft swiftly turned tail and headed back for Sicily.

The guns ceased firing and shortly afterwards, I saw three Spitfires chasing and attacking the Ju88s. I could hear the staccato of fire from the Spitfires' cannons. One of the Ju88s was set aflame; it turned over to one side and plummeted towards the sea. This was followed by three parachutes, blossoming up in the sky, in quick succession. One of the other aircraft's engines emitted a stream of black smoke and the aircraft spun down towards the water, until it was hidden from view by buildings.

Hurricanes now joined the Spitfires in the fray. But immediately, a flight of Messerschmitt 109s came at them out of the sun, like hawks. Soon enough, one of the Hurricanes was hit and spiralled down, trailing smoke. I then witnessed one of the cruellest episodes of the war. While the Hurricane pilot, who had managed to bale out, was drifting down, dangling under his parachute, one of the Messerschmitts machine-gunned him and made a very close pass over the parachute. The plane's slip-stream collapsed the parachute and the poor pilot plummeted down into the sea, parachute and all.

The dogfight lasted a few minutes and then the aircraft dispersed; the enemy towards Sicily and our fighters back to their airfields. When everything was back to normal, I emerged from my cover and ran back to the Bofors gun. The soldiers told me, that they had had a very close shave. The bombs that had fallen on the barracks had caused many splinters and debris to fly in their direction. In fact, one of them, who had not taken proper cover, had been wounded in the arm by a flying rock and had to be attended to.

Round about 12.30 pm, I headed back for home to have some lunch. On arriving near the Nazzarene Church, I saw the Air Sea Rescue launch speeding into harbour and I hurried to its mooring place, to find out who had been rescued. It berthed in its usual place near Marina Street, at The Strand, where an ambulance, a military lorry and the usual bystanders were already waiting. Three German airmen disembarked under armed escort, shoved into the lorry and driven off to the prisoner-of-war camp. Stretchers were then brought ashore from the launch. The first casualty was wearing a British uniform and appeared to be dead. All I could see was the sleeve of the uniform jacket with three chevrons and a crown showing that he carried the rank of flight sergeant. The second stretcher was completely covered and I could not tell whether the dead airman was one of ours or not.

The Royal Air Force had an Air Sea Rescue Unit at The Strand in Sliema and this was billeted in the ground floor houses, between Marina Street (Sacro Cuor Street) and Belvedere Terrace. The High Speed Launches (H.S.L.s), were sixty-eight feet long and could achieve a top speed of thirty-eight knots, They were armed with .303 Lewis machine-guns mounted in aircraft-type double gun turrets and were used to recover air crews who came down by parachute or from ditched aircraft, in the sea around the Islands and sometimes, even from far out at sea. It was easy to tell when they were putting to sea by the loud noises made by their powerful Napier engines. Whenever I heard this noise, I ran down to The Strand to find out whom they had rescued. Whenever it happened to be a British pilot, all bystanders would break into a round of applause. But, if the person fished out of the sea happened to be Italian or German, he would stand no chance of living to tell the tale, were it not for the armed escort and the police. The enemy airmen would be harassed as soon as they set foot ashore.

There was another Bofors gun at Qui-Si-Sana, at the junction with Dragut Street. I often went there too. The soldiers manning it were billeted in the garages in the corner, which were also used as ammunition stores. Below the gun, on the fore-shore, there was a concrete pillbox, where the Plevna Hotel swimming pool now stands. Tigne' heavy anti-aircraft battery was about 300 yards further up the road, near Tigne' Barracks. A short distance out to sea lay the wreck of a Royal Air Force Maryland reconnaissance and torpedo bomber, which had ditched sometime before.

It had formed part of No. 69 Squadron, and had been attacked on the 13th January 1942, by two Me109s, after returning from a reconnaissance sortie. The two Messerschmitts had swooped down from the clouds like two hawks and machine-gunned it. They never gave our aircraft the time to defend itself. Squadron Leader J.H. Dowland, who was at the controls of this unfortunate aircraft, managed to ditch it safely into the water and except for him, all its crew were saved. The Bofors guns and some other machine-guns around that part of the coast had opened fire on the two Me109s, which had attacked the Maryland and these quickly turned tail and fled. Given half a chance, they would have dived down on its crew and machine-gunned them while they were floating on their rubber dinghy. It had become common for fanatic German pilots to shoot at British pilots who had survived a shot-down aircraft while they were still descending by parachute or floating in the water.

After the first storm, many pieces of the Maryland had been washed ashore on the rocks beneath the Bofors gun, at Qui-Si-Sana and we frequently went to gather some souvenirs. I remember having carried an entire aircraft hatch home. This was the biggest relic I ever managed to obtain for my war-relics collection. Unfortunately, in those days, few people had time for these mementoes and, at home, I used to be told that they should be dumped. The aluminium hatch and other similar souvenirs were eventually thrown away, together with other unwanted things by mother, during a general spring-cleaning of the house.

Once, while we were looking for flotsam on the shoreline, one of my friends found an instrument panel dial. While we were curiously inspecting it, the guns of

131

Fort Tigne' which were almost on top of us, opened fire. We were so frightened that we could barely run for cover on the rocks. Then we heard a strange noise and the screech of falling bombs. We took cover inside the pill-box, deafened by the noise from the bombs, exploding all around us. We were so terrified that one of us became hysterical and started yelling and, had we not held him back, he would have gone out into the open.

I looked out of one of the slit windows of the pillbox and saw the splashes where the bombs were exploding in the water. Fort Tigne' could hardly be seen through the smoke and dust clouds. We heard rocks crashing down on the roof of the pillbox. Inside, the air was full of dust smoke and the smell of high explosive and cordite was suffocating.

When it was all over, we rushed out and climbed up to the road above. The first thing we saw was the Bofors gun covered in rocks and dust. Two soldiers had been hit by flying rocks. Another one was suffering from shell shock and was staring vaguely in the distance, trembling. I could see many buildings razed to the ground in Dragut Street and McIver Street. The British officer in charge of the Bofors gun told us off, in no uncertain terms, for being there as the area was very vulnerable to enemy aircraft attack. A few weeks later, I realised how right he was, as the gun received a direct hit and all the crew manning it were killed.

I remember when a bomb fell on Prince of Wales Road between St. Albert Street and Prince of Wales Junction. It was about 10.30 am on 7th March 1942. I was on my way to the shelter with mother and Victor, when we came to the cross-roads between St. Mary Street and Prince of Wales Road. There, I saw a Ju88 flying low, in our direction, from Valletta. The roar of the guns was deafening. Bofors shells were going up in clips of eight. I urged my mother and brother to run as fast as they could, but mother was not as fast as we were. I could not get my eyes off that 88 and soon saw two or three bombs being dropped from the approaching aircraft. I pulled mother and my brother into a wide recessed doorway and, from where I stood, I could actually see buildings collapse and stones and beams fly in the air, amidst a cloud of dust. I felt the blast hit me and I would have been overwhelmed and thrown to the ground, had I not had my arms clasped around the iron gate of the doorway. My eardrums felt as though they were about to burst with the blast. As usual, this explosion was followed by a shower of debris from the sky and had I not squeezed further in, where my mother and brother had taken cover, I would surely have been injured. I heard a loud noise of something falling and rolling over about ten yards from where I stood and, on looking in that direction I saw a huge stone which had been thrown up into the air by the explosion of the bomb, two blocks away.

Mother was beside herself with fear and hugged my younger brother. I tried to calm her down, telling her that it was all over and that she need not panic. I pointed out where the bomb had fallen, but she retorted that there were two explosions. She was afraid that the other one might have been close to my father's office. I reassured her that when the danger was over, I would run up and find out for myself. On running up to see what had happened, I met father who was likewise hurrying down the road to check if we were all safe and sound.

Chapter X

MISERY AND HUNGER

By early 1942, foodstuffs had become almost unavailable. The bread ration had been cut down drastically to ten and a half ounces, per head, daily. There was a one-pint bottle of goats' milk to each family, daily; kerosene was distributed according to the size of the family on presentation of coupons and one had to "queue" up for everything. The word "queue" was a new word which had entered our vocabulary during the war. There were no new clothes to buy, particularly no shoes. We had been reduced to a state where we had to scour demolished buildings, in the hope of finding a pair of shoes which were still usable. I remember, once I was lucky enough to find a pair of shoes similar to those my father wore when he was a kid. They were in fairly good condition and, in my excitement I even thought that they fitted me. I wrapped them up in a piece of cloth and ran back home, very proud of my find.

First, I tried to clean off the caked dust that seemed glued to them but, of course, no shoe polish was available. I went into the kitchen, got some lard and some soot, mixed them on the fire and when the mixture had cooled down again, I used it as shoe polish. The shoes became black all right, but you could hardly say they had a shiny finish. At least they were much better than the shoes I was wearing. The following day, I proudly put them on for a trial run. Alas, after I had taken a few steps, I felt them pressing on my feet like a clamp, because they were the wrong size after all!

Luckily, as it was summer, I did not have to wear these 'new' shoes very often, firstly because I was trying to keep them for the rainy days and secondly, because they really hurt my feet. Instead, I used to wear a pair of sandals, made from a wooden sole and two pieces of sack cloth crossed over each other. Not to make too much noise, I covered the soles with a layer of rubber from old car tyres. This type of footwear had actually become quite fashionable. We even wore shoes with soles made of rope, instead of wood and nobody was ever embarrassed. There were no longer any social or class or age distinctions in attire and everybody had been reduced to the same common denominator.

I had forgotten how butter and good margarine tasted. The latter was also severely rationed, and was very rancid. We ate bread with a spread of lard, which mother obtained from meat fat. I had grown so accustomed to eating bread without any spread on it, that I still do so to this very day. The bread was nothing to write home about and if it were not eaten on the same day, it would get mouldy. It had a sour taste and, very often, it was of a dark colour because the flour was mixed with bran. Potatoes were also added to the dough and this caused it to rot very quickly.

135

This acute scarcity of foodstuffs, clothes and drinking water, particularly when some reservoir was hit by bombs, was becoming the most telling factor of the siege. Many were so hungry that they could even be seen foraging for scraps of food in rubbish bins. We even chewed carob seeds which we picked from the many carob trees in the valley known as Wied Għomor, at St. Julian's. If anyone left a pound note lying on the floor, he was more likely to find it again than he would have found a piece of bread he left lying around for a few seconds.

In March, 1942, the authorities set up victory kitchens to distribute warm meals, to the general public. The kitchens served vegetable soups, goat meat stews, tinned sardines and herrings, beans and macaroni, and the 'menu' changed every day. The amount of food dished out depended on the number of members of each family. To obtain food from the victory kitchen, one had to present coupons previously acquired from the kitchen itself, costing sixpence per portion and show one's ration book to prove that he was entitled to the rationed items.

There was a victory kitchen in a house in our street, near the junction at St. Trophimus Street. The main purpose behind the setting up of these kitchens was to cut down on the consumption of kerosene. A new regulation was issued prohibiting people from collecting wood from demolished buildings as it could only be used in the victory kitchens and bakeries.

A friend of father, who lived in Rabat, had offered him his own ration of bread. He could not eat it himself, because of some diet he was on. He had told father he could send for this bread whenever he needed any. Although this was against the law, hunger compelled one to do things which normally one would not do. As father could not go and fetch the bread himself, being busy at work, like my elder brother Joe, and as my youngest brother Victor was still too young, I was assigned this task. As a result, I had to go up to Rabat almost daily, as we could not afford to lose such a golden opportunity.

Going up to Rabat was no picnic. I had to have an early lunch and then hurry down to The Strand, take a ferry to Valletta, walk to Floriana and then, down to Porte Des Bombes, to the bus terminus. The roads leading to Valletta were all bombed and blocked with craters and demolished buildings. At noon, I would catch the first bus to Rabat. This would only take me as far as the road leading to Ta' Qali airfield, where it stopped to save on petrol consumption as buses ran on petrol, not diesel, in those days. I then had to walk all the way up the hill to Rabat. As I was fond of walking, this did not bother me very much and there were always interesting things to see on the way, like R.A.F. personnel at work and aircraft flying low above me, about to land on the airfield.

The fields around Ta' Qali airfield were full of aircraft dispersal pens, some even extending as far as the fields on both sides of the Rabat road and on to the road leading to Zebbug. In these pens I could make out some of the first Spitfires that had been flown in from the aircraft-carriers *H.M.S. Eagle* and *H.M.S. Argus* on the 7th March, 1942. These pens were meant to protect aircraft from bombs falling close by. They had three walls and were U-shaped. At first, they were built with sandbags filled with earth, but it was soon noted that these were inadequate, as they were not blast proof. Later, building stone from demolished sites was used. After further experimentation, it was discovered that the best pens were those that were made of petrol cans filled with earth and tied to each other with strands of wire. There was no shortage of used petrol cans on the Island!

Petrol was no longer carried in bowsers as there were hardly any such vehicles left. Instead of being shipped to Malta in tankers, this was carried in five-gallon tin cans or forty-gallon drums which could be carried in any kind of transport. Petrol cans were brought over on cargo ships, warships, submarines or even on aircraft.

The pens had very thick walls and no top cover, apart from camouflage nets strewn with tree branches, to try and make them less conspicuous from the air. There were no hangars of course, as the only ones that had existed on the Island, at Luqa and Hal Far airfields and at Kalafrana Seaplane Base, had all been destroyed by bombing.

At first glance, one may have thought that it was easy to construct these pens but this was not the case. To begin with, there were no bulldozers or other similar heavy, earth-moving machines, existing at the time. Everything from rock cutting, to levelling the ground, to the transport of building stone and filler, had to be done manually. Suitably level terrain had to be found to erect these pens and taxi-ways had to be cleared through a maze of rubble walls.

Considerable effort went into the building of these pens. The three sides each measured ninety feet long by fourteen feet high. The thickness of these walls tapered from twelve petrol cans at the base to two cans at the top. Each can measured approximately ten by ten by eighteen inches. Sixty thousand petrol cans went into the building of the three walls and these were filled with

3,500 tons of earth. Two and three quarter miles of wire were used to tie them up together and this involved 39,600 man-hours (two hundred men working for eighteen hours for eleven days). If only half a dozen of these pens had been built in one week, it would have been no mean feat but in February and March, 1942, some forty pens a week were being built and, by the end of April, 1942, there were three hundred and fifty completed pens all over the Island, one for each aircraft, petrol bowser, control van and steam roller.

Air Vice Marshal Sir Hugh Pughe Lloyd, Air Officer Commanding Malta, wrote:

"Soldiers had constructed the larger part of the pens. There were always 1,500 working on the aerodromes and very often we had 3,000. Civilians also helped. The fact that everybody put in, at least, one hour of work a day, was highly appreciated. Officers, clerks, photographers, store-men, wireless operators, cooks, air crew, ground crew and whoever else had an hour to spare, used to work on these pens undeterred by bad weather or enemy action. It was a Herculean effort and it definitely helped considerably in the final outcome of the Battle of Malta."

Back to my Rabat escapades; very often, I would have to take a long detour after getting off the bus, just off the road leading to Ta' Qali airfield. This was due either to some aircraft taxiing across the Rabat road to its pen, or due to bomb craters caused by recently exploded bombs. These detours made it possible for me to get an even closer look at the newly-arrived Spitfires on my way.

The Point de Vue Hotel, on Saqqajja Square in Rabat, had been requisitioned from Mr. Joseph Vella by the

R.A.F. and turned into a Mess for R.A.F. Sergeant Pilots stationed at Ta' Qali. The Officers' Mess was situated at Palazzo Xara in Mdina, which was later to become the Xara Palace Hotel. Although all were in R.A.F. uniform, these pilots did not come exclusively from Britain. There were Australians, Canadians, New Zealanders, Polish, Norwegians, South Africans, French and Greeks. A few also came from the United States of America and had served with the famous Eagle squadrons. They had volunteered to join the Royal Air Force at the outbreak of war. Although most of them were still very young, they had considerable aerial combat experience and were acquainted with German tactics, as they had already seen action in the Battle of Britain.

As I was always fascinated with anything that took to the skies, I simply loved watching the activity around Ta' Qali. To me, pilots were what pop stars are to modern youths. I used to make the most of the time I had before having to go back to Sliema and, very often, I would accost one or two of these pilots and try to engage them in conversation. I soon became quite friendly with one of them. On one of these visits to Rabat, I was walking up to Saqqajja when the siren sounded. I ran up breathless to the Point de Vue Hotel, from where I could hear gunfire in the distance. I approached a group of pilots who were looking down from the walls. One of them pointed skywards. Fifteen Ju88s, in formations of three, were approaching from the direction of Luqa. Nine Spitfires scrambled from Ta' Qali to intercept them and climbed towards the Junkers which, according to these pilots, were coming in at an altitude of between 15,000 and 18,000 feet. Above them, I spotted the fighter cover, weaving from one side to the other like flies and from what I overheard, these were Messerschmitt 109s. These pilots had very good eyesight and never missed a thing. This is what kept them alive after all!

In an attempt to start a conversation with the pilot next to me, I asked him whether the Spitfires would be able to intercept the enemy before they unloaded their bombs. The pilot replied that, if they maintained their rate of climb and speed, they would probably attack the bombers from below. He added that if they used this tactic, the enemy would never know what had hit them and the fighter cover would discover the attack too late to be of any use in defending the bombers. He also told me that German pilots often resorted to new tactics during dog-fighting and that was why he and his friends would watch the combats from down below and observe what was happening in the skies, when they were off duty.

One after the other, the Ju88s dipped their noses and started their shallow dive down to a height of some 10,000 feet, towards Ta' Qali airfield. The anti-aircraft gunfire was now at its peak. A Ju88 was hit before it released its bomb load. There was a huge ball of smoke and plenty of falling aircraft debris was raining down from the sky. The aircraft following it, quickly changed course to avoid the debris of the stricken aircraft. Amidst cheering from the other pilots, the one next to me pointed out that some of the Spitfires were engaging the Messerschmitts while the anti-aircraft guns were con-centrating their fire on the Junkers. I watched a few Spitfires entering the flak, putting themselves at great risk and setting upon the last formation of Junkers. The staccato of machine-gun fire mixed with that of the ack-ack. Another Junkers let off a plume of black smoke, dipped to one side and crashed in the sea off Madliena. Another released its bombs to lighten its load, changed course and flew out in the direction of Filfla Island. Its bombs could be seen exploding in the fields near the Rabat Road, close by the mental hospital. The other Junkers, which managed to dodge the anti-aircraft fire or the Spitfires, released their bombs on Ta' Qali, by then completely obliterated from view by the smoke and dust clouds hovering above it.

While I was completely engrossed in this ferocious attack on Ta' Qali airfield, I felt somebody violently grab me from the shoulder and throw me to the ground yelling: "Down!"

A split second later came the sound of a low-flying aircraft and machine-gun fire. All of us were all face down on the ground. The pilot I had been speaking to was pinning me down with his strong arms. When it was all over, he calmly gave me a useful bit of friendly advice: "Whenever you're watching enemy action, don't just keep looking in one direction, but keep an eye on what might be coming from behind you." I made a mental note of this and remembered it all my life!

I thanked him. He smiled back and asked me what my name was and when I replied "Carmel", he quickly put in, "Oh! Charles you mean!" From that day my name was changed from Carmel to Charles. It was a custom for R.A.F. air crews to find new names or nicknames for their pals. Hardly any of them were ever referred to by their real name. It was a sort of a call sign. There was a pilot by the name of Bye, who used to be called "Bye-Bye", Bye. Another young looking pilot was known as 'Willie the Kid' and the ace pilot George Beurling who had the habit of saying "screwball" became known as

'George Screwball Beurling'. The pilot I had befriended was an Australian called Peter but he asked me to call him Pete, as he was known by his pals. He belonged to No. 185 Squadron, which was stationed at Hal Far. At times, when that airfield became unserviceable, the Squadron moved to Ta' Qali and operated from there and the air crews were billeted either at Rabat or at Mdina.

Pete asked me where I came from and I replied that I lived in Sliema and that I only came to Rabat to obtain some bread. He paternally lectured me on the importance of being careful and taking cover during air raids because, very often, German aircraft would come in unexpectedly and strafe anything that moved or came in their sight or else they would drop a random bomb and then turn tail, back to their base. He also warned me about booby traps and told me that if I saw any unidentified object on the ground, I should never touch it, as this could be very dangerous and could cost me my life.

These booby traps came in all shapes and sizes. Some looked like fountain pens and exploded when one tried to remove the cap. Others were shaped like thermos flasks which, on being moved, would blow up and kill whoever was close by. The oval-shaped butterfly bomb was slightly larger than a tin of condensed milk and was dropped from aircraft in a canister, containing twenty-four small bombs. This opened up in mid-air and released its deadly contents which then glided down to earth, hanging by a piece of steel wire from a pair of wings. On the way down, the wings, which flared out from the outer casing would start to revolve, priming the detonator and, on landing, the bomb would be ready to explode at the slightest movement. The butterfly bomb was extremely dangerous and effective, causing many fatalities and casualties. It was used mostly as an anti-personnel bomb.

I remember one very tragic incident when a boy came across one of these bombs. He had been trailing behind his parents on a hike, in the countryside. When he called to show them what he had found, his father shouted out that he should not touch it. Nevertheless, the boy threw the object to his father to enable him to see for himself and, a split second later, the boy was an orphan!

Once, some Maltese labourers at Ta' Qali airfield found a mysterious canister and tried to open it up. An R.A.F. sergeant, who was an explosives expert, saw what they were up to and ran in their direction yelling and warning them not to touch it as it was a bomb. For some reason or other, the workers ignored him and, when he saw that they were not heeding his warnings, he left them to their fate. Other workers gathered round to see what was going on. The bomb suddenly exploded and four of them died on the spot. Such stories were common in those days.

But, there was also the funny side to these grisly episodes. Once an officer from the Bomb Disposal Unit, on his way to Hal Far airfield on a bicycle, spotted a fountain pen lying in the dust on the roadside. "This must be one of them," he thought and alighting from his bicycle, took out his handkerchief, looped it round the pen and, very gently, lifted it up. In order not to jerk the fountain pen, he stood the bicycle against the rubble wall and walked all the way to Hal Far, paying great attention not to drop the pen and detonate it. On arriving at the workshop, he clamped it into the workbench vice and surrounded it with sandbags so that, if it were to explode, he would not be injured. Carefully, he began to unscrew the cap with a special tool. It never exploded as it was a real fountain pen after all!

Time flew while I was talking to Pete and I would have missed the route bus back home had Pete not offered me a lift down to Ta' Qali, on an R.A.F. lorry, carrying pilots who were relieving those that had just landed, after the interception that we had seen earlier on. Pete hurried into the mess and, shortly afterwards, emerged wearing a leather flying jacket. He took something out of his pocket and handed it to me: "This is yours. When we meet again, I'll give you another one. Now hop onto the truck. Let's get going." It was a bar of chocolate. I was delighted as I had not had a bar of chocolate for ages. I was about to devour it, but then I had second thoughts and decided that it would be much nicer if I took it home and shared it with the rest of my family.

When the lorry arrived at the Ta' Qali Road junction, I jumped out and Pete waved to me and asked me to look him up whenever I was at Rabat again. I suddenly remembered that I had forgotten to get the bread, which I had purposely gone to fetch from Rabat, but I had no time to race up the hill again to get it, as I would have missed the route bus to Valletta.

By the time the route bus arrived, the Spitfires in the nearby pens started up their engines one by one and taxied towards the runway for take off. This was known as a 'scramble' and meant that enemy aircraft had been detected approaching the coast. In fact, soon after, the siren sounded. There was no shelter nearby, but I spotted a small room further up the road and decided to take cover in it. Not that it would have protected me from a direct hit but, at least, as Pete had just told me, it would have protected me from shrapnel and splinters from falling bombs. Besides, I could hide from low flying aircraft which machine-gunned anything that moved. The Spitfires took off in quick succession and swiftly climbed in the direction of Delimara.

Some ten minutes later, I again heard the noise of low-flying aircraft. For a moment, I thought that our fighters were returning to the airfield and therefore, I emerged from my cover. But, on stepping out, there was a sudden burst of machine-gun fire from an aeroplane strafing the fields around the hut. I identified it as a Me109 about to attack Ta' Qali airfield. Two others quickly followed it in. A column of thick black smoke rose from some structure on the airfield but it was not a bomb, as no explosion had preceded it. Afterwards, I learned that a petrol bowser, that was standing by to refuel the Spitfires upon landing, had been hit and caught fire. Then, two Spitfires swooped down out of the clouds like birds of prey, upon the Messerschmitts and opened fire on them. I saw part of a Messerschmitt's wing fly off as though it had been sawn off and spin down to the ground. The aircraft flipped on its back and plummeted down. The pilot took to his parachute which looked like a big, white, silk umbrella and the wind carried it in the direction of Naxxar, while the aircraft appeared to have crashed in the sea beyond Dingli Cliffs.

Besides fetching bread from Rabat, I also had to buy fresh goats' milk from Mensija Hill. To get there, I had to walk from Sliema to St. Julian's and up to Ta' Ġiorni Ridge, past an anti-aircraft battery, situated near the present-day government housing estate. This country path took me between two gun emplacements, each housing a 3.7 inch anti-aircraft gun. As the battery was on top of the ridge, it commanded a view of three-quarters of Malta on one side and of the sea on the other. The guns in the reinforced concrete emplacements, the command post and the predictor, which was an instrument to calculate the height, range and velocity of attacking aircraft, were all below ground level, to make them inconspicuous from a distance. They were also covered with camouflage netting to be hidden from enemy aircraft.

Very often, on my way to Mensija, I would spend some time watching the gun crews cleaning their guns and sometimes, I would venture closer and chat with them. They would explain how the guns functioned and I was always very interested in what they had to say. Occasionally, I was offered a mug of tea which I drank very reluctantly. They called it: "bloody washing water." And believe me; it did taste awful!

This battery at the time was manned by British soldiers of the Royal Artillery. They never sent me away on the pretext of security and, as long as they were not on alert, they let me stay there as long as I wanted. However, as soon as an alert was sounded, the battery sergeant major would bark the order: "All civilians, Out!"

Once when I asked a sergeant why I could not hang around to see the guns in action, he replied that it was very dangerous because the battery was very vulnerable to air attack. He explained that besides, when the guns fired, the blast and the noise could very easily damage my hearing. I confirmed this from bitter experience later on. Those, who at some time or other, manned guns, eventually became hard of hearing and suffered from what the British soldiers called "gunners' deafness" which, though not total, it impeded one from distinguishing certain fine notes and sounds.

On 19th March, 1942, in the afternoon, I was walking up to Mensija to buy milk. I had put a wine bottle in a sack-cloth and set out on my way. When I arrived on the present-day site of Ta' Ġiorni College, the air raid siren sounded. It was about 2.15 pm. I trudged on through the path between the gun emplacements and, soon enough, the sergeant yelled out, ordering me to go and take cover. The only available shelter was in the battery itself and, obviously, I could not use it. So, I hurried on towards Mensija and entered the first rural shelter I came across, about four hundred yards away from the battery. I could easily see the guns from there. Orders were given out to the gun crews regarding bearings, elevation and deflection. With every order, the guns changed elevation. They were brought to bear in the direction of Luqa airfield and the cry: "Target in sight!" was heard. Immediately after that came the order: "Engage... Commence fire." Five tongues of fire leapt out of the muzzles of the guns at Ta' Ġiorni Battery.

Looking in the direction where the guns were pointing, I made out about thirty Ju88s already starting their dive on Luqa. There were also some eighty Stukas. A huge pall of smoke hung over Luqa airfield. I felt safe enough to come out of the room where I had taken cover, as the target seemed to be far away. The Ju88s headed straight for Ta' Qali at a height of some 10,000 feet. When they were above Luqa, the Stukas started their dive upon Ta' Qali in groups of three and released their deadly loads. I could not see the airfield at Ta' Qali from where I stood, but the smoke from bomb explosions was clearly visible as it mushroomed high above the Naxxar skyline. It appeared that larger bombs than usual were being used, because the thuds of the explosions could be heard easily, despite the long distance. There was something ablaze on Luqa airfield as black smoke was rising up in the sky and I could actually see the fire.

The Stukas were still following each other and releasing their bombs in quick succession. The gunfire from Ta' Ġiorni Battery was incessant. A Ju88 was hit and exploded in mid-air, bombs and all, and just disappeared in a big, black puff of smoke. A Stuka, which was diving down, collided with another one which was flying quite low and both exploded in mid-air. Another was seen trailing smoke and then crashed into the sea. Two parachutes opened as the crew had bailed out and were drifting down towards the water.

After about ten minutes of this ferocious attack which, to me, seemed more like an hour, the guns at Ta' Ġiorni and Tal-Qroqq Batteries ceased firing. However, there was still sporadic gunfire from other batteries in the distance and the smoke over Luqa was thicker then ever. My eardrums were numbed with the sound of gunfire and I could only hear a funny whizzing noise. I thought it was all over and was about to continue on my way to Mensija when the guns suddenly opened up again. From the door where I stood, I saw a Ju88 approaching from the direction of Ta' Qali, flying rather low, at about 3,000 feet, and heading straight in my direction. The Bofors quickly engaged it. Red tentacles of fire from tracer could be seen reaching out for the aircraft, which took evasive action, weaving from side to side. Smoke started coming out of its starboard engine and, soon after, I saw two bombs falling on Ta' Ġiorni Battery. I shrank back

149

into the room, the foundations of which immediately shook with the tremendous blast. One of the gun emplacements suffered a direct hit!

I edged as far into the room as I could to get away from falling splinters, stones, chunks of concrete, pieces of metal from the gun and blood from the butchered bodies of the unfortunate gun crew I had got to know so well. I was terrified, and as the enemy aircraft disappeared, I fled the room in a hurry.

In a flash, I reached the farmhouse from where I used to buy the milk. Frenc and his wife Nina were waiting at the door and, on seeing me sprinting up the hill, realised what I had just been through. They took me in and Frenc told his wife: "Give him some black coffee, because he is as pale as a ghost." Then, he turned to me and scolded me gently: "Why didn't you come straight up here, instead of remaining in that room?" Of course, I couldn't say anything to that, apart from describing what I had just seen near the battery.

Nina handed me the milk and advised me to hurry back home so as not to worry my parents. She suggested that I should avoid passing by the battery again and take the pathway in Wied Għomor instead. This led down all the way to Spinola Bay, near the Rockyvale. I politely refused to take this alternative route as it was much longer and opted to go back the same way.

On reaching Ta' Giorni Battery, I found utter confusion; half a corpse was hanging on a tree; a soldier's leg protruded from beneath a rubble wall; in a field, there was a body of a headless soldier with his clothes ripped off. Although by this time I had become accustomed to such gruesome scenes, I felt my stomach turn. A soldier was gazing blankly into the air, sitting on a stone nearby and trembling all over. He was obviously shell-shocked. Officers, NCOs and other ranks were frantically looking for casualties and human remains.

Four soldiers had died and four others were wounded in this attack. From that day onwards, my parents never sent me to Mensija to buy milk again and we had to settle for the one pint-bottle allowance given to each family.

When this was not enough or unavailable, we made do with powdered milk. We had become accustomed to consuming food which had been dried up or dehydrated, such as potatoes, eggs, fruit, cabbages, onions, and other greens. There were simply no fresh vegetables around.

The authorities requisitioned many buildings including stores, houses and garages which were vacant, in order to store foodstuffs. Just opposite our house, there was a garage which was used for this purpose. A former shoe shop, further down from our house, in the corner with Prince of Wales Road, was also taken over for storing beans, peas, sugar and other similar foodstuffs. These were stored in sacks. Whenever lorries came to load or unload, adults and children used to arm themselves with tins or cardboard boxes and collect whatever fell to the ground. When we could do so without being noticed, we pierced one of the sacks and this, of course, ensured that there was much, more to "sweep" off the ground. Very often, I managed to fill a whole tin-full of beans or peas!

Chapter XI

BLACK CARNIVAL!

O nce, my pilot friend Pete asked me if I could accompany him to Valletta to show him round St. John's Co-Cathedral. We agreed that on his first off-duty day, we would meet and go to the city together.

This day fell on the 15th February 1942, which, had we been living in peacetime, would have been "Carnival Sunday". The air raid alert was on throughout the day. The first one had started at 2.00 am and ended at 7.30 am. After only a 30-minute break, the second air raid alert was sounded. I met Pete near the Point de Vue Hotel, at Saqqajja at about 3.30 pm. We were lucky to hitch a lift on a Royal Air Force 15 cwt truck that was going to Valletta. It dropped us off at King's Gate, now known as City Gate.

We walked by the Royal Opera House which was still standing in those days. It was yet to be destroyed by enemy bombs on the 7th April, 1942. I described to Pete the scene in Valletta in pre-war days, telling him about the crowds and the merrymaking which went on in the streets on Carnival day. I described the parade of grotesque masks and carnival floats which carried couples in fancy costume, singing, dancing and blowing whistles; the pelting with "*perlini*"; (sugar-coated almonds), and '*Kosbor*'; (sugar studs) and cheese cakes; the brass bands, with their lively, happy music; as well as the mosaic of different coloured carnival costumes and the masked balls, which used to take place at the Opera House,

We then arrived at St. John's Co-Cathedral, which had not been damaged, in spite of the fact that all the buildings around it had been demolished by enemy bombs. When Pete saw the Cathedral's facade, he did not seem very impressed but, on entering, he was simply overwhelmed by its beauty. He could not take his eyes off the frescoes on the vaulted ceiling painted by Mattia Preti. His gaze then drifted down to the floor and I explained that the most distinguished members of European nobility were buried there. We toured one side-chapel after another, until we came to the one dedicated to the Nativity, which was slightly damaged by enemy action. The chapel belonged to the German Langue of the Order of St. John. He half smiled and remarked: "It's amazing how these Germans can even go for something built by their ancestors!" Ironically enough, the only damage sustained by the Co-Cathedral of St. John was in the German Chapel.

We left the Cathedral and proceeded to Merchants Street and, on approaching some demolished buildings I explained that once my father's office had been situated there. Along the way, our conversation again fell on the Knights of St. John, and I remember telling him that history seemed to repeat itself. In fact, just as the Order had been made up of knights coming from different European nations, the Royal Air Force squadrons, besides being manned by British and Commonwealth personnel, also counted among their ranks, men from the U.S.A., Poland, Belgium, Holland, France, Greece and Norway. All these airmen shared the same ideal — that of ridding the world of tyranny, in the same way as the Knights of the Order were intent on defending Christian Europe from the Turkish Ottoman and Muslim threat.

Pete observed: "Indeed, there is little difference. However, the Order was composed of knights who had to prove their noble descent for eight generations and who shared one common religion, the Catholic Faith. Today, religion, class or race, do not matter. In the modern military service, particularly in time of war, servicemen, who in civilian life have important jobs or are in a position to order their dependants, share the same work and dangers as their subordinates. Now things had changed. Of course, there was nothing wrong about this, because everybody pulled the same rope, with one objective — that of destroying the enemy before the enemy destroys us. During the times of the Order, every Langue lived in a separate Auberge. Today, the members of the Services, with different religions, creeds or race, all work, eat and sleep together, without distinction."

We then turned towards Old Theatre Street and entered the Governor's Palace. In Prince Alfred's Courtyard, I showed my friend the famous clock at the top of the building. We did not linger there for long because the red flag was rapidly hoisted on the Palace tower.

Pete said it would be better if we took cover because Valletta was a target area and he suggested that we should run to the shelter in the old railway tunnel. When we got to St. Francis Church, there was a sudden commotion and many people started running in the direction of the tunnel, upon hearing the rumble of gunfire. This was a sure sign that the enemy was fast approaching.

Although there had been many attacks on Valletta, particularly when ships were in harbour, some shops, cinema theatres and other outlets were still open for business and many people, particularly off-duty servicemen, would flock into Valletta to watch a film show or have a break in the Command Hall, where they could entertain themselves; playing billiards, table tennis, or practice their shooting in the .22 rifle shooting gallery. This old building, which during the war also housed a spacious theatre and cinema, had been the hospital of the Knights and is now the Mediterranean Conference Centre.

I was hoping that this alert would soon be over because I did not want to return home late. I had not told my parents that I was going to Valletta as I did not want them to worry about me.

We finally made it to the old railway tunnel where many people were jostling to get inside, through the narrow entrance. Men and women were tugging at their children and old and sick people, wrapped in blankets, were also trying to make their way inside.

It was then about 5.45 pm and the gunfire from nearby batteries at Fort Manoel and at Marsa could be distinctly heard. The latter battery was situated on Jesuits Hill, where the Marsa Power Station stands today. We made our way into the tunnel, which was packed. The smell was unbearable — a smell of dampness mixed with that of urine and other body odours. The more the gunfire seemed to increase, the more people crowded in. I was getting out of breath and gradually edged closer to the entrance to be able to inhale some fresh air. Pete stopped me, as he thought that I was going outside again.

The entrance was only about ten feet deep and, from where I stood, I could hear a man reciting the Rosary from the lower part of the tunnel. Somebody else interjected, "Jesus, Mary, Joseph, make the bombs fall in the sea and in the fields."

Then I heard the screeching of falling bombs. The floor of the tunnel shook with the deafening explosion and the blast threw me inwards. The few electric light bulbs which dimly lit up the tunnel went out. There was general panic with women screaming, terrified children crying and men trying to calm people down. Some women quickly lit the candles which they always carried for such emergencies. Then the tunnel was filled with acrid smoke and dust, smelling of TNT. It was clear that the bombs had fallen very close. An air raid warden, who had just entered the tunnel, informed us that the bombs had fallen in Kingsway (Republic Street), near Queen's Square (Republic Square).

When some sort of order was restored, Pete and I left the shelter and saw many servicemen, police, A.R.P. personnel and ambulances heading down Kingsway, towards the Governor's Palace. Pete asked one of the soldiers what buildings had been hit and the reply promptly came, "The Regent Theatre!" Peter looked at me with a frozen expression and whispered quietly: "My God!"

We hurried down Kingsway to the bombed theatre and what I had just been telling Pete about pre-war

Carnivals, flashed back to my mind. Those scenes of past merrymaking which I had described, had suddenly changed into scenes of sorrow and despair. There was a grim parallelism between the gory scene that evening and the scene on a peacetime Carnival Sunday: Carnival floats now turned into ambulances racing down Kingsway; grotesque masks now assumed the shape of faces and corpses of the mutilated victims; instead of the whistles blown by girls in fancy dress, we could hear the screeching of the destructive bombs; *"Perlini"* and *"Kosbor"* were now replaced by red-hot shrapnel which killed or tore up whoever they hit; the percussion of the brass bands was replaced by the drumming of intense gunfire and the kaleidoscope of spectacular colours was replaced by the dull, cement-grey colour of dust, blown up by high explosive and the red of the casualties' blood!

With these sad reflections in mind, I realised that we had reached St. Lucy Street. We were stopped from going further by a police officer but as Pete was in uniform and I was in his company, we were allowed to go through. We trod very warily on debris, wooden splinters, stones, bits of furniture, beams, showcases, windows and bent iron railings from balconies. I spotted a leg and an arm sticking out from beneath the rubble. Rescue workers were already working relentlessly to dig out people buried underneath this devastation. Their screams and cries for help could be heard coming from beneath the demolished buildings. There were groans from those who were still buried and who were hoping against hope to be rescued, before the demolished buildings caved in on them and buried them forever. Other rescuers were carrying stretchers up and down the mounds of debris, transporting the dead and wounded between the fallen girders that had previously supported the roof of the Regent Cinema. It was obvious that there had been many serviceman casualties, from the uniforms many of the victims were wearing.

On reaching Queen's Square, we were faced with a grim sight. There were rows of corpses covered with sheets or blankets and doctors and nurses were milling around the casualties. Priests and monks were administering the last rites to the casualties and the dead, among who was Fr. Gerald Pace, the Prior of the Carmelite Community of Valletta. We saw *Karrozzini* blown up and dead horses with parts of their bodies spattered along the walls. There was a huge bomb crater in the Square, by the side of the Palace, in front of the Casino Maltese, where one of the bombs had fallen. One of the wings of the Palace was pock-marked with splinters and the other wing, close to the Casino Maltese, had been demolished. Nothing was left of the shops on that side of the Square. Everything had been reduced to rubble. Another bomb had fallen in Prince Alfred's Courtyard, near the clock we had just been admiring.

On that "Carnival Sunday" there were no hawkers selling sweets and *'Perlini'*, masks, trumpets and funny hats. There was no dancing either. The only thing that survived from the pre-war scene was the statue of Queen Victoria, who appeared to be gazing with a look of concern at the destruction which had left more then one hundred dead, in one fell swoop. Only few who had been inside the theatre had survived that attack and most of these had perished in the following days, after they had been painstakingly rescued from beneath the debris.

The Regent Theatre was situated on the present site of Regency House, in Republic Street. On that fatal

Sunday, it was screening the film: "North West Mounted Police", starring Nelson Eddy and Jeanette McDonald. It was packed! Very few people in the audience had left the theatre to seek cover when the "red flag warning" was flashed on the cinema screen. Luckily, the Capitol Theatre, next door, was empty, because the show had just finished and people had got out in time.

This disaster subsequently gave rise to much debate and many blamed the authorities for allowing such places of entertainment to remain open during air-raids. Others also ventured to say that the enemy seemed to be aware that these places were crowded with service personnel at certain times of the day and that the bombs had been purposely dropped on the theatre. It was true that among the dead and wounded there were many service personnel but there had also been many civilians. Not only those who happened to be inside the cinema perished, but many were killed in the street outside. As far as I can remember, this was the biggest wartime tragedy in Malta. It was certainly the one that claimed the largest number of victims in one air-raid. At least a hundred people had perished but, to this day, no one knows the exact number.

As it was getting dark, I told Pete that I would have to take leave of him otherwise, I would not find transport. Pete replied that he wanted to go to Sliema as well, to meet a friend from the squadron he had served in, when he was still in England. We sadly walked down to the landing place at Marsamxett and caught the last ferry-boat to Sliema, where we parted at The Strand. Pete headed for Għar id-Dud and I trudged up Prince of Wales Road. The horrible scene I had witnessed in Valletta was still vivid in my mind.

Mother was beside herself when I arrived home and said that she was very worried about my brother Joe, as he had not yet returned home. As far as she knew, he had to go and see a film in Valletta, with his friends. She was already aware of the tragedy in the Regent Theatre, because news like that travelled extremely fast. As she was not aware that I had been in Valletta after going to Rabat, I decided not to mention it, not to worry her even further.

Mother told me that father had already gone to enquire after Joe, at a friend's house. She sent me to another family, to find out where he and his friends were. At about 8.00 pm, I found Joe at his friend's house and told him to come back home immediately because mother was worried sick, thinking that he was at the film-show in Valletta. On the way home, I related all that I had seen and told Joe not to mention anything to mother, except for the fact that he had never been to Valletta and that he had been at his friend, Edwin Overend, all the time.

We had other air raids during the night. One started shortly after Joe and I got home and lasted until about midnight. That night, I did not venture outside as I was still very impressed by what I had seen in Valletta, earlier on that day. We had been under alert for twenty hours.

Carnival Sunday, indeed!

Chapter XII

THE BOMB BY THE POLICE STATION

Since the autumn of 1941, the Germans had withdrawn many squadrons from Russia, to recuperate and, by the end of February 1942 the Luftwaffe was estimated to have about five hundred Stukas, between two hundred and three hundred Me109s and a formidable force of Ju88s, on Sicilian airfields. The Commander-in-Chief of the German forces in Italy, Air Marshal Kesselring had stated on Rome Radio: "There is more than one way of taking Malta!"

Part of the enemy's plan was to stop all British aircraft from using the airfields on the Island and British ships from putting into our harbours. After neutralising the airfields and the harbours, Malta would then capitulate automatically. Accordingly, the Germans now concentrated their attacks, more then ever before, on the airfields.

It was normal that, whenever there was one of these night attacks, the Germans would wake us up earlier than usual and we would emerge from under ground, like ants leaving their hill. I used to go to church to serve Mass. Masses were said at the Sacro Cuor Church between 5.00 am and 8.00 am during weekdays. Although my friends and I were young men, aged mainly between fifteen and eighteen, we were still very keen on serving as many Masses as possible; something which unfortunately young lads are no longer so keen on doing nowadays.

The war had taught us many things which were to be useful in life. We learned to suffer and undergo hardship. It taught us to help each other in times of need and, above all, that, in times of danger we should seek God's help.

It was Tuesday, 17th March 1942 and after an air raid at 6.00 am, I went to church to serve the 6.30 am Mass, said by Fr. Diego. I was helping him to don his vestments, when Albert Mifsud, one of my friends, asked me whether we could serve this Mass together. I told Albert that he could do it himself and I would then serve a later Mass, but Albert still insisted that we should serve together.

After Mass, we walked up to the friary for the usual bowl of sugarless, black coffee in the company of Fr. Diego. We then accompanied him to his cell, where he showed us some tools he had been given by his brother. Albert left us as it was time for school. He attended Stella Maris College, in Gzira. I stayed in Fr. Diego's room, watching him repair a Primus-stove from the friary's kitchen. He was showing me how to clean the burner of the stove, as new burners were unavailable in those days. When the job was complete, we went down to the kitchen of the friary and proudly handed the repaired stove to Friar Cherubim, the cook.

At 7.45 am, mother sent me to my father's office, with some papers which he had forgotten to take with him to work. On arriving at the junction between St. Trophimus Street and St. John the Baptist Street, the alert sounded. I turned back and ran to the Friary and came across Fr. Diego in the corridor, heading for the roof.

When we were half way up the spiral staircase, the guns opened fire. Fr. Diego took out his telescope and hurried on upstairs, to make sure that he would not miss seeing any enemy plane crash. At the top of the staircase, just before emerging onto the roof, he heard the usual sound accompanying falling bombs and turned back, and shouted, "Run down! They are coming down very close!" I had barely gone down six steps, two at a time, when a huge explosion and a tremendous blast bent me double. I covered my head with my hands. Fr. Diego, who was closer to the roof door, dropped his glasses and these fell at my feet. I was afraid that something had happened to him and I was only relieved when I heard him asking whether I was all right. I looked out of a slit window, in the spiral staircase and saw a huge grey cloud mushrooming up from where the Sliema Police Station stood. The red flag on top of the police station building could no longer be seen and I could hear pandemonium and women shouting and screaming in the streets. I handed Fr. Diego's glasses back to him, telling him that most probably the police station had received a direct hit. He decided to rush down to the church, get the holy ointments for Extreme Unction and hurry off to assist the casualties.

We met a woman who lived close by and she informed us that there were many dead and wounded near the police station. I asked her to inform mother that I was with Fr. Diego and on the way to my father's office and not to worry about me.

We rushed up St. Trophimus Street and came to the junction with Rudolphe Street. On the opposite side of the road, where houses had front terraces, there was a row of stretchers with wounded people. Fr. Diego rushed to them at once, reciting the Holy Rites and giving them absolution. He first approached a man whose face was covered in blood from a big gash in his head and whose clothes were tattered. This man was moaning and groaning and calling out a woman's name. I could not tell his age. Then we went to assist another who had part of his thigh torn out by shrapnel. He was in great pain and had to be pinned down by A.R.P. personnel and prevented from moving, until he was given first aid. A.R.P. personnel, monks, doctors, nurses, police and other volunteers, most of them covered in blood, were working incessantly at the rescue operation.

After we had done our best to help the wounded, we came to a group of corpses, completely covered with blankets or sheets. This row of corpses took up the whole length of the pavement, from the corner with St. James Street, all the way to Prince of Wales Road. The majority of the wounded were rushed to the Blue Sisters Hospital, while the dead had to wait their turn.

Fr. Diego started uncovering the faces of the dead, mumbling a short prayer and making the sign of the cross on their forehead or some other part of their body, if he could not do it on their forehead and covered them again. Some of them were so disfigured that I had to turn my face away.

Others had half of their head blown off altogether. One man had his stomach torn out and all his intestines were visible. A woman had her breasts crushed and her clothes torn to shreds. Fr. Diego gently uncovered another corpse — that of a young man who was about fifteen years old. His face was livid and his eyes were wide open, in a frozen gaze. I could not recognise him because of his unusual colour. He did not seem to be suffering from other wounds though his face was also slightly swollen. Fr. Diego knelt down to make the sign of the cross, with holy ointment, on the youth's forehead. Then, he suddenly pulled back and stood up, clasping his forehead and with a suppressed cry, whispered: "Maria Santissima. Haven't you recognised him?"

"No I cannot," I replied hesitantly.

"Albert! It's Albert!" cried Fr. Diego.

"What Albert?" I asked.

"Albert! You two were serving mass together this morning!"

I was suddenly overcome by a cold sensation and remained transfixed looking at the corpse. I felt a lump in my throat and started to cry. Fr. Diego, who was usually a pillar of courage, had tears in his eyes. He knelt down again beside Albert's inert body, made the Sign of the Cross and muttered some prayers in Latin. He then gently covered Albert's face again with the blanket.

A few feet away from where Albert was lying, I saw his school satchel on the ground with some books strewn around it. On picking up one, I found that it had his name written on it.

We got closer to the police station and the scene there was not much better. The first thing that struck me was a *karrozzin* blown up by the explosion. The horse was lying dead in a pool of blood. One half of the cab driver was lying on the pavement and the other half on the road with half of his head blown off by a splinter.

165

The walls were spattered with pieces of flesh and blood. The glass kiosk, which covered the entrance to the public toilets situated in front of the police station, had been completely obliterated and one could only see the remains of the iron framework. Even this looked as if it was about to collapse. The public convenience, which was situated below ground level, was also used as one of the entrances to the underground rock-shelter. A spiral staircase led to it and this was awash with the blood of dead men, women and children, lying on top of each other.

Part of the police station, on the Prince of Wales Road side, had been blown up and there were many other damaged buildings. The bomb had exploded right in the middle of the road and had left a huge crater in front of the building, today housing a branch of H.S.B.C. Bank. I could smell a strong odour of gas and, at one point this caught fire, ignited by some electric spark.

Fr. Diego noticed that my father was waiting at the corner, in front of Sajjan Street. We went up to him and I handed him the papers. He let me know that he had been very concerned about me, because he knew that I was on my way to meet him. He quickly sent me back to reassure mother that everything was all right with me.

Just one enemy aircraft and one bomb, which did not seem to be of an unduly large calibre, had caused all this havoc, which was out of proportion with what I had seen in other places. Twenty people had died including Police Sergeant 89 Charles Lanzon, Police Constable 547 Alfred Vella, Special Constable 152 Joseph Bartolo and twenty-two others were wounded in this raid.

In my opinion, the majority of bombs that fell on Sliema and caused such havoc were strays. They were not meant to fall there, but were usually aimed at some military objective nearby. Sliema was surrounded by five anti-aircraft batteries, at Fort Manoel, Fort Tigne', Fort Spinola, Ta' Giorni Battery and Tal-Qroqq Battery. The submarine base was also in the vicinity.

Chapter XIII

THE CRUELLEST MONTHS

March and April, 1942 were months of incessant bombing, and we had to spend entire days and nights down in the shelter. Housewives barely had time to cook a quick meal or do some housework during the day. Children had to go without schooling. Waves upon waves of enemy aircraft were continuously attacking the harbours and the airfields. Twice the tonnage of bombs that fell over London during the worst twelve months of the blitz was dropped over Malta.

April was the cruellest month. Statistics for this month were astonishing:-

Axis sorties	9,600
Air raid alerts	282
Bombs dropped	6,729 tons
Building demolished	6,000 houses
Killed	300
Seriously wounded	329
Slightly wounded	305

It was calculated that it took twenty-two tons of bombs to kill a civilian and some ten tons to cause a serious injury. Heavy anti-aircraft guns fired over 77,000 rounds and light anti-aircraft guns fired 88,000 shells, during this month.

The invasion of Malta appeared to be more imminent then ever. More preparations for the defence of the Islands were undertaken: barbed wire fences surrounding the coastline were doubled; more pill-boxes were constructed; trenches were dug in the roads; anti-tank defences were constructed and land mines were laid. These were like man holes made of cement. Mines were laid inside them which were then camouflaged with dust or loose gravel. I remember there were some of these holes near Porte Des Bombes and in St. Anne's Street, in Floriana. Others were laid in St. George's Road at Spinola Bay, in St. Julian's. Service personnel had strict orders to carry their fire-arms wherever they went in case of emergency and leave had become very restricted.

Due to the imminent danger of invasion, all English currency notes were withdrawn from circulation and, instead, the authorities printed the Emergency Bank Note Currency in denominations of one pound, ten shillings, five shillings, two shillings and one shilling. Silver coins were also withdrawn from circulation. Copper coins like pennies and half pennies became very scarce and I.O.U. coupons were issued instead of small change from shops, bars and cinemas. The new currency notes would have no international value, in case that they fell in enemy hands.

The civilian population had been given instructions on what to do in case of an invasion. Everybody was to leave his house or place of work and take cover in shelters. The few remaining British families on the Island were evacuated and sent back home. The Home Guard was formed from members of the Volunteer Corps. These were civilian volunteers, of all age groups, but mostly older people and those who, for some reason or other, did not qualify for military service.

Had the Germans invaded Malta and come face to face with these 'soldiers', which the British called Dad's Army, it would have been quite possible, for the majority of the soldiers of the Wehrmacht, to become prisoners because, on seeing this motley lot, they would have burst their sides with laughter and dropped their weapons in uncontrollable fits!

At first, these Home Guard personnel had no uniforms. They only wore an armband with the letter 'V' (Volunteer), and later on, the letters 'HG' (Home Guard). Whoever happened to have some weapon like an old shotgun or some other fire-arm which was still functioning, had permission to carry it about. I remember two occasions when members of the Home Guard were seen carrying a blunderbus and a flintlock musket.

As the invasion loomed, these units were better organised and were issued with army uniforms. Instead of obsolete arms, they were issued with proper Lee Enfield Rifles, like regular soldiers. They were trained to use these weapons and other small arms as well as to throw hand grenades. In case of an invasion, the signal was to be the sounding of sirens and the peeling of church bells.

The armed forces in Malta, at that time, numbered about 30,000 men, who lived on a diet of a slice and a half of bread and jam and a mug of tea in the morning, boiled beef and a slice of bread at noon and the same diet in the evening. At times even water was rationed.

The arrival of Field Marshal, Lord Gort, as Governor and Commander-in-Chief of the Armed Forces in Malta, in early April 1942, stirred a great deal of speculation because, in 1940, Gort was responsible for the successful evacuation of the British Expeditionary Force from Dunkerque.

According to official German documents, Colonel Deichmann, The Chief of Staff of Air Corps II, under the Command of Air Marshal Kesselring, laid out a plan for the carpet bombing of all military installations in Malta, with the objective of neutralising them. Apart from attacks on gun emplacements and anti-aircraft batteries, all dive bombing had to come to an end and instead, all bombers had to work together on this plan, which had been approved in the beginning of March 1942, after much debate and discussion. The priorities of the plan were:

1. To strike at and destroy in a surprise attack, all fighter aircraft on the ground, at Ta' Qali.
2. To attack the bases of Luqa, Hal Far and Kalafrana, where bombers, torpedo bombers and seaplanes were based.
3. To attack the harbours, the dockyards and the naval base.

Reconnaissance aircraft appeared in the skies more frequently. It seemed that the Germans were bracing themselves for an all-out attack but something went amiss. When stencils, which had been used to make copies of the plans, were found by a German security officer as they were being carted away by a refuse collector, the operation was postponed until it could be ascertained whether the British were aware of this information. Reconnaissance photographs taken over Malta showed that Spitfires and Hurricanes were still based at Ta' Qali and Hal Far airfields.

On Friday, 20th March, 1942, I happened to be at Rabat, near the Roman Villa. I do not remember the exact time. I only remember it was late in the afternoon and the sun had almost set, when the air raid warning signal sounded. I decided to go to Mdina and watch the air raid from the bastion, which had the same view I had previously enjoyed from Casa Depiro. There, I found many R.A.F. personnel mostly pilots, together with some civilians eagerly waiting for the spectacle to commence. Although I did not expect to meet my friend Pete, I looked round to see whether he was there, just in case. I heard a man in uniform tell his pals that he was going to take cover as he had heard Fighter Control warn, that the Malta radar was reporting big air activity over Sicily and they were expecting a large air raid by enemy aircraft, approaching from the East of the Island. I was not quite sure whether to take cover or remain there, as I did not want to miss an attack like this. If all these aircraft were coming in, where were they going to attack? There were no vessels in the harbours. That left no other alternative except the aerodromes and, if they were going to attack Ta' Qali, I would get a grandstand view of this attack. After all, Mdina was not a target zone and it was quite far away from the airfield. I decided to stay on and see what happened - the folly of youth!

We did not have to wait long for the anti-aircraft batteries to open up. The enemy was approaching from the direction of Delimara. This was evident from the puffs of smoke from the anti-aircraft barrage. Above Hal Far airfield, I could see columns of smoke and dust rising from the bomb explosions, on the ground. Similar columns of smoke could be seen rising to the sky above Luqa airfield and they hung there for a considerable amount of time, as it was a windless evening. Then I noticed anti-aircraft fire above Grand Harbour and I spotted twelve Ju88s flying at a height of some 14,000 feet. They were flying in two formations of six. Soon after, they broke formation to present less of a target to the curtain of anti-aircraft shells that was rising to meet them.

I did not see a single R.A.F. aircraft in the sky. They must have just landed from a previous scramble. It was almost dusk and Spitfires and Hurricanes did not operate at night. The Ju88s started diving down, one by one, to a height of approximately 4,000 feet and released bombs of all sizes on Ta' Qali airfield. I then saw another fifteen aircraft following the first group in and diving down to a lower height. They started machine-gunning everything in sight on Ta' Qali airfield, among the bursts of the bombs and the sound of gunfire. The blast of the bombs, particularly from the large calibre ones, could be distinctly felt from Mdina.

The sun had set by now and as it was almost dark, the gun flashes going up from all over the Island were even more visible. Tongues of fire were rising up from petrol dumps, bowsers or aircraft which had been hit at Ta' Qali. The red tracers of the Bofors, rising to the sky, added to this terrific spectacle. It was just like one grand fireworks display from one of the pre-war *festas*. The large number of incendiary bombs resembled a *fjakkolata* or lights coming from a thousand torches. The bright, white light emitted by the incendiaries illuminated the target, for the attacking aircraft. The huge pall of smoke

CHARLES B. GRECH

that hovered above Ta' Qali airfield glowed from the many fires on the stricken airfield. Other fires were visible over Luqa airfield.

It was soon completely dark but another wave of aircraft came in to sow their seeds of destruction. The thick dust cloud gradually drifted towards Mdina and the acrid smell of high explosive filled my nostrils. Suddenly, there was a flash traversing the sky. It was a Ju88, which had been hit and plummeted into the sea, beyond St. Paul's Bay. Yet another ball of fire shot up from a petrol bowser that had received a direct hit on Ta' Qali. Another aircraft could be seen aflame in the sky; its bomb load went off as soon as it hit the ground on Ta' Qali airfield.

This ferocious attack, the likes of which I had never seen to that day, lasted for about forty-five minutes. I was so engrossed and excited at this unprecedented sight, that it never dawned on me that I was in great danger and that I could easily have been hit by shrapnel or some stray bomb. I remained there reassured by the presence of the servicemen around me, who were equally engrossed at this spectacle of destruction. I thought that they would be capable of sensing any imminent danger if there were any. I still remember one civilian in his sixties looking aghast, mumbling to himself, lifting his pipe up to his mouth but never actually putting it in and staring at the terrible scene. The R.A.F. servicemen, who must have felt rather helpless and angry on seeing their airfield being pulverised, jumped for joy whenever they saw an enemy aircraft come crashing to the ground.

Back to reality, I overheard one of these officers tell his friend, "I have never seen such a terrifying inferno. The Battle of Britain was a joke compared to this. I think that the invasion of Malta must be imminent." I was overcome by fear at this last remark and as soon as the air raid died down, I hurried towards Saqqajja. I was lucky to thumb a lift on a military lorry, which was heading towards Sliema, when I got to the Y junction that leads to Zebbug.

The ride was not without its own small share of adventure! Very often, the driver had to slow down to a crawling speed or even stop to remove some obstacle from the middle of the road, which was strewn with boulders, tree branches and splinters from falling bombs. I admired his skill in driving through that confusion in pitch darkness. Further down the road, we were stopped by somebody. I do not remember whether it was a policeman or some serviceman, as in those days, everybody wore the same khaki battledress and steel helmet. This man warned the driver to be very careful because, besides craters in the road, there was the danger of unexploded bombs.

According to German records, sixty Ju88s, with a heavy escort of Me110, twin-engine fighters, had taken part in that raid. The same records also state that this was the first carpet bombing attack, which the German Air Force had ever carried out.

The following morning, a reconnaissance aircraft flew over the Island. The enemy wanted to gauge the results of the attack of the previous evening. The photographs were taken in stereo, giving a three-dimensional effect, when viewed through twin-lens viewers. When the photo-interpreters of the Luftwaffe and their intelligence officers carefully studied the results of the attack, they discovered that Spitfires and Hurricanes were still on the aerodromes, even though the airfields at Hal Far,

Luqa and Ta' Qali appeared to be holed like a sieve and were covered with craters of all sizes, some of them even as much as forty feet in diameter. This must have made the photo-interpreters scratch their heads in surprise, until one of them detected something odd!!

A sort of ramp could be seen projecting from a rocky outcrop at the south-western end of Ta' Qali and it appeared to be coming from a tunnel under the rock. The German officers concluded that the R.A.F. must have excavated hangers in the living rock.

This 'discovery' soon led to yet another, even more determined attack. Ju88 bomber formations from Kamfgruppen 606 and 806 from Catania, I/KG from Gerbini and 2 Gruppen KG 77 from Comiso were armed and loaded with 2,000 lb., armour-piercing rocket as- sisted bombs, which descended at great velocity and penetrated forty-five feet of solid rock. These were heav- ily escorted by Me109s from JG.3 (Udet) and JG.53, and another squadron of Me110s from III/ZG26.

All in all, two hundred German aircraft were mus- tered for this second raid. Ta' Qali was again the target and it was again pulverised a second time in twenty-four hours. This raid was so fierce that the thud of the explosions on Ta' Qali could be heard from Sliema. It resembled the continuous rumble of a thunderstorm. The barrage from the anti-aircraft guns was again very intense and fearsome.

The second phase of the Deichmann Plan had to be interrupted however, because a convoy of ships with supplies of munitions, food and petrol was approaching Malta. The Italian Fleet put to sea, to intercept it but it had to turn back to its bases when it was repulsed by a British force composed of four cruisers and sixteen destroyers.

This Italian naval threat, however, caused the convoy to be delayed and instead of reaching the harbour during the night, it only arrived the following morning. Before reaching the safety of Grand Harbour and when it was still about twenty miles off Malta, the convoy was attacked by the Luftwaffe and the rumble of the battle could be heard very clearly from Sliema. They promptly sank the vessel *Clan Campbell*. Another ship, the *Breconshire* was hit off Zonqor Point and was subsequently towed round to Marsaxlokk Bay, where it finally went to the bottom on the 27th March, 1942, after three days of repeated air attacks.

Meanwhile, however, on Monday, 23rd March, 1942, the two other surviving vessels, *Talabot* and *Pampas*, succeeded in entering Grand Harbour and began to unload. Their cargo of about 5,000 tons represented only about one fifth of the entire load of the convoy.

The Luftwaffe went berserk over the presence of these two vessels in Grand Harbour. At about 2.30 pm, during a heavy air attack on Grand Harbour, a stick of bombs straddled the *Pampas* and a heavy calibre bomb went straight through the funnel, into the engine room and exploded, causing heavy damage and flooding it. The vessel started sinking rapidly and fires were also started in other parts of the ship but the vessel was later beached to prevent her from sinking.

Talabot, which was berthed in front of Pinto Stores, was laden with supplies, mainly petrol and ammunition.

It was early in the afternoon, on the 26th March, 1942, and I had just got to Porte Des Bombes on my way to Rabat to fetch the usual 'blessed' loaf of bread. The air-raid warning sirens sounded their plaintive wail. As the area was considered a danger zone, all traffic quickly came to a stop and everybody ran for cover to the nearest shelter. I ran to the old railway tunnel together with some others. The tunnel had an entrance at Porte Des Bombes. Part of it was used as a broadcasting station for Rediffusion and another part as the Central telephone exchange. The Services telephone exchange was also housed in the bowels of this one-mile long tunnel.

We soon heard the anti-aircraft guns in action, particularly those of the Marsa Battery at "Ta' Ċejlu", on top of Jesuits Hill. The rhythm of gun fire increased and I got that creeping feeling of fear which would come over me whenever I was inside a shelter and could not see what was happening outside. Gradually, I started wedging my way out to get the occasional peep outside the tunnel.

A special constable at the entrance to the shelter, who stood there to prevent anybody from going out during an air raid, stopped me and asked: "Where do you think you are going? Don't you know what's going on out there and what is raining down from the sky?"

I replied, "I am afraid inside here, unable to see what is happening."

"My son, it is better to be afraid then dead because out there, even if you are not killed by a bomb, it is very likely that you will be hit by falling shrapnel. Listen to me and remain in here. Even I would much rather be out there but I have to remain inside as well."

I had to obey him, very reluctantly but I knew he wished me well. I remained inside, sheltering behind the blast walls.

The blast from the bombs was like sudden gusts of wind. The attack was on Grand Harbour and the targets were those two cargo ships. Whenever bombs fell into the sea and exploded underwater, the earth trembled. Most of those, who had taken refuge in that shelter, were men going back home from work. They appeared calm and were commenting on what they were hearing outside. They were either dockyard workers or service employees, who were used to heavy bombing. They made it sound as if nothing unusual was going on. This helped me pluck up some courage and dispel my irrational fear.

Gradually, the gunfire subsided and finally came to an end. It was followed by the usual dead calm. The special constable crept outside and I promptly followed him. The first thing I saw, was a huge pall of thick, black smoke rising to the heavens above Grand Harbour, behind the church of the Capuchin friars. The S.C. sadly remarked that the smoke was most likely coming from *Talabot*. As I had never seen a ship on fire, I hurried up to the Capuchin friary but I was quickly stopped in my tracks by a policeman, who told me that I could not go on the bastion. I therefore headed towards the playground, but there, I found another policeman telling people to keep off as there was a chance that the ship, which was laden with ammunition, would blow up at any moment. So, I walked on to the Duke of York Avenue (Triq Ġlormu Cassar), leading up to Castille Place and, from there, I could see the entire grim spectacle.

Tongues of fire, as high as the Floriana bastions, were leaping up from *Talabot*. They transformed themselves into a thick, black column of smoke, rising hundreds of feet high. Tug boats and other light craft, plying around the vessel, were trying to extinguish the enormous pyre. I had not been there long when yet another policeman came along and sent me off. The smoke now assumed a reddish hue, reflecting the light of the setting sun, while the smoke immediately above the vessel glowed from the huge flames rising from the ship. It was quite late by now and the bus service had stopped running. I had to go down to Marsamxett and catch a *dghajsa* to take me across the creek to Sliema.

All that night, the Floriana skyline, particularly Sarria church and St. Publius church, were silhouetted against the glow from the fires on *Talabot*. The vessel was ablaze for two days and finally it had to be scuttled in Grand Harbour, to prevent the fire from reaching the holds, laden with ammunition. Luckily, some of its cargo, particularly the sugar, had been saved. I remember this well, because, for many weeks, we had to consume wet sugar, salvaged from its holds. Later the ammunition was raised to the surface by divers and could be used. However, petrol and oil supplies were totally lost.

It is only fit and proper to mention the outstanding courage shown by Commander D.A. Copperweath and his small team of men, who, while *Talabot* was ablaze from stem to stern, managed to flood the holds and sink the vessel. They very courageously placed explosive charges, which were then detonated from ashore, before the fire could reach the ammunition holds. In this way, a gigantic explosion, which could have caused havoc to Floriana and the surrounding areas, was avoided. Commander Copperweath was awarded the George Cross for his valour.

Many blamed the inefficiency of the Royal Air Force for the failure of this convoy to deliver its load safely but few were really aware of the difficulties that the pilots and the ground crews of the Royal Air Force had to face in those days. There was a shortage of aviation fuel, ammunition and aircraft spares and, very often, aircraft mechanics cannibalised bombed aircraft, for spares. Aircraft could not take off, due to the large number of craters on the runways, after determined strikes by the Luftwaffe. Moreover, exhaustion was now also increasingly taking its toll on pilots and ground crews.

The fast minelayer, *H.M.S. Welshman*, had often succeeded in eluding the German and Italian forces. It used to arrive in Grand Harbour during the night, disguised as a French destroyer, unload its small cargo of supplies and ammunition and depart in the shortest time possible. This warship and a few submarines had now become the Island's only remaining lifeline.

The first day of April, 1942, happened to be Wednesday of Holy Week, when special functions are held in church, marking the start of the religious ceremonies. After lunch, I went out to meet my friends and we decided on what church service we were to attend. One of us had a wooden rattle and wanted to try it out as soon as the last candle had been extinguished, during the service. The friars were not keen on allowing us to use these rattles. So, as a prank, we got a little boy to clack it, telling him: "Now, when you hear the monks chanting away in the choir, start clacking the rattle as hard as you can."

This little boy dutifully carried out our instructions and started clacking the rattle with a vengeance. The din did not last long as he was quickly bodily evicted from the church and the friar gave him a hiding with the rope he wore around his cassock, shouting out at him: "Why don't you go and clack it next to your mother's ears!"

At about 2.10 pm, the air-raid warning signal sounded again. "Air raid, let's go and take cover," said Franky,

"We don't want to join those who have just died near the Police Station, do we?"

"I am going up to the friary, as I had to meet Fr. Diego, and then I will come down for the service and see you there," I replied and left.

On arriving at the junction of St. Mary Street with St. Trophimus Street, where there is a niche dedicated to St. Mary, Fort Manoel's guns engaged the enemy. I looked skywards to see whether anything was visible. I saw a Ju88 approaching from the direction of Valletta, at a height of about 3,000 feet. I wanted to run for cover but I had no time so I remained where I was, clinging to the wall. I did not dare move from there, lest I would be machine-gunned. I saw the aircraft releasing two bombs above the submarine base at Manoel Island. Then, the same aircraft released another two bombs which appeared to be of a dark green colour with red and yellow bands painted on their warheads. These were plummeting straight in my direction. I mumbled a quick Act of Contrition and clung to the corner of the block, almost as if to stop the building from falling on top of me. Then two huge deafening explosions and a tremendous blast flung me to the ground. There was a big cloud of dust and smoke. Pieces of glass and wood were flying in all directions. Balconies fell into the street and doors and windows were blown out, to the opposite side of the street. All this in one split second! I was so terrified that, instead of running away, I froze like a statue and remained fixed to the spot, as if glued to the ground, still hugging the corner and deafened for a few seconds. I was covered with glass which fell from the bulbs adorning the statue of St. Mary, hanging above me in the street corner. The cuts I received from the glass, soon brought me back to my senses. I could not see further than five yards up the street, because of the thick dust cloud and the dense smoke and could not tell where the bombs had fallen. The only thing I could gather was that they must have fallen very close by and, most probably, not more than a block away. I heard the shouting of men and the screams of women and I had a premonition that the bomb had fallen near our house. I therefore hurried back home, fearing the worst, because my mother and Victor were still at home. On reaching the house, I saw with relief that it was still standing. The door had burst open. I called out for my mother and Victor but there was no reply. There was glass and dust all over the place, the garden door had been blown in and a small chandelier, which had been hanging in the hallway, lay shattered on the floor. When I got no reply, I ran out into the street and sprinted to the shelter, hoping to find mother there. On entering the shelter and arriving at the bottom of the steps leading to one of the compartments, a woman told me to hurry and go near my mother, as she was very anxious about my safety.

I was covered in dust and looked as if somebody had emptied a sack of cement on top of me. Whenever buildings were bombed down, a greyish dust was stirred up. While descending the steps of the shelter, I was repeatedly asked where the bombs had fallen and could only reply that I did not know exactly where, but that I thought that they must have fallen pretty close to the church, because I had not seen any demolished buildings in St. Mary Street. Mother had been crying and telling people that I must have been killed, as I had gone to church. Strangely enough, my news that the bombs might have fallen near the church, reached my mother down below, even before I arrived beside her. On seeing me, those around her quickly reassured her, "Here he is, safe and sound."

Mother quickly pulled herself together and scolded me severely but hugged me to her nonetheless. "Where have you been? You've driven me sick with worry! Look at you! You look like a chalk statue!" she sobbed.

Hoping to calm her down, I assured her that the house was still standing as I had been there a few moments before and that the only damage sustained was broken glass and the blown-in garden door. An Englishman, Billy Hamer, who lived close by and who was serving in the Royal Navy, told me, "I thought that was the last time I would see you alive because after the explosion, the dust cloud hid you completely. I thought that the building you were sheltering under had collapsed!" Then he added: "The Sacro Cuor Church has received a direct hit." This news immediately spread to the four corners of the shelter.

People, who had relatives living close by the church, shot out of the shelter without waiting for the "raiders passed" signal while others broke into uncontrolled panic.

Mother did not want to go out and would not allow me to leave, even though our front door was open. I wanted to go and see what had happened because even I had some friends living there, but I dared not leave mother alone after all the anguish I had put her through earlier on, during the raid. A quarter of an hour later, father came on the scene looking very worried. He had good reason to be. From his office, he had seen the bombs fall on the church and he immediately feared for our safety. He told us that besides the church and the friary, many other buildings had also been damaged and that there were dead and wounded everywhere. I immediately thought of Fr. Diego.

As I felt that father could take good care of mother and my brother Victor, I left the shelter and rushed towards the church. As I turned from St. Mary Street into St. Trophimus Street, I came upon a scene of total devastation. There were fallen balconies blocking the road and masonry strewn everywhere. The shop windows in front of the church had been obliterated. Houses had been demolished, and there were people running hither and thither. In the corner of Church Street, there was a row of demolished houses. The road was completely blocked with rubble and impassable. I proceeded further and saw a number of corpses lying in the street leading to the friary. Among these, I recognised Police Sergeant 184 Michael Riviera. Afterwards, I learnt that he had died when he was giving first aid to a casualty and a damaged wall had collapsed on top of him. Groups of people appeared to be looking for relatives under a demolished house, belonging to the Cassar family. I saw the solicitor, Gerald Cassar, being taken out from under the debris. He had survived, but his sister was killed. Among those helping the wounded, was my friend Manuel Zammit, later to become Fr. Raniero, Chaplain of the Malta Police Force. A dog called 'Prince' was lying on the road with its head crushed under a stone. Prince was a very popular dog and he was always on guard at its owner's bazaar, 'Ta' Zaqzaq'. Whenever somebody blew a raspberry in its direction the dog would face him and keep barking until its tail was stroked. Then, Prince would chase his short tail until it got tired, bolting to the shelter whenever it heard the alert sounded. That day, it did not make it in time and, sadly, the bombs overtook it before it could make it to safety. Not even dogs like dear Prince were spared by the enemy!

The closer I got to the friary, the more dead men, women and children I came across. Rescue workers were doing their best. I do not remember having spoken to any one, as I was speechless at what I was seeing. I was thinking how lucky I was not to have been in the friary when the bombs fell, as I would surely have been one of those lifeless bodies or buried under the debris. It appeared that the bombs had mostly mowed down those who were heading for or entering the friary shelter. There was a boy, my age, lying dead, his face downwards under the pavement. When I got closer to him, I recognised him as one of those friends I had planned to meet at Fr. Diego's, later on that day. A young woman with a little child lay dead near the church's side entrance. Children were bemoaning the loss of their parents and wives were crying for their missing husbands or children.

I came across Fr. Alessandro Azzopardi outside the oratory and asked him whether any of the friars were killed or injured. He sadly replied that that Fr. Diego was still missing. Fr. Lino Mamo had managed to get away slightly wounded on his forehead by a flying stone, while he was leaving his cell. Fr. George Xerri, the parish priest, was wounded and still lay buried under some debris. He then asked me to accompany him to administer the last rites to the wounded. The other friars were performing the last rites in various parts of the bombed site, while A.R.P. personnel were still working hard to extricate the parish priest from beneath the fallen masonry.

Fr. George had been hearing confessions of women parishioners when the bomb fell. The confessional was situated under the nave which took the direct hit. Those who were confessing or awaiting their turn to do so were all buried under the huge chunks of masonry that cascaded on top of them. Two hours later, they managed to extricate Fr. George, who was suffering from a grievous head wound. Two women, Ophelia Colombo and Concetta Mifsud Ellul, who had come for confession all the way from Gzira and a fourteen year old girl, Giusa Tabone had been killed by falling masonry. Fr. George and another wounded woman were rushed to the Blue Sisters Hospital. Those who were in other parts of the church however escaped with little or no injuries. Fr. George died two months later.

The crystal chandeliers, which had been bought some two years before the war, were shattered. Luckily, the painting of St. Gerolamo, a masterpiece by Giuseppe Cali', only suffered a minor scratch from a wooden splinter. The pulpit which is a masterpiece in oak, mahogany and bronze and which was considered to be one of the most beautiful in Malta was surprisingly left unscathed, even though the nave opposite had collapsed. It would indeed have been a great loss had it been destroyed. The large church organ sustained slight damage in the pipes which were displaced. It was indeed a miracle that the beautiful and artistic titular statue of Our Lady of the Sacred Heart of Jesus was undamaged, even though the bomb had fallen just behind its niche and all around it had been blown up.

I felt somebody nudging me on the shoulder and, on turning round, I found Friar Paul, who was a very holy man. He asked me calmly, "Are you still alive? I thought you were at Fr. Diego's." I asked him whether he had any news of him, and he sadly replied that Fr. Diego was still missing. He also whispered that some of my friends were looking for Fr. Diego and that he was going to join them and asked me whether I wanted to accompany him. We walked up to where the friary once stood and tried to pass through where the main door had been, but the rescue workers told us not to go that way, as people still lay buried under the debris. They were extricating those who were blocked in the wooden shelter. Fortunately, all those who had taken cover in this shelter survived to tell the tale. Many of those who were buried alive had been caught either in the entrance to the friary or in front of the entrance to the wooden shelter. Others were trapped on the steps, connecting the friary to the church. We walked round to Carmel Street and entered the friary's garden. From what I could make out, the bomb had hit the main staircase of the friary, next to Fr. Diego's cell and that wing was completely obliterated. There was now little hope that Fr. Diego was still alive. The other friar, Fr. Lino, had survived because, when the friary was collapsing, he was just about to leave his cell and instead, had stood there while all his surroundings crumbled down. He only sustained a cut on his head from some falling stone which fell when the ceiling collapsed.

A woman was taken out dead from beneath the rubble, clinging to a baby, which was still alive. Another pregnant woman was also rescued alive from beneath the ruins. They tried to save the baby, but to no avail. We could hear moaning and groaning from beneath the rubble until it was dark and the rescue operation continued after nightfall.

I do not remember ever having handled and moved so many stones in my life. I discovered a hidden strength that day. Every now and then, I unearthed some of the tools which Fr. Diego kept in his room and I put them aside together with others that we had found but, alas, Fr. Diego himself was nowhere to be found!

While I was frantically searching and turning debris over, I heard my brother Joe call out to me. He left work to see what had happened, when he heard that the church had been hit. He knew that I was always there or at the friary. Joe was employed at the Command Pay Office, situated at Villa Rosa, in St. George's Bay. He breathed a sigh of relief on seeing me safe and sound. Who knows? Perhaps it was the statue of Santa Maria, in the niche above my head that had spared me!

This tragedy is considered to be by far the worst one in my home town. Twenty-eight people had died and twenty-three others were seriously injured. During this air-raid, *H.M. Submarine, P36*, which was berthed at Lazzarett Creek, had also been sunk, as well as another submarine, *H.M.S. Pandora*, together with the drifter *Sunset*, in Grand Harbour.

It was indeed the Wednesday of Holy Week — The day of darkness!

Chapter XIV

A FAMILY TRAGEDY

T he next day, Thursday, 2nd April, 1942, we got up very early, as we had a lot of damage in the house to see to, after the previous day's air raid. Mother made some coffee and prepared a small lunch pack for Joe, who used to sleep at grandma's house. Before going to work, he would always pass by to collect his meagre lunch pack. Father and I set to work to fix the back door while mother was busy sweeping the dust and broken glass that was strewn all over the place. Mother saw Joe off to the door and hurried away. Father left for work about half an hour later. My brother Victor, who was still very young helped, as best as he could, with the tidying up of the house. Mother continued with her daily chores. Meanwhile, I started stoking the *Patalott*, a contraption like a brazier, made from a one-gallon, paint-container and a piece of iron pipe, jutting out on the side, at the base. Saw dust was pressed inside it and soaked in kerosene. When ignited, it gave out a smoke-less flame. It was very economical but it could only be used outdoors. It was mostly used to boil the water for the laundry. Later, when we could no longer get carpenters' saw dust and kerosene, we had started to use an old stone brazier (*Kenur*), which we found in the house amongst the old bits and pieces belonging to grandma and which had not been used for many years.

We only used this stone brazier to boil the washing because it emitted clouds of black smoke which then settled all over the house, in the shape of soot and ashes. We used kerosene only for cooking food, because this was strictly rationed and we could not afford to waste the gallon and a half allotted to us once a week.

At about 10.15 am, there was the habitual air-raid warning signal. As the red flag had not yet been hoisted, mother and I continued with our chores. She was doing the washing and I was still stoking the fire. At about 10.30 am, we went up on the roof to hang out the day's washing. The sky was quite overcast and, for a time, everything seemed normal and quiet. As usual, we could hear orders being given to the gun crews at Fort Manoel and I told mother: "We had better hurry because although the red flag had not yet been hoisted, the Fort's guns are already elevated in the direction of Valletta." We soon heard the droning of enemy aircraft in the distance but I could not spot them because of the clouds. The guns remained silent and I said to myself: "They must be ours."

The cloud base that morning was not higher then 2,000 feet, but there were gaps in it. For a moment, I forgot what I was meant to be doing up there and scanned the skies to try and spot the approaching aircraft. Then came the sound of a diving aeroplane and a Ju88 suddenly appeared through the clouds, coming down to about 1,500 feet. The guns of Fort Manoel and other batteries immediately engaged it.

Mother screamed: "Hurry down!" I replied that there was no need for that because, even if the aircraft released its bombs, it was not flying in our direction. Now the guns of Fort Tigne` and Tal-Qroqq and Ta' Giorni batteries were also in action. The pilot of the Ju88 was not deterred by all this gunfire and pursued his course, in the direction of St. Andrew's Barracks.

"He's dropped them!" I called mother.

"God have mercy on their victims!" mother exclaimed, looking transfixed at the sight of that fatal stick of bombs screeching down, until they disappeared behind the skyline. Immediately afterwards, we heard the explosions.

"I think Fort Spinola has copped it, because that's where I saw them fall!" I exclaimed.

Then, the lone aircraft changed course and disappeared in the direction of Sicily. We did not give that attack much thought and continued with our work.

When we had finished with our household chores, I left for the friary to find out if there was any news of Fr. Diego. Rescue workers were rummaging among the debris, looking for those who were still missing. They were being aided by some friars and other volunteers, including some of my circle of friends.

I quickly joined them but it was not long before Tony, one of my friends, shouted: "Here! Come here! I can see parts of his cassock, under the stones!" Everybody rushed to him and, very carefully, we started lifting one stone after another. To our great disappointment, it was only one of Fr. Diego's tunics, which was still hooked on to a door.

The column of smoke rising above the Sacro Cuor church and the friary on 1 April, 1942.

The ruins of the Friary of the Franciscan Fathers after the same air raid.

A bird's eye view of the Franciscan Friary after it was demolished by bombs.

The confessional of the Parish Priest, Fr. George Scerri, after bombs had fallen on the church on 1 April 1942, killing four women, who were waiting for confession. The monk seen kneeling is Fr. Odoric Grima, the astronomer still remembered for his almanac.

Bomb damage at the Nazzarene Church and Friary.

Although parts of the Parish church of our Lady Of the Sacred Heart had been demolished, the church remained open for religious services.

A pall of smoke hangs over the background of Spinola Bay from bomb explosions, after the attack on St Andrew's Barracks.

The author's brother Joe, 17, killed by enemy action on 2 April 1942.

The Royal Opera House in 1939 (top), and after it received a direct hit on 7 April 1942 (bottom).

A newly arrived Spitfire Mk. Vc, at Ta'Qali Airfield.

The Italian Cant that was captured (hijacked) by the crew of the RAF Beaufort, over the Adriatic, seen here moored at St Paul's Bay.

The tanker "Ohio" being towed into Grand Harbour on 15 August 1942.

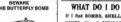

BEWARE
OF THE BUTTERFLY BOMB

Many people in Malta last Monday found in their fields, their gardens, courtyards and on their roofs, a queer yellow contrivance consisting of a small round box with vaned wings attached. It was a 'present from Jerry'. A "Yellow butterfly bomb", as this type of German anti-personnel bomb is called. To move it meant death.

The yellow butterfly bomb is a small round yellow box, shaped like the top of a jill gun and three inches in diameter. It is attached by about six inches of wire to four curved metal fins, two of them with red bars painted across them. The bomb is a delayed action one and may explode within 30 minutes of reaching the Earth. If it does not explode then it will do if it is moved. ON NO ACCOUNT TOUCH IT. Report its presence to the police who will send for the Bomb Disposal Officer to deal with it.

It is important to warn children about this anti-personnel bomb which the enemy scatter in the hope of killing a few more of us. Parents and teachers should describe the appearance of the bomb to the children.

WHAT DO I DO

If I find BOMBS, SHELLS, MINES, bits of AIRCRAFT or any unusual object?

(1) I DO NOT TOUCH THEM, but report them immediately to the Police.

(2) I remember that lives have been lost through tampering with objects which contain explosives.

(3) I remember too that even things which may not be explosive often provide the authorities with information which may be very important.

WARN
YOUR CHILDREN ABOUT THIS

CUT THIS OUT—AND KEEP IT!

Issued by the Information Office

Space presented to the Nation by
Messrs. Jerem Buchanan & Co., Ltd., Glasgow
Agents for Malta: Simonds-Farsons Ltd.

The Luqa wartime Control Tower.

Warnings against anti-personnel bombs and booby-traps were frequently published in The Times of Malta and il-Berqa.

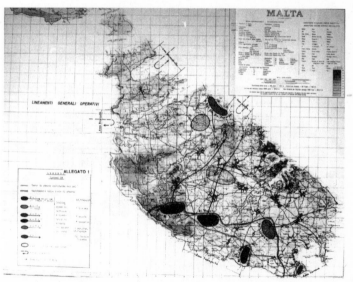

Landing zones for Operation "Hercules" or "C3", the planned invasion of Malta.

Service personnel toiling at bomb craters on one of the airfields.

Servicemen reconstructing aircraft pens after an air raid.

The author, in
Royal Air Force
uniform.

A 3.7 inch anti-aircraft gun being towed for embarkation,
prior to the invasion of Sicily, July 1943.

Invasion barges and landing craft at Pietà (top), and at Ta' Xbiex (bottom) moored to hards built by Maltese workers, summer, 1943.

Air Vice Marshal Sir Keith Park drives Gracie Fields - the
"Forces' Sweetheart" – out of Luqa Airfield in his MG.

Pilots of No. 185 Squadron, R.A.F. at Hal Far, 1943.

The Sacro Cuor friars in a thanksgiving procession after Italy's surrender, September, 1943.

Celebrations in Valletta on the same occasion.

Crowds made up of civilian and service personnel celebrate at The Strand, Sliema, 8 September 1943.

An English sailor being helped onto a "Dghajsa", after jumping into the water at The Strand, Sliema, during the same celebrations.

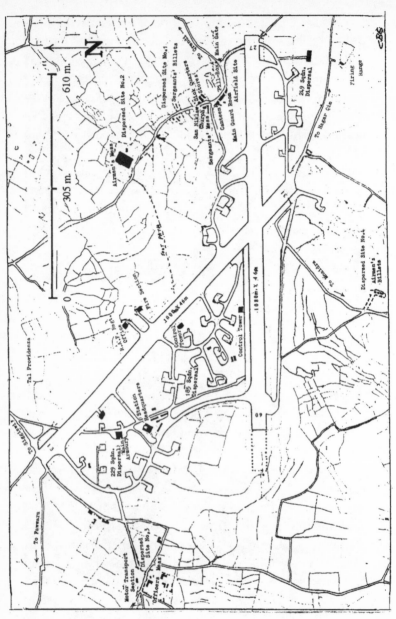

Qrendi Strip, 1943.

At about 12.30 pm, another one of the rescuers called out excitedly. This time a lifeless foot, shod in sandals, was showing from beneath the debris. Very quickly, we started removing the stones, with A.R.P. personnel directing the rescue operation. On removing some more fallen masonry and dust, we sadly unearthed the corpse of Fr. Diego. We carried him away and laid him in the garden path. Fr. Diego was no longer one of us and our group of friends had lost a great mentor. Many owed their safety to his decision to dig a shelter in the living rock. Had this refuge not been excavated, the number of fatal casualties in Sliema would surely have been much larger.

I meekly returned home and broke the sad news to my parents who were both stunned, particularly father, who had been an intimate friend of Fr. Diego.

Although I had lost my appetite, I ate something light as, in those days one could not afford to miss out on any food that came one's way. I noticed that father looked very anxious. He was not eating at all and was unduly silent. I thought he must be thinking about Fr. Diego's death!

To break the ice, I described what we had seen from the roof earlier that morning. When I told him that I thought the bombs had fallen on Spinola Battery, he mumbled back that that was not quite where they had fallen. "They had been dropped on Villa Rosa." Mother apparently did not quite understand what he had just said and interjected: "Aunt Mary went to live just there." Father retorted curtly, "What has this got to do with your aunt Mary? Villa Rosa! Not Villambrosa! That is where Joe works!"

Mother suddenly froze, dropped everything and quickly rushed upstairs to change and go out. When she ran down again, she told father that she was going to see Sur Guze', as his son-in-law Leslie Beckett, a corporal in the Royal Army Pay Corps, who lived with him, also worked with my brother at Villa Rosa.

Mother and Sur Guze's daughter, Lina, hurried down to The Strand, took a cab and left for St. George's Bay. On arriving there, they found a complete shambles. Mother asked for her son and Lina for her husband. Nobody gave them any information, as this was a military area. Indeed, they were even asked to leave. Finally, an English sergeant took them to the Commanding Officer, Major Howell, to see if he could be of any help. When mother and Lina told him the reason for their being there, Major Howell informed Lina that her husband had been wounded and conveyed to St. Patrick's Military Hospital, at St. Andrew's. Then he turned to mother and, with great kindness, explained that her son was still missing. My mother fainted on the spot and the medical orderlies of the Army Medical Corps, who were standing nearby, had to give her first aid.

When she recovered, Major Howell told her that it would be better if she went back home and that he would phone her or even come to our house himself to give her any news. But mother insisted on remaining there. Major Howell was adamant however and told her that, if she remained there, she would do untold damage to the morale of the soldiers, who were still looking for Joe. My brother was the only one still missing. Major Howell, who knew my father well, sent mother home in a military vehicle.

Meanwhile, back home, we had all become extremely anxious for any news of my brother, Joe. When our relatives heard about what could have happened, they

194

also flocked to our house. They looked after father who, by then, was fast losing his composure. At about 5.00 pm, an army car pulled up in front of our house and an English sergeant helped mother out of the car, escorting her to the main door. From the way she looked, we at once realised that it could only be bad news. While my uncles and aunts milled around mother, father invited the sergeant in and asked him for the latest news. He offered him a tot of whisky, out of a bottle he always kept for that 'special' occasion. In order not to depress father unduly, the sergeant told him that other clerks had said that they had last seen my brother Joe under the staircase and that it was therefore possible that he might still be alive, because, although the building had been demolished, the staircase was still standing.

That Maundy Thursday we did not pay the traditional visits to the seven churches. Instead, relatives and friends came to visit our house. Everybody turned up to console my parents. There were those who tried to raise their morale by telling them that there had been many who had been found alive, even after lying buried under bomb debris for days. We had not told grandma what had happened and when she asked why Joe was not sleeping at her house, my uncles told her that he was ill and would be sleeping at our house that night.

There were some air raids during that night but none close to Sliema. Whenever she heard gunfire in the distance, mother muttered to herself: "Who knows how terrified Joe must be." or "How cold he must be feeling tonight!"

That night, instead of the usual light-heartedness, in the smaller shelter there was great anxiety. Sur Guze's family was very much in the same boat. Leslie was seriously injured and might not have lived to see the light of day. In the larger shelter there was as much gloom and sadness because many had just lost their relatives in the Sacro Cuor tragedy.

These were indeed days of darkness and of sorrow for many people. If my brother's number was up, this would be the third loss of life from enemy action in my family. The first to die had been my cousin, who had gone down with *H.M.S. Royal Oak*, at Scapa Flow. Next had been my uncle, father of this same cousin. He died in Naxxar, where he was staying as a refugee, when a bomb exploded on his house just as he was on his way to the shelter. Now, it seemed, it was my brother's turn!

No church service could be held in our parish church of Sacro Cuor the following day, even though it was Good Friday, as the church was now in ruins. I went back there in the morning to help the monks salvage whatever they could from amongst the debris.

Only few of my friends turned up however. Some had lost their lives on Wednesday. Others lay wounded in hospital and others simply could not be bothered because they had just lost their dearest ones. We picked up the pieces of the crystal chandeliers and placed them in wooden boxes, hoping that, one day, they could be put to good use again.

The friars now had been given alternative accommodation in a house, at number 151 Rudolphe Street, near the junction with St. Trophimus Street. They remained there until the bombed friary was rebuilt two and a half years later.

At about 4.30 pm, when we were at home drinking a cup of tea, the door bell rang and I went to open the door. It was a policeman. He asked me whether father was in.

I replied that he was still at work and asked him whether he would like to leave a message with me. He told me quite bluntly that they had found Joe dead and that his body was lying at the St. Julian's Police Station.

Mother overheard everything from the hallway. You can imagine how she reacted! She wanted to leave there and then for St. Julian's, but her sisters stopped her. They sent me off to tell father. The road from our house to my father's office seemed endless and it appeared much longer than usual. I was all the time wondering how best to break the news to my father.

With every brisk step, thoughts crossed my mind in quick succession. I was pondering whether my brother had suffered any pain before dying; whether he was maimed; I thought about our childhood; our games when we were still very young; how relieved Joe had been, on finding out that I had not been hurt in the bombing of the Sacro Cuor Church... and now, less than twenty-four hours later, he was dead himself! I could vividly picture him going out to work for the last time; an eighteen year-old boy, full of youthful energy. Now I would never see him again ..... It was like sequences in a slickly edited film.

I finally arrived at father's office and as soon as Ganni, the messenger, saw my bloodshot eyes, he at once realised why I was there and showed me in. Father immediately understood and asked: "So they've found him dead after all, haven't they?" He uttered this before I even had time to open my mouth.

I broke into tears. Mr Ganni Bencini, my father's senior officer and a great friend of his, walked in and kindly told father to go home. Mr. Bencini was extremely sorry for Joe as he had taken to him like his own son. My brother had even spent some time working in that office on a voluntary basis, before taking up his job at the Command Pay Office.

Father asked me to accompany him to St. Julian's Police Station but, on arriving there, we were told that the corpse had already been taken to the mortuary in Floriana. As it was getting too late by then, we decided to return home.

My uncles advised father not to go to Floriana to identify my brother the following day, telling him it would be better if he stayed at home with mother and made the necessary preparations for the funeral. Uncle Eddie offered to go to Floriana instead and I begged him to take me with him. Father and mother would not hear of it, as Floriana was very vulnerable to air attacks. Finally, however, they reluctantly let me go.

That Easter Saturday afternoon, we took the route bus and alighted at Porte Des Bombes, where the buses to Valletta used to stop in those days. As we approached St. Anne Street, we came across a scene of great devastation, as some bombs had just fallen there. Many buildings, including the Capuchin friary, had been blasted out of existence. As we were in no mood to look at the damage and as these were the worst days for Floriana, we made straight for the Central Hospital, which, in those days, was inside the building which today houses the Police Headquarters.

Uncle Eddie enquired where we could identify my brother's body, and one of the orderlies led us into a large hall full of corpses and slowly guided us around the rows of bodies. Whenever there was a corpse which was unrecognisable, we read out a tag attached to it. After walking round this hall of death without success, we walked into another hall which was also full of corpses.

There were still some of the victims of the Sacro Cuor tragedy among the dead in that room and I recognised some of those that had not yet been buried. In those days it was not all that easy to bury one's dead, as even coffins were extremely scarce. Very often, corpses remained in the mortuary for three or four days before burial, until the family could finally lay its hands on a suitable coffin.

We went through the whole lot until we finally came to my brother Joe. It was indeed a macabre scene and, had it not been for my determination to see my brother for the last time, I would have bolted out of there. There were dead bodies of all ages and from all social classes; people who had died crushed under falling masonry and others who had been butchered by bomb explosions. Some had barely any resemblance to the human form left and were badly maimed or had parts of their bodies missing. Others appeared seriously burnt. In one corner of the room, there were dismembered limbs of people, which could not be identified.

There were other bodies which did not appear to bear the slightest scratch, except for the fact that their face, or part of it, was completely black. These had died of bomb blast and my brother was one of them. The orderly explained that his was an instantaneous death and that at least he did not suffer. My uncle appeared somewhat reassured on seeing that my brother's corpse was not disfigured and motioned me to leave the room. He told me not to mention anything at home about what we had witnessed at the mortuary. I was only to say that Joe had died of bomb blast and that no wounds were visible.

Father tried hard to get someone to make a coffin for Joe and, two days later, he found an undertaker from

Rabat. But, this wretched man did not bring the coffin to the hospital in time and left us waiting there. Shortly afterwards, one of the hospital orderlies came around with a telephone message he had received and informed us that the funeral would have to be cancelled, because the fellow who was transporting the coffin had been blown up by a bomb: cart, donkey, coffin and all. As my brother had been dead for quite some time and was fast decomposing, the health authorities warned father that if my brother was not buried within the next twenty-four hours, they would have to take care of the matter themselves and bury him without a coffin. Providentially, at the eleventh hour, father found someone else who sold him a coffin there and then.

Joe did not get the decent funeral he deserved. In those dark days, it was unheard of to have a funeral with the pomp with which they are held today. The only persons who attended his funeral at the Santa Maria Addolorata Cemetery were my father, two uncles, three friends of Joe and myself.

The cemetery itself had been the target of heavy bombing during the previous night and, even there, I witnessed other macabre scenes. Graves had been blown up or open, while others had caved in. Coffins had been blown out of them and corpses, in the worst state of decomposition and letting off the foulest of smells, were to be seen all over the place.

"Don't these fiends have any mercy on the dead?" I mused. Meanwhile, other dead were continuously being brought in for burial.

Joe was laid down to rest in the family grave which, luckily, had not been hit during the previous night's air raid, although a bomb had fallen only a few yards away.

It was a very brief ceremony and then we sadly took a cab back to Sliema.

Two other Maltese civilians, Edgar Zahra and Walter Farrugia, a British officer, Lieutenant F. Harwood and three soldiers, Privates C.P. Davies, A.A. Golledge and A.C. Pullan had perished together with my brother Joe. Sur Guze's son-in-law, Leslie, died the following day at St. Patrick's 45th General Hospital.

My mother cried her heart out for months on end. Father always kept a brave face, not to make matters worse for mother. To this day, I can still hear, echoing in my ears, my mother's words of foreboding on the roof, as we looked up at the falling bombs that were to kill Joe:

"God have mercy on their victims!"

Chapter XV

FOR GALLANTRY

In a broadcast to the people of Malta on the Rediffusion Relay System, the Governor, Sir William Dobbie announced, that he had received a message dated 15th April, 1942, from His Majesty King George VI. The brief but historical message said:

> "To honour her brave people I award the George Cross to the Island fortress of Malta to bear witness to a heroism and devotion that will long be famous in history."

Coming when it did, at a time when garrison and civilians alike where at the end of their tether, this royal appreciation of the trials and tribulations of the Maltese was a great morale booster.

For the first time, this great honour was bestowed on a whole nation. The majority of the Maltese have always greatly cherished this award for gallantry and have proudly displayed it on their National Colours and coat of arms for the past sixty years.

The George Cross medal itself took some time to reach these Islands. It is reputed to have been brought over by Lord Gort himself when he flew out from Gibraltar to assume the Governorship of these Islands. However, a relatively unknown R.A.F. pilot also insists that he was entrusted with flying out the original award and that the one brought out by Lord Gort was only a replica! Be that as it may, the George Cross medal and ribbon are one of the most treasured possessions of the Maltese nation.

On the 20th April, 1942, forty-seven Spitfires were flown off to Malta from the American aircraft carrier, *U.S.S. Wasp*. These brand new aircraft flew in without incident and landed at Ta' Qali and at Hal Far, with little fuel to spare. However, the Luftwaffe in Sicily was shadowing their arrival through radio monitoring. Twenty minutes after the last of the Spitfires had landed, a rain of bombs exploded on Hal Far and Ta' Qali airfields and, within an hour, only twenty-six of the forty-seven new fighters remained serviceable.

The situation in Malta was going from bad to worse. Starvation, exhaustion from lack of sleep and the many diseases related to malnutrition, were now taking their toll on the population. Everybody smelt of mould and dampness from long nights under cover, in the wet shelters. The signs of strain and exhaustion could even be seen on the soldiers' faces. In spite of all this, however, the soldiers' morale was still high and they looked quite prepared for any emergency. The air crews used to go down to Sliema to relax, when they were off duty. They stayed at the Modern Imperial Hotel, the Meadow Bank Hotel, the Crown Hotel at Fond Għadir and the Adelaide Hotel on the waterfront, and in other large blocks of flats, including Balluta Buildings in St. Julian's. A house in the lower part of Victoria Avenue (Borg Olivier Street) was used as Sick Quarters. Another house was used as a Rest Camp and a large number of men in R.A.F. uniforms were often seen strolling along the promenade. The officers' Rest Camp was in a house in St. Paul Street, at St. Paul's Bay.

In summer, the rocky beach at Fond Għadir was very popular with bathing servicemen. Had it not been for them, we would not have been able to go to the beach at all and we would have had to swim inside the harbours. The coast was surrounded by barbed wire but there was a small gap at Fond Għadir which was opened up during the day and was closed again after sunset.

Apart from the girls whom they dated and escorted to the cinema or other social occasions, servicemen had little else to distract them from the daily dangers they had to face. Sometimes there was that occasional dance too. Girls had a field day in those times. They vied with each other in befriending and dating pilots. Some ended up getting married to English servicemen. Others were not so lucky, because their friends died, went missing or became prisoners-of-war on enemy territory.

I remember one girl who lived in our street and who was engaged to get married to a Spitfire pilot. Whenever he was off duty, they spent most of their time together on the roof of her house, which enjoyed a very wide view. When this pilot was on active duty, we would know right away, because this girl would stay alone on the roof, scouring the skies for any sign of her loved one. Often when he was returning from some mission, he would make a low-level pass over our area and dip the Spitfire's wings twice as a sign that he was all right. When the pilot went missing, the girl had remained hopeful and for many weeks, she could be seen on the roof top, reading and gazing at the sky, hoping to see his aircraft fly over. The poor girl ended up dying of sunstroke.

There were other similar love affairs and all ended in different manners. Another girl, who lived down the road, was dating a young man who lived close by and who was a corporal in the King's Own Malta Regiment. Whenever he was off duty, all the neighbourhood would find out, as he would play a trumpet to announce his arrival. Besides alerting his girlfriend he also invariably annoyed everybody else. This couple ended up getting married and raising a family.

Attacks by the Axis forces, particularly on the airfields and the harbours, increased in intensity. Anti-aircraft gunners were now completely exhausted and gun barrels were getting worn out faster. They had been ordered not to engage the enemy uselessly as no more spare gun barrels were available. The stocks of ammunition were dwindling fast and guns were rationed to five rounds per gun, for each air raid.

The Germans must have sensed that the air defence and the density of the anti-aircraft barrage were getting weaker and weaker. This made them even bolder in their sorties over Malta. It is reported that there were German fighter aircraft which had even performed "touch - and - go" landings and take offs on the runway at Ta' Qali, where they were only met with small arms fire. There were also reports of hand grenades being thrown by low flying aircraft onto gun emplacements or on small gatherings of people.

To deal with the intensity of these air attacks, anti aircraft guns started using a new weapon which, if the rumour I heard was true, was being produced at the naval dockyard. Apparently, this consisted of a shell which did not detonate on reaching a certain height, like other anti-aircraft shells. Instead, a parachute attached to it, would open up and the shell would than float down, until, hopefully, it got entangled on some enemy aircraft and would then explode or self-destruct after a pre-set time. The idea seems to have been borrowed from the Star Shell, but instead of releasing a parachute flare to illuminate the target, it released the parachute for slow descent. German pilots apparently found this new weapon quite baffling and had to take evasive action, whenever these "secret weapons" were fluttering down to earth in front of their aircraft. Very often this new type of weapon would not explode in mid-air but would land back on the ground. I remember having seen one of these contraptions hanging from an electric cable, in the cross-roads of St. Mary Street and Prince of Wales Road. It was later removed by personnel of the Bomb Disposal Unit.

R.A.F. personnel were no less exhausted than their Army counterparts. The air crews and ground crews had been stretched to their limit. Of late, whenever I passed by Ta' Qali airfield, I noticed intense activity the likes of which I had never seen before. Spitfires were taking off and others landing, some of them riddled with bullet holes and others trailing smoke. Some would crash on landing. Once, I saw the ambulance and the fire tender racing to the spot where a Spitfire had just crashed. The pilot survived the accident and he was very quick to get out of the cockpit and clear of the aircraft. I remember another Spitfire, with one of its wings partly clipped off and with a spluttering engine, doing a belly-landing in a trail of dust and soil. The crash-line crew raced in its direction and the pilot emerged from the cockpit covered in blood and apparently very seriously injured. He was immediately carried off in an ambulance to hospital on nearby Mtarfa Hill.

I often saw fitters running towards the returning aircraft and start inspecting the engine, even before they had come to a stop. Armourers checked the guns and reloaded the magazine boxes with belts of 20 mm cannon shells. Other airmen, on the remaining few petrol bowsers, were busy refuelling the aircraft with precious aviation fuel, which was daily getting scarcer and scarcer. There were men in uniform and civilians, who had the never-ending job of filling in bomb craters. This work was performed in record time in order to ensure that flying operations were not interrupted.

Whenever Ta' Qali airfield was heavily bombed and it was not possible to fill in the craters in time, the aircraft stationed there would have had to land on another airfield, either at Hal Far or Luqa. There was also the constant danger of unexploded bombs, anti-personnel bombs, or delayed action bombs which went off much later and well after air raids had ended. Men from the three services were engaged in repairing aircraft pens which had been hit. All this work had to continue unabated, even when bombs were raining down on the airfield.

Aircraft, which needed major repairs, such as the changing of aluminium plates on the fuselage or wings or an engine change, could not be repaired on the blitzed airfields. The smaller fighter aircraft, like Hurricanes and Spitfires, were loaded on a sixty foot long trailer-truck, nick-named "Queen Mary" and taken to the Aircraft Repair Section of No. 137 Maintenance Unit, in what today is Gasan's Garage at Gzira. They could be manoeuvred through the narrow roads once the aircraft wings were dismantled.

Muscat's also near the old Empire Stadium, at Gzira, had also been taken over by the Royal Air Force as stores, while Mamo's Garage had been requisitioned by the Royal Electrical and Mechanical Engineers (R.E.M.E.) as a workshop for the maintenance of guns, searchlights, motor transport and other army mechanical equipment. Aircraft, which had just been repaired, would then be spray painted beneath the iron, grandstand steps, at the Empire Stadium.

My friend Pete, the fighter pilot, had come down to Sliema for a rest as the Rolls Royce Merlin engine and the Spitfire which he usually flew were being given a general maintenance and overhaul at Gasan's Garage. One day, he asked me to accompany him on a visit to the repair works and I was impressed with the scene of feverish activity in the workshop, where the aircraft was being serviced. A flight sergeant and chief technician had allowed me to sit in the cockpit of the Spitfire. My face lit up with joy and then Pete explained all about the functions of the controls and the different instruments on the panel. He then led me round the workshops, where many Spitfires and three Hurricanes were having their engines overhauled. There were other aircraft riddled with German bullets and with missing parts. Airframe fitters and riggers were working on a number of aircraft and mending the torn or holed aluminium panels. Armourers substituted machine guns or cannons and there was a deafening noise of banging and hammering on metal and the sound of riveters in action.

Reconnaissance aircraft did not take long to spot the tell-tale signs of this activity and during the night of the

8th May 1942, at about 2.00 am, the Germans bombed Muscat's Garage.

Later on that morning, at about 7.15 am, whilst R.A.F. personnel were rummaging through the debris to salvage aircraft spares from the stores, a time bomb went off and killed thirteen of them, including one Maltese, aircraftman 2nd class John Farrugia Gay. Many others were wounded.

According to Luftwaffe records, the period between the 20th March and the 28th April, 1942, had seen the highest level of aerial activity: 5,807 bomber, 5,667 fighter and 345 reconnaissance sorties had been flown to Malta, and 6,557,231 kilograms of bombs, almost as many as had been dropped during the entire Battle of Britain, had fallen on these Islands.

In nearby Sicily, Marshall of the Luftwaffe and Commander of Luftflotte II, Kesselring was now ready for Operation Hercules, the invasion of Malta. The Italians had code named this operation "Operazione C3". General Kurt Student and the XI Air Korps, had been preparing for this Operation for many months. Student had at his disposal excellent aerial photography of the Island which showed the fortifications, coastal and anti-aircraft batteries and other defence positions in great detail. The enemy even knew the exact calibre of our guns and to what extent and how many degrees they could traverse.

On dark nights, Italian Frogmen were despatched to reconnoitre for obstacles beneath the surface of the water, around the coastline. There was also an unconfirmed rumour that two groups of Germans had even succeeded in landing on the Island, from rubber dinghies launched from submarines offshore, and that one group had been caught but the other had managed to get away and returned to Italy, without obtaining any vital information.

The only known case of an Axis spy landing on the Island was the failed attempt made by Carmelo Borg Pisani, a young Maltese, who, before the war, had been studying art in Italy. On the outbreak of war, he had embraced the Fascist cause and even joined the Italian armed forces. He was chosen to be sent out to Malta in a submarine, to report on the location of stores, ammunition dumps and the state of fortifications, prior to the Axis invasion, planned for some time in July 1942.

On 17th May, 1942, he was shipped to Malta in an Italian submarine, reaching the coast on the night of the 20th May. Borg Pisani was landed under a stretch of steep, rocky cliffs at Ras id-Dawwara, in rather stormy weather. The cliff proved to be too difficult to scale. After remaining stranded for some hours on a rocky crag, exposed to the force of the elements, he finally decided to cry for help. He was soon spotted by a coast patrol of the King's Own Malta Regiment, who, taking him for an Italian flier in a pretty bad shape, signalled for help from a R.A.F. Air Sea Rescue launch, to take him off the rocky ledge he was on. On being brought ashore from High Speed Launch 128, the prisoner was promptly dispatched to the Military Hospital at Mtarfa, under armed escort.

A Royal Army Medical Corps orderly, Private 60306 Charles Debono, who on that night happened to be on duty as receptionist clerk at the hospital, many years later gave me a first hand account of how Borg Pisani was unmasked on being admitted to hospital. This led to his being convicted for treason and his sentencing to death by hanging, some months later.

Private Debono recollects: "One night in May 1942, while I was on duty at the reception, one of our Austin ambulances, number 161, pulled up outside the main entrance. A squad of King's Own Malta Regiment men jumped out and informed us that they had brought in a prisoner who needed medical attention. An English NCO and I rushed out to the ambulance to take down the patient's particulars. Inside the dark ambulance we found a young man huddled on a stretcher wet to the bone. A short while later we were joined by Colonel, then Surgeon Captain Thomas Warrington, the duty Medical Officer.

On seeing Captain Warrington, the patient exclaimed in perfect Maltese: *"Int mhux Tommy mill-Isla?"* (Aren't you Tommy from Isla?) to which the doctor replied: *"Issa qed ngħarfek. Int mhux Borg Pisani? Mela int mhux imsiefer?"* (Now I'm recognising you. Aren't you Borg Pisani? Weren't you supposed to be abroad?). The game was up for Borg Pisani, who was quickly carried inside on a stretcher."

Debono continued to tell me: "Months later, I happened to be smoking a cigarette in our front garden at Attard chatting with my sister Mary, when up the street came the hooded mendicants of the Confraternity of the Holy Rosary, responsible for collecting alms for the needs of prisoners sentenced to death. On asking them who the condemned person was, the mendicants replied that it was none other than Borg Pisani. I was taken aback and that night I could not sleep!"

Borg Pisani's case stands out as the only instance of a Maltese who actively opposed the Allies cause, as the Maltese, almost to a man, including those with pro-Italian sympathies before the war, wholeheartedly supported the war effort and indeed many paid for it with their lives on the anti-aircraft batteries, on the airfields, in the naval dockyard and in their homes.

General Kurt Student then decided to send one of his high-ranking officers on an aerial reconnaissance mission over Malta, with instructions to draw up a detailed report about the Island and the most advantageous places where troops could be parachuted and landed from the sea. On his return, this officer had reported very optimistically. Although it was somewhat difficult to make use of gliders for an airborne assault because of the small size of the fields; the rather high walls surrounding them and the small size of the Island which made the defence more compact and concentrated, Malta could still be taken, provided that the landings would be preceded by intensive attacks on the airfields and on the gun batteries. Once these were neutralised, it would be safe to launch an airborne assault.

The senior Italian officer in charge of the operation was Marshall Count Cavallaro. Besides the German XI Air Korps, the Axis also had the Italian Folgore Parachute Division, which had been trained by General Bernhard Ramcke. Kesselring was very impressed by their efficiency. The order of battle also included the Italian 'Superga' Division, which was trained in aerial assault. In all, 70,000 men were earmarked for the planned invasion. The total number of the attacking force exceeded by five times the number of men engaged in the German assault on Crete, in May 1941.

General Conrad, who was responsible for the airborne transport of the assault troops, was allotted ten Groups, comprising of five hundred Junkers Ju52 transport aircraft, three hundred DFS Gliders, which could carry ten fully-equipped troops each and two hundred Gotha Go 242, a new type of glider, capable of carrying twenty-five fully-equipped troops. The airborne assault was planned to commence immediately after the last massive air raid. The seaborne assault would follow a few hours later.

The final plan provided that a large number of landing craft and ships from the Italian Battle Fleet would leave their harbours in Italy and sail for Malta. In the meantime, two airborne divisions, one Italian and the other German, would be dropped from the air over the South-West areas, ranging between Zurrieq, Qrendi, Siggiewi and Dingli. A small group of paratroops had to be dropped early in the morning, before dawn, to establish a bridge-head. This would be followed, later on, by the first wave. The second wave would come in about five hours later and the third wave of parachutists would be dropped in the afternoon.

There were also plans to drop dummy parachutists to confuse the defence and draw away vital detachments from more strategic positions, to engage these dummies. These 'parachutists' had to be dropped on areas far away from the real invasion drop zones. After landing and forming up, the two airborne divisions had to occupy the airfields at Ta' Qali, Luqa and Hal Far. One of these aerodromes had to be repaired in the shortest possible time and made serviceable, to allow transport aircraft to land with more troops, stores, guns, ammunitions, petrol and other supplies.

Gozo had to be invaded right away and without much effort as this Island was undefended.

The ships of the Italian fleet had to shell the coastal fortifications, particularly those of Delimara, Benghajsa, St. Leonard, Tigne', Madliena, Campbell and Bingemma which were all armed with nine-inch coastal guns. When the naval bombardment ceased, two Italian divisions were scheduled to land in Marsaxlokk Bay, Birzebbuga, St. Thomas Bay and Marsascala. After neutralising the many small fortifications and smaller defences spread out over that area, particularly the pill-boxes, these two divisions would then join up with the two German divisions and occupy the remaining part of Malta. The final assault would be on the capital city, Valletta.

Both sides expected heavy casualties if the invasion were to take place, although the Germans and the Italians were perhaps not fully aware how bad the situation of the defenders was, particularly with regard to stocks of ammunition for anti-aircraft guns, aviation fuel and foodstuffs. The only positive factor was the determination of the defence force and the high morale of the Maltese population.

The invasion was scheduled to take place between the last week of July and the first days of August, 1942.

Hitler had never been very keen on the invasion of Malta. His priority was to occupy Egypt and head for the oil wells of the Middle East. He summoned Student to the Fuhrer's General Headquarters at Rustenburg. Student gave a full report of the preparations and the plans for the invasion and Hitler is reputed to have listened without uttering a word. When Student had finished, Hitler exclaimed:

"And then what? The British fleet will sail from Gibraltar and Alexandria and the Italian fleet would not be able to stop it. As soon as they receive radio reports of the British approaching, they would turn their tails and steam back to their bases in Sicily and they would leave you and your troops in the lurch, on an Island in the middle of the Mediterranean!". *

Student remained speechless. After all that detailed planning! Hitler prohibited Student from going back to Italy and had him transferred to Berlin.

A few weeks before the scheduled date for the invasion, Field Marshal Rommel finally took Tobruk and entered Egypt. When the German High Command realised that victory in North Africa appeared to be within its grasp, it postponed Operation Hercules, the planned invasion of Malta. When the pendulum of war in North Africa again swung against the Germans, after the famous Battle of Alamein, launched by General Montgomery in October 1942, it was too late to try again and the last opportunity to invade Malta had slipped by.

Operation Hercules would never again see the light of day!

(*see Cajus Bekker: The Luftwaffe War Diaries.)

Chapter XVI

HELP AT LAST

L ord Gort arrived in Malta in the early hours of 7th May, 1942, to take over the governorship of these Islands from the tired Sir William Dobbie, who left the Island with his wife and daughter Sybil, on the same Sunderland flying boat, bringing Gort in. Gort was to preside over a scene of utter destruction. Two years of almost incessant bombing had reduced the streets, in various towns and villages, to mounds of rubble.

The Luftwaffe and the Regia Aeronautica ruled the skies. Maltese and British anti-aircraft gunners and a handful of R.A.F. fighters, battling against hopeless odds, were struggling to hold Kesselring's air fleet at bay, but barely just! The harbours were littered with wrecks. The remains of burnt-out cargo ships gave an unmistakable foretaste of what was to come in the approaching summer. Warehouses around the harbour were in ruins and the three ships that made it to Malta in the March convoy had been sunk at their moorings, by hand-picked, Luftwaffe crews.

Lord Gort's immediate task was to save Malta from looming starvation and ultimate surrender. He at once ordered a stock-take of all essential commodities. Cuts were announced in the sugar and rice rations. All surplus animals, including sheep and goats, were to be slaughtered, due to the shortage of fodder. The pasta ration was withdrawn completely and the bread ration further reduced. A "target date" was set, signifying when these supplies were calculated to run out. After that date, surrender would be inevitable.

The Governor's other very urgent task was to place fairly and squarely before the War Cabinet in London an accurate picture of Malta's dire needs in supplies and fighters for the Island's air defence.

Thanks to Gort's standing and to the first-hand evidence of experts who had been flown out of Malta, a maximum effort started being set in motion in Britain, to save this vital outpost, while there was still time.

For some time, rumours were spreading that more Spitfires were reaching Malta soon and many preparations were afoot on the airfields. One thing, that seemed to confirm that something was about to happen, was that I did not see Pete around for about three days. He was now back at Hal Far, after a short period during which his Squadron was operating from Ta' Qali, as Hal Far had been non-operational due to heavy bombing. The increasing activity I was seeing at Ta' Qali, on my way up to Rabat, also fell in line with these rumours.

On the 9th May, 1942, I was up in Saqqajja Square at Rabat and, at about 9.00 am, I heard the drone of aircraft engines in the distance. I looked towards Luqa airfield, expecting to see aircraft about to take off from there, but I could not see anything from the vantage point near the

Point de Vue Hotel. Then some R.A.F. personnel rushed out of the Hotel, shouting excitedly, "They are here...! They are here!" They ran down the road below the Square, which leads to Mosta. I followed them, eager to see what was happening. A sergeant pilot shouted above the rest: "There they come; twelve of them, over St. Paul's Bay." All the airmen started cheering. I saw what looked like twelve specks flying low, at about 1,000 feet, approaching Ta' Qali airfield. The R.A.F. boys were beside themselves with joy. All were by now shouting, hugging each other, throwing their caps in the air, and waving their hands, at the fast-approaching new arrivals. In a few seconds, those twelve 'specks' I had seen in the distance, materialised into a squadron of twelve new Spitfires. When they were above Ta' Qali, these aircraft banked, swung round on their port wing, leaving the formation, lowering their undercarriage and landing on the runway in quick succession. Shortly after, another squadron appeared in the sky and then another; planes kept coming in for the best part of that morning. Some of the Spitfires also landed at Luqa and others at Hal Far.

In all, sixty-four brand new Spitfires, for the defence of Malta, had been flown in from the British aircraft carrier, *H.M.S. Eagle* and the American Carrier, *U.S.S. Wasp.* The enemy did not sit back and watch during this entire operation. Every now and then, the Me109s would be seen high up in the sky. Occasionally, two of them would swoop down and attack a Spitfire coming in to land. However, the Hurricanes from Hal Far were ready for them and drove them off. Strangely enough, there where no Ju88s about on that day. Usually, they raided the Island at just about that time of day.

The following morning, I again went up to Rabat. I wanted to see Pete very badly to find out all I could about the arrival of these new Spitfires. When I met him, the first thing he told me was that his Squadron was converting to the new Spitfires Vc. He explained what kind of detailed organisation had gone into the arrival of the new aircraft. Pete had been on duty, standing in for a pilot from another Squadron at Ta Qali.

Wing Commander Edward John "Jumbo" Gracie, the Commanding Officer of Ta' Qali, was a man of great discipline and ability. He drew not only the admiration of his superiors but also that of his subordinate officers and other ranks. Pete told me that had it not been for his grit and determination, no aircraft would have been able to use Ta' Qali, in those difficult days.

Wing Commander Gracie had also stirred up some controversy in the course of his command of R.A.F. Station Ta' Qali. In order to give a grim warning to those who were responsible for pilfering material from the airfield, he had set up a symbolic gibbet and entered the following warning in the Daily Routine Orders;

"A gibbet has been erected on the perimeter road leading to the caves. Any man, woman or child, civilian or service personnel, found guilty of sabotage, theft or, in any other way, hindering the war effort, will be shot, and will then be hung from this gibbet, as a warning to all others."

Somebody, probably one of the pilots, took a photograph of the gibbet and smuggled it out to England and it was published in a London newspaper. This raised a hornet's nest. I was told this story by my friends who had seen service in those days at Ta' Qali, when I later joined the Royal Air Force.

219

When Wing Commander Gracie was informed of the arrival of the new Spitfires, he had summoned all his officers and pilots to a general conference in the Officers' Mess, at Xara Palace, in Mdina. He outlined his plans and told them what he expected from each one of them when the fighters arrived.

He made it quite clear that, whoever would be caught skiving or taking cover in a shelter, during an air raid, would be shot and that he would be the first to execute the order. Each officer and pilot was given a paper with detailed instructions as to what he had to do, when a new aircraft arrived in its allotted pen. Each pilot was assigned to a pen and he was to ensure that there was enough petrol, oil, glycol coolant, ammunition and ground crew to refuel and perform any necessary maintenance on the new aircraft.

Despatch riders, on motor cycles, were to guide each Spitfire to its appropriate pen, according to its serial number. As soon as the new aircraft entered its pen and turned off its engine, the pilot would leave the cockpit and be taken to the mess, while a fresh pilot would take his place in the cockpit. Then, a team of technicians and armourers would check the engine, the wireless set and the cannons, while others would load the magazines with ammunition belts. Soldiers and policemen would help refuel the petrol tanks.

Ground crews vied with each other to turn round the aircraft in the shortest possible time. The operation was so successful that one squadron of twelve Spitfires was back in the air after a mere seven minutes. When the enemy approached our Islands, that afternoon, it was faced with three fresh squadrons of Spitfires and the few enemy aircraft which managed to reach the coast were heavily engaged by anti-aircraft fire.

The following day, now remembered as, "THE GLORIOUS TENTH OF MAY", witnessed a day-long air battle over the island, when the gunners and the new Spitfires claimed to have shot down over sixty-three Axis aircraft in pitched dog-fights.

War historians consider this day as the turning point of the air war over Malta.

Towards the end of the war, when I was serving with the Royal Air Force, I met Christina Ratcliffe, who had been a decoder at the Lascaris underground Sector Operations Room, No. 8 S.O.R. At that time, she was still coming to terms with the loss of her boyfriend, the famous Malta reconnaissance pilot, Wing Commander Adrian Warburton, who had died in action some months previously.

Once during tea break, in one of our spells of night duty, I asked her around for a chat and our discussion drifted to what had happened down in the operations room on 10th May, 1942. Flicking her long blonde hair to one side, cigarette in one hand and a mug of tea in the other, she began to relate what happened on the day, when the R.A.F., after months of bitter frustration and impotence, was at last in a position to match its strength against the Luftwaffe and the Regia Aeronautica.

She told me that the alert had gone off at dawn and everybody felt tense and waited for the inevitable raid. On the airfields, everything was quiet and no reports of aircraft taking off were coming in. Gradually a lone approaching aircraft was picked on the radar screens. It was "George", the Ju88 reconnaissance plane on its usual early morning flight. Although all anti-aircraft ammunition restrictions had been lifted that day, the enemy plane was not engaged, perhaps to lull any suspicions that the enemy had, that the defenders were ready for the fight.

At about 10.00 am the state of readiness was up-graded. In the labyrinth of tunnels and chambers, dug deep down under the Upper Barrakka, at Lascaris, the radar stations reported: "One hundred plus milling over Comiso." As instructions flowed in from the Filter Room, the Operations Room came to life, with girl-plotters receiving instructions from the controller. The girls, armed with sticks like billiard cues, started putting "counters" on the huge map, red for enemy and black for friendly aircraft. The map measured some eighteen feet by twelve feet and it showed the Maltese Islands and part of Southern Sicily, as well as the main enemy airfields. It was marked off into lettered squares, each sub-divided into numbered grids.

The Ground Observers were also brought to 'readi-ness' and the anti-aircraft guns were brought to 'Alert'.

Outside, nothing happened for about fifteen min-utes, until the first Spitfires started scrambling from Hal Far, Luqa and Ta' Qali airfields. About five minutes later the anti-aircraft guns started blasting away on a very high elevation.

Christina remembered that there were too many one-way tracks on the plotting table; too many hostile plots pointing towards the Island. The amount of traffic on the table had hitherto been unparalleled. Two pairs of hands were simply not enough to cope with the mass of plots between Malta and Sicily and a girl helper was posted to each end of the table to rake off the old tracks and set up fresh blocks. There was no time to change over. The girls themselves, by that time all Maltese, were grateful for this opportunity to show their mettle and explode the myth that they would panic when put to the real test. They carried out their task so well that Group Captain A.B. "Woodie" Woodhall, the Officer in Charge of the Operations Room, during a lull in the afternoon, came down from the "Shelf" and thanked each girl-plotter personally for the "very fine show" she had put. The "Shelf" was a sort of balcony above the plotting table where the Controller, Ops. B. and the Gunnery Liaison Officer sat. Among all the happy faces on the "Shelf" that day, perhaps none beamed quite so brightly as that of Group Captain Woodhall. At long last, he had available squadrons of real aircraft, manned by genuine, dyed-in-the-wool fighter pilots to put up against the approaching enemy hordes.

Very soon, the girls in the Ground Observers Room began receiving the first visual reports from the five observation posts in Malta, located on top of St. John's Cavalier in Valletta, Tas-Silġ, Dingli, Għargħur and Torri l-Aħmar at Marfa Ridge as well as from the Gozo Station. "Visual: fifty plus bombers and hundred plus fighters. Hostile, now crossing Gozo," came the first urgent report.

Outside, in the glaring sunlight, the sky gradually filled with Messerschmitt 109s, followed by wave upon wave of Ju88s, which started unloading their bomb loads on the airfields. Then, radio-telephone signals revealed that the Spitfires were descending upon the raiders, out of the sun. The new Spitfires mixed in with the bombers with guns blazing mercilessly, while those which had taken off earlier circled in to land, covered by those with sufficient fuel. The Spitfires refuelled and re-armed in an incredibly short time, rolled off, taxied to the runway end and took off again to meet waves of other incoming enemy aircraft.

The noise of the battle filtering into the operations room continued throughout the late morning and early afternoon, sometimes deafening and sometimes quieting off, but never ceasing. The Germans appeared to be trying to swamp the defence with wave after wave of fighters. In the afternoon, the Italians gave a hand with planes bombing the airfields from some 20,000 feet, but missing their targets. At about 6 pm, some Ju88s were reported to have broken through and to have dropped time-bombs on Ta' Qali, which cratered the runway. It was immediately filled in again and repaired by men of the 8th Battalion of the Manchester Regiment. In fact, all airfields remained serviceable throughout the day.

Christina paused. It was time to get back to work. She half smiled and turned away. "After 10th May, it was never the same again!" she muttered.

Chapter XVII

CLOSE SHAVES

Four days later, on 14th May, 1942, I was woken up at 3.15 am, by the siren wailing an air raid warning. As the gunfire appeared to be quite distant, instead of going underground, I lingered in the street near the entrance to the shelter, chatting with some friends. There was very little anti-aircraft fire during this raid, apart from the sporadic salvo from the guns of Fort Manoel and some other anti-aircraft batteries around Sliema. They only seemed to want to remind the enemy flying overhead that they were still alert to repel any attack.

It was still pitch dark. The only faint light came from the stars that studded the sky. The silence was only broken by the subdued whispering of a group of people standing by the entrance to the shelter. At times, one could hear a ripple of laughter at some good joke. The distant drone of aircraft engines, high up in the sky, gave you the feeling that you were being watched or stalked in the darkness. I looked up at the sky and strained my ears to listen to that tremolo drone of engines, which at times, seemed to be drawing nearer and, at times, seemed to dissolve into the distance. I half expected to hear the usual screeching noise of falling bombs and the terrible explosions that invariably followed. However, that night, nothing of the sort was happening. We only kept hearing the drone of the engines and, occasionally a salvo, fired from the anti-aircraft guns. This went on until dawn and we put it down to one of those nuisance raids.

When the "raiders passed" signal was sounded, everybody started emerging from these latter-day catacombs to go back home, either to sleep in the comfort of his bed or to go to work. I went home as well, washed and changed to go and hear the 6.00 am Mass at the Sacro Cuor Church. I met Fr. Alessandro on the church parvis and, after exchanging greetings, I entered to serve Mass.

Fr. Alessandro was already in his surplice and ready for the Mass, when the siren came on again. I asked what he intended to do and he replied that we should carry on regardless of the impending raid and leave it to Our Lady of the Sacred Heart to take care of the rest.

The Mass commenced. When we reached the prayers after communion, I started hearing gunfire in the distance. I looked around to judge the reaction of the congregation and spotted my father sitting in the front row. Some started fidgeting in their pews and others gradually edged sideways to the relative cover of the naves and the belfry. The bolder ones kept to their seats, as if nothing was happening. Perhaps, they felt much safer in the House of God! The Mass which was being said on the main altar continued. We were on the side-altar, dedicated to St. Joseph.

The Mass had, by then, reached the concluding stages. Suddenly, there was a tremendous explosion and a

strong blast which deafened my ears. The church trembled from its very foundations. Most of the glass panes
that were still on the windows were blown in and some
pieces of masonry fell from the ceiling. A cloud of dust
filled the entire church and there was panic. Women
began screaming and some of the chairs were over-
turned. Father came up and pushed me to a corner of the
church near the altar. Fr. Alessandro took cover in the
other corner of the same altar. The Mass which was being
said on the main altar also came to an abrupt end. The
noise of the explosion had been amplified by the acous-
tics of the church itself. Some shouted that the bomb had
fallen outside, in the street and others were saying that it
fell in St. Mary Street. On hearing this, I asked my father
to go and check whether it was true. We ran out of the
church and headed for St. Mary Street but on arriving at
the street corner, we could see nothing except an all-
enveloping cloud of dust up the street. It was about 7.00
am. We rushed back home to see if mother was all right,
and found her safe and sound but very jittery, with my
younger brother.

Father and I raced up to the roof to find out where the
bomb had fallen. From the roof of the washroom, we
could see the dust cloud was still hovering over Stella
Maris Church. At first, father thought that the church
had been hit again and he said we should go and see for
ourselves. We turned into Carmel Street and, as we came
to St. Dominic Street, we were stopped by the police from
going any further. The bomb had fallen in Annunciation
Square and on buildings in St. Vincent Street between
Carmel Street and St. Nicholas Street. We turned back,
walked up to High Street and came down to Annunciation Square, through St. Paul Street and were able to look

upon the disaster from the Stella Maris Band Club side of the square.

Corpses, covered in blankets, were lying on the pavement, all around the square, just outside the verandas of some houses on the opposite side of the square. The wounded were being given first aid. Other casualties had already been taken to hospital. Police and civilians were helping Civil Defence men in the rescue operation and were removing fallen masonry, to extricate those still buried underneath the debris. There were many people in the square. Some were just curious onlookers and others were awaiting news of relatives reported missing. Someone said that it had not been an aerial bomb but a torpedo. Others said it was a mine, because it was seen having a longish shape as it was coming down. Whatever it was, it had certainly demolished many buildings, injuring many people and caused seven fatalities!

One Sunday in May, we had some air raids on Luqa airfield during the night. There had been another air raid at dawn. I was in the company of some of my friends, near the entrance to the shelter and at about 6.45 am, four rounds from the guns of Fort Manoel made us jump. Our eyes probed the skies. In the distance, I could make out about fifteen Ju88s, flying in, at about 15,000 feet, coming in from the seaward side. They were flying in sections of three and appeared to be heading for Luqa airfield.

As it appeared that there was no imminent threat to our part of the Island, Vince, George and I ran down to The Strand but, by the time we got to the bottom of Prince of Wales Road, these aircraft were already flying past Marsamxett Harbour. The guns of Fort Manoel were no longer engaging them as the aircraft were directly overhead and the gunners obviously could not bring their weapons to bear on them at that angle. The guns of other batteries however, were still engaging the enemy relentlessly and soon after, one of the Junkers broke out of the formation, belching fire and black smoke from one of its engines. It side slipped and started losing height, descending in the direction of Hal Far. I could count three parachutes open up beneath it.

Meanwhile, the other aircraft started diving to drop their deadly load. Six of them diverted their course towards Ta' Qali and the remaining eight flew onto Luqa. They were now being engaged by Bofors and machine-gun fire as they had come down to a very low altitude. The sky was criss-crossed with tracer shells. Huge columns of black smoke and dust could be seen over Luqa airfield. One of them, in particular, was greyish in colour and mushroomed high above the rest. The noises reaching us in Sliema were comparatively loud and sounded like a continuous rumble of thunder. Then we heard an even louder noise, accompanied by a strong blast, which was unusual, considering the long distance between us and the target area. It must have been an ammunition dump which had received a direct hit and exploded. This pall of smoke continued rising to a height of some 10,000 feet and, as there was no wind, it hung up there, like a gigantic mushroom rising even higher and higher. Although we could not see Ta' Qali from the Sliema Strand, we could hear explosions coming from that direction as well.

In those hard times, it was not uncommon to overhear complaints about our fighter defence and people were not happy when our aircraft did not intercept the enemy out at sea. To a certain extent, these complaints were justified. But few knew that our aircraft were very short of petrol and that many Spitfires and Hurricanes were unserviceable because of the damage suffered in the air and on the ground as well as the shortage of spare parts. Sometimes, there would not be more than four serviceable Spitfires to take to the air and this is only because of the unstinting efforts of the mechanics and ground crews, who cannibalised spare parts from other damaged aircraft and patched up those which could fly again. The enormous amount of craters on the airfields and the complete lack of equipment to level the airfields again, also kept our fighter aircraft grounded, even though Maltese and British servicemen were working non-stop and at great risk to fill in these craters.

Our fighter pilots certainly were not at all happy to have their aircraft grounded on such occasions, when they knew that their duty was up there in the skies, intercepting the enemy before it reached our shores. I noticed that when these pilots were caught on the ground, they got very frustrated and they made this very plain to me on a number of occasions, when I spoke to them. Very often, when this happened, these pilots appeared to go berserk and run here and there, firing at low flying enemy aircraft with their service revolver or some rifle they found close at hand. This also happened when some of their colleagues where shot down and died. They worked so closely with each other and depended so much on one another that whenever one of them perished, they felt as though they had lost part of themselves. When they were flying together, an error on the part of one of them could cost the life of one or two of his pals.

I heard a story of two Spitfire pilots who were patrolling over the Island. There had been no air raid warning or signs of approaching enemy aircraft. However, while these two aircraft were flying over Grand Harbour, two Messerschmitt 109s appeared from nowhere. The leader was looking ahead as he normally did. His number two, who was supposed to keep an eye on the rear and the sides, got distracted and did not keep a proper lookout. In a few seconds he was hit. A thin wisp of white smoke started leaving his aircraft. The Spitfire dipped its nose downwards and crashed somewhere in the vicinity of Għargħur. The other pilot managed to get away and landed at Ta' Qali, with an aircraft riddled with bullet holes.

On 21st May, 1942, just before noon, I asked mother for some food before going up to Rabat. I told her that probably I would be back late, as I was meeting my friend Pete. She was not to worry if I returned home slightly later than usual. Needless to say, that this was followed by umpteen warnings to be careful should I find myself in a dangerous situation. On board the route bus to Rabat, I overheard two men talking about the Hotel Point de Vue. They were saying that it had been hit by a bomb in one of that morning's air raids. Later I learnt that a 1,000 kilogram bomb had fallen just outside the hotel and caused great havoc. Six R.A.F. pilots: Flight Lieutenant A.A.V. Waterfield, Flight Lieutenant C.H. Backer, Flying Officer J.C.M. Boothe, Flying Officer J.J. Guerin R.A.A.F., Pilot Officer W.C.H. Hullet and Pilot Officer E.E. Streets had died, while others had been wounded. Twenty other civilians, including a young girl, were also killed at Rabat during the same air raid.

At about 12.30 pm, while I was trudging up to Rabat on foot, the sirens gave their usual warning. Three Spitfires swiftly took off from Ta' Qali and disappeared in the distance. There was absolute silence and nothing could be heard, except a lone sparrow's song and the crunch of my own rapid footsteps and those of a few others, who were following me up the hill, after alighting from the same bus. When I had stopped briefly to watch the Spitfires taking off, these persons overtook me on their way up the hill. I heard the drone of aircraft engines, high up, coming from the direction of the sun. I tried to spot them but the blinding glare of the sun prevented me from seeing anything. I tried to shield my eyes with my hands but it was to no avail. From the sound of their engines, I could tell these were small fighter planes. I strained my eyes almost to the point of tears, but still could not see a thing. Shortly afterwards I heard machine-gun and cannon fire, high up in the sky. It was obviously a dogfight between the Spitfires I had seen taking off and enemy aircraft. But still there was nothing to be seen in the sun's blinding glare.

I jumped into a field nearby, where there was a country room, and took the wise precaution of taking cover from stray shells, bullets or empty cartridges that might fall from the sky. I still continued to search the sky and finally, I made out a thin line of smoke. This enabled me to locate where the dogfight was taking place. The aircraft were very high up, probably about 30,000 feet. They looked like small mosquitoes and I was unable to identify friend or foe.

Then there was a loud wail as an aircraft fell from the sky, spinning out of control. Initially, I thought it was going to crash close to where I was but, when it descended to 5,000 feet, the pilot seemed to have regained control and levelled out. The sound from the engine was still very erratic and I could hear it spluttering and cutting out a number of times.

It was one of our Spitfires and it glided down to land in the direction of Ta' Qali. When it lowered its undercarriage, only one wheel locked into place while the other remained retracted. The pilot circled the airfield hopefully but it was to no avail, as one of the wheels would not come down. The engine kept spluttering all the time; cutting out and coming to life again. I prayed to God to bring this pilot down safe and sound. He then made a final attempt. It seemed that he did not want to lose his precious Spitfire. Indeed, losing a Spitfire was just not on, even if the pilot had to risk his own life to bring it in safely. The aircraft was now at the end of the runway. It levelled out, and glided gently, engine cut, touched down on one wheel and, after some fifty yards, its wheel folded in and the Spitfire skidded on its belly for another hundred yards, until it came to a stop and disappeared in a cloud of dust, off the runway.

Three vehicles sped to the crashed Spitfire. The outline of a man could be seen emerging from the dust cloud. It was the pilot who had escaped unhurt. I thanked God for hearing my prayer and sparing that poor pilot's life. When the dust cloud subsided, I saw the Spitfire lying on one side, with its nose dipped into the ground and its tail pointing skywards.

Meanwhile, the dogfight, high above, was still raging on, although, by this time, it had moved onwards beyond Rabat and I could neither hear nor see any signs of the battle above. I decided to move on and proceed up the road to Rabat. When I had crossed the field and come to the road the other two Spitfires came in over Ta' Qali. One of them performed a Victory Roll over the airfield. This was the sign to those on the ground that he had shot down an enemy aircraft. I wonder how he fared with his

Commanding Officer after landing, as Victory Rolls were against regulations!

After getting the bread, I walked straight to the Point de Vue Hotel. There was a huge crater in front of it and the building was very badly damaged. I waited at Saqqajja Square, where I was to meet my friend Pete, for about half an hour, until finally I saw Pete's friend Harry, approach. I asked for Pete. He replied that Pete was at Mtarfa 90th General Hospital, as he had been slightly injured in that morning's air raid. He said I could go and visit him and as he was going there himself, he asked me to accompany him. I accepted the invitation right away, so we walked together all the way to the next hill of Mtarfa, with Harry describing what had happened, on the way.

As we entered through the main gate and walked up the drive to the hospital, Harry exclaimed: "Look! There he is, coming this way, with his head bandaged." Pete was walking towards us with two other pilots. One of them had his arm in plaster and the other, limping and resting on a walking stick. After thanking me for going to see him, Pete introduced me to the other two, whose names I do not recollect. He told me that the medical officer had released him from hospital but the other two pilots had to stay on for a few more days to recover. Both pilots had been injured when their aircraft crashed. I asked what was wrong with him and he replied that he had no serious injury. He only had a slight contused wound on his head, caused by a glancing blow from a small bomb splinter, while he was running towards his aircraft. He also told me that he was lucky he did not reach his aircraft in time, as this had been blown up by the same bomb. Pete had four stitches on his head.

After taking our leave from the injured pilots, Pete, Harry and I started to walk down to Ta' Qali Airfield on the Mosta road. When we reached the crossroads near the Mtarfa Military Cemetery, there was an air raid signal. Harry suggested that we should take cover as we were very close to the airfield. We had walked for about twenty-five yards when Pete shouted, "109s …109s…coming in very low over St. Paul's Bay." I saw five Me109s flying at tree-top height, machine-gunning everything ahead of them. They flew straight on to Ta' Qali, strafing the airfield and flying so low that, anti-aircraft guns could not engage them. Only solitary machine-gun fire met the intruders. Pete, Harry and I took cover behind a rubble wall and buried our faces in the soil. When the aircraft had flown past us, we picked ourselves up and ran to a room about two hundred yards away. The 109s were still circling the area and diving in turns down to strafe Ta' Qali and whatever they set eyes on in the vicinity. I then spotted one of them coming back at us from the direction of Naxxar. Pete was running some 10 feet ahead of me and Harry was following me. We were right in the middle of the field, sprinting for the blessed room which seemed to be getting further away. The Me109 opened fire and I saw Pete leap to the ground and I instinctively did the same, swallowing a mouthful of earth. The precious loaf of bread flew out of my hands. Bullets whined close by and I was peppered with a shower of small stones and earth sods.

I heard a sudden cry of pain from one of my friends, but I could not tell from whom as I was still hugging the ground with my face literally buried in the soil. When I raised my head slightly and opened my eyes to see what was happening, I saw one of the Me109s with its yellow-

235

painted nose, diving straight at us again, with a terrifying roar and then it quickly disappeared behind Mtarfa hill.

I looked in Pete's direction and saw him begin to get up. He asked me whether I was all right and I replied in the affirmative but, on looking back, I realised that Harry was gripping his leg and wincing in pain. He called for help as he had been hit. We ran towards him and saw that his shorts were covered with blood from a thigh wound. Pete asked me to hold Harry from the back, until he figured out what best to do. He then whisked out a field-dressing first-aid kit from his tunic pocket and bandaged his wound. Pete told Harry that he had a .303 bullet wound in his thigh and that he was going to leave him with me, while he ran back to Mtarfa Hospital to fetch help.

He had not gone far when an army lorry appeared on the Mosta Road, coming in our direction. We soon had the assistance of two other men, who helped carry Harry on to the lorry which took us all back to Mtarfa Hospital. We left Harry there for further treatment - he was to spend ten days in hospital and he was also grounded for another week. He was more disappointed because he could not fly rather than because he had been wounded. Before we left the hospital, the medical orderly asked us to go to the Medical Inspection Room, where we were treated for shock.

Later that day, Pete broke the news that his Commanding Officer had informed him that his tour of duty in Malta had come to an end and that, the following night, he was to go to Luqa airfield to catch an aircraft back to the United Kingdom, for a well earned rest. He would then be posted to another squadron. He asked me whether I wanted to go to Ta' Qali with him to take leave of some of his friends in 229 and 249 Squadrons. I very readily accepted, of course. This was the first time I had an opportunity to go into the airfield. We walked into a dispersal hut, where a group of fighter pilots were awaiting orders to scramble. They were playing cards on a small table or reading books or magazines and discussing one of their recent dogfights with the enemy. When Pete appeared at the door, he was warmly greeted and one of the officers asked him who I was. Pete introduced me as one of his Maltese friends and informed the officer that I had just lost my brother through enemy action. The officer promptly shook hands with me and expressed his sorrow at my brother's death. I was then introduced to the other pilots. Pete pointed to four of them and admiringly gave me their score of enemy aircraft shot down. These pilots were what were popularly known as "Aces" and their names have remained famous for their skill in aerial combat to this very day. A sergeant pilot quickly offered me a mug of tea, as there was nothing else they could offer us. Then they went on to brag about their escapades and I was all ears.

One of these pilots was relating how two days earlier, on 29th July, 1942, they had been scrambled and had intercepted a large Italian Cant Z506b. This three-engine seaplane was flying between Malta and Sicily and appeared to be heading for Malta. The Spitfires swooped on it like hawks and the enemy seaplane dived down very low over the water until it was practically skimming the surface. It then came down on the sea and stopped. A member of the crew emerged on the wings, waving a white piece of cloth, signalling that it was out of the fight. The pilot went on to say that after his friends returned to base, he had remained circling over the Cant, until an Air Sea Rescue launch came out and towed it into St. Pauls Bay.

This was only the happy ending to a very gripping episode. On 28th July, a Bristol Beaufort aircraft of 217 Squadron had taken off from Luqa, on an anti-shipping sortie. Such attacks were launched on Axis shipping, supplying Rommel's Afrika Korps with men and war material. After the Beaufort had torpedoed and sunk a ship, it was hit by return fire and it ditched into the sea. Its crew of four boarded their rubber dinghy and were, after a while, rescued by an Italian seaplane, which flew them to the Italian airbase on the island of Levkas, lying off the west coast of Greece, between the islands of Corfu' and Cefalonia.

The following day, the crew of this Beaufort were ordered to board a Cant Z506b on their way to Taranto, in southern Italy. They waited for an opportunity to over-power the guard and the Italian crew of the aircraft and, after a short scuffle with the crew, succeeded in disarming them, forcing the pilot to change his course for Malta. At first the pilot refused because he feared they would be shot down by the Spitfires but when he felt the cold steel of a pistol against his head, he decide it was safer to obey the orders given to him by the new 'skipper'.

The Cant survived the 'attentions' of Malta's Spitfires, despite having suffered some twenty .303 bullet holes and another eight from 20 mm cannon shells on the wings. Fortunately, none of these missiles had hit the fuselage because, had that been the case, some of the nine people on board would inevitably have been hit. This was probably the first recorded hijacking in the history of aviation!

Coming back to my narrative, I wished time would stop still to be able to remain on this airfield with my new acquaintances. But time does not wait for anyone and soon afterwards, we had to return to Rabat. When we arrived at the Mess, Pete asked me in and gave me a bottle of beer and a small bag to take to my family. This contained two tins of boiled sugar sweets, about four packets of Wild Woodbine cigarettes, two bars of chocolate and some service biscuits - a treasure-trove in those days!

Pete and I shook hands for the last time. We said goodbye and promised to write to each other when we parted for the last time. I was never to see him again! After I had written to him twice, my second letter was returned to me with the words: MISSING IN ACTION stamped on the envelope. Months later, I learned from one of Pete's friends, who remained on the Island, that Pete had been lost in action, whilst flying over enemy-occupied France.

Chapter XVIII

THE LURKING FACE OF DEATH

I have always strongly believed in the saying that one cannot escape one's fate! During the war, one could have taken cover in the strongest and deepest shelter and still not survived. When someone was killed by a bomb, a shell or a bullet, the British used to say, "It had his name written on it." This is exactly why I chose to remain outside during most air raids. I can relate many strange incidents of death and equally of people who escaped death by a hair's breadth.

In Mosta, for example, in Gafa' Street on 21st March, 1942, at 14.30 pm two bombs seemed to have been hand-placed at the two entrances of rock shelter No. 71, which was full of civilians most of them workers, returning home to Mellieħa. Although the shelter did not cave in, the blast from the bombs killed forty-eight and left seventy-five seriously wounded, when all of them, presumably, had their minds at rest that they were perfectly safe down there. A survivor from this tragedy relates that the blast moved along the shelter like a fireball.

Some of the dead bodies were found shrunk to the size of babies.

In Gzira, a shelter was hit by a bomb and part of the rock-covering caved in. An old woman was trapped by a large rock that caught her leg so she could not move. The same bomb burst the main water pipe and a large quantity of water flooded the shelter. Many attempts were made by the rescuers to free her. They even considered amputating the woman's leg on the spot, to save her life, but the water level rose and soon filled the shelter. The poor woman drowned.

On Tuesday, 24th March, 1942, at about 4.00 pm, a bomb fell on some houses in Rinella Street, Kalkara. Two entrances to a shelter were blocked with masonry from the overlying buildings and twenty-two people, including the entire Coster family, some of whom had returned to their Kalkara residence after experiencing the Mosta tragedy, three days earlier, perished when a gas main burst and water from a nearby well, cracked by the force of the explosion, flooded the shelter and drowned all the people there, who had already been overcome by gas fumes. Only one person survived to tell this horrible tale. Three of the victims; Gustav and his younger brother Joseph Coster and a friend Guzi Camilleri, who all worked at the nearby Bighi Naval Hospital, on hearing that bombs had fallen in their street, rushed home only to find their home in ruins and rescue people trying to clear one of the shelter's entrances from the rubble. As Mary Coster, Gustav's and Joseph's mother, their grand mother Carmela Mintoff and their aunt Filippa Mintoff were taking refuge in the shelter, Joseph decided to go down the shelter, to rescue any survivors who might still be alive. Gustav followed soon after. When they both failed to come up again, Guzi Camilleri decided to go down himself. None of them ever saw the light of day again. The three were overcome by the gas fumes which were leaking out from the damaged mains gas pipe.

At Safi, a bomb had ricocheted off a wall and went right through a shelter's entrance, exploding down below and killing more than thirty civilians.

Hardly a day would go by without some similar episode being reported. Death had become the main topic of conversation. Danger lurked everywhere, all the time. On a fine day a person would decide to go out for a walk in the countryside. His foot would hit an object and, in a split second, he would be blown up to kingdom come. If he were accompanied by a friend, his action would kill his friend as well and they would both keep each other company in the afterlife! Children were the ones who mostly fell victim to these incidents. Today we read about children who die or get injured with some 'festa' petard. In those days it was bombs and steel splinters that killed them.

In April, 1944, when the tide of war was fast receding from our shores and when one would have expected that life would gradually come back to normal, a terrible tragedy befell six Sliema boys. On Sunday, 9th April, large waves were breaking on the foreshore beneath Tower Road, between St. Julian's Tower and Fond Għadir. At about 2.30 pm, a large, round, conical-shaped object was sighted bobbing up and down and being thrown on the shore and drawn back out to sea by the waves. A large wave finally deposited this strange object firmly on the rocks and clear of the water. Some children, who happened to be on the rocks at the time, were intrigued by this mysterious object and slowly approached to examine it from a close distance. They were promptly cleared from the area by a police constable. A naval officer who was strolling by was asked by the constable to have a look at the object, in case it was dangerous but the officer declined, stating that there were specially trained people who could do the job better than him and walked on.

The constable then asked some sailors who were passing by, to identify the object. They seemed to conclude that it was nothing more than a buoy. They lifted it up and deposited it close to the seawall, beneath the promenade. When a police inspector came over, he was also satisfied that the object was a buoy. He later reported the matter to the District Superintendent and no further action was taken.

Unfortunately, two days later, the curiosity of six boys got the better of them. Eric Frendo (15), George Debono (5), Victor Debono (9) and Frank, Albert and John Giorgio aged 12, 11, and 9 respectively, came upon the object while playing at soldiers on the foreshore. This find promised to be something special so they decided to examine it and possibly take it to their "camp". They probably assumed that, had the thing been dangerous, the authorities would not have left it lying around and unguarded. They also noticed that the object had been moved from where some of them had seen it the day before. Instead of being close to the sea-wall, it now lay in a hole half way between the wall and the sea. Albert Giorgio and Victor Debono were struggling to pull it by means of a rope. They had barely moved it a few meters when the device exploded, killing George Debono and Albert and John Giorgio. Eric Frendo died in hospital later, while the other two boys sustained serious injuries.

I am more inclined to believe that this had been an anti-personnel bomb, a booby trap or a land mine which exploded on being moved. I do not think it was a naval-mine as it was rumoured, because there had been no damage to the adjacent buildings and not even window glass panes were shattered. Moreover, had it been a mine, the detonation of seven hundred pounds of TNT would have completely obliterated those four boys, considering the damage such mines caused when they accidentally came down on land, destroying entire blocks of buildings. I knew Eric Frendo, as we were often together at the Salesians Oratory. Normally, he was a very cautious boy. They were all aged between seven and fifteen and they must surely have had enough sense not to approach a mine, let alone meddle around with it. Besides, it was improbable that the soldiers stationed a few yards away at St. Julian's Tower and at the Sliema Point Battery, would not have spotted a large sea-mine which had been washed ashore. These soldiers, guarding the foreshore, were usually very alert and they kept a watchful look-out for sea-craft, mines, corpses or strange objects which drifted ashore.

Constant watch was kept from these outposts and pill-boxes, all around the coastline, for saboteurs or spies, who might try to come ashore from some submarine on rubber dinghies. Whenever these guards spotted a stray mine on the water surface, they would report its position and it would then be exploded with machine-gun fire from a Royal Navy minesweeper.

Mines were often the cause of considerable loss of life and sea-craft. One such tragedy took place on the 8th April, 1941, when, shortly after 5.00 pm, the mooring vessel *Moor* sank after striking a mine in Grand Harbour.

Only one crewman, Diver Anthony Mercieca survived. He was blown inside the ship's cabin and struggled out as the ship sank. Twenty-four others perished. The destroyer H.M.S. *Jersey* was steaming out of Grand Harbour, when she struck another mine and sank at the harbour entrance on the 2nd of May, 1941. On 29th December, 1941, at about 4.00 pm, the Gozo boat *Marie Georgette* struck a mine off St. Julian's tower and was blown up. Out of a crew of eleven, two were missing and the other nine were injured.

Before he had left for Britain, Pete had told me a story of a Spitfire which was on its way back from a mission over Comiso, in Sicily. The release mechanism of one of the under-wing bombs, a two hundred and fifty pounder which it was carrying, jammed and the bomb remained dangling on the bomb rack. The pilot tried every manoeuvre in the book to release the bomb from its rack into the sea but he simply could not jettison it. He realised that his only hope lay in taking to his parachute and abandoning his aircraft, bomb and all, over the water. He did not want to do this however as he wanted to save his aircraft. A Gozo boat happened to be on its way to Malta with cargo from Gozo, its crew feeling quite safe, as there had been no air raid warnings. They were actually watching and enjoying the aerobatics display being given by this Spitfire pilot, in his efforts to release the bomb. At one point they saw the Spitfire flying very low in their direction and they eagerly waved at it, as was the custom in those days, whenever a friendly aircraft flew over.

To their great chagrin and surprise, however, a huge column of water suddenly erupted from the sea about fifty yards away, accompanied by a big explosion. The bomb had finally been freed and dropped to the water when least expected. Luckily, no damage was caused, except for the shock suffered by the poor crew. Instead of waving, they now clenched their fists and swore at that Spitfire pilot.

The Pilot saw none of this and glad to have finally succeeded in releasing the bomb, headed for Ta' Qali. On leaping out from the cockpit, he found his Commanding Officer waiting for him. He stood to attention with a beaming smile, gave a smart salute to the C.O., expecting to be congratulated for his feat in getting rid of the bomb and saving the aircraft. Instead, he was severely told off for having almost blown up a Gozo boat carrying precious food. Protests about the incident where an R.A.F. Spitfire had "bombed" a Gozitan boat had already been sent in by the Civil Authorities. When, however, the reason for this "bombing" was given out by the Service Authorities, the explanation was accepted.

On another occasion, a shell got jammed in the breech of one of the 4.5 inch anti-aircraft guns of Fort Spinola. The gunners tried their very best to unblock the breech and as they were trying to force open the lock of the breach, to get the shell out, the gun suddenly went off and the shell shot out of the muzzle of the gun, hitting one of the houses in Tower Road, in front of the Carmelite friary in Balluta Bay, St. Julian's. It left a gaping hole in one of the walls and brought the ceiling down. Luckily, nobody was injured. My Uncle Eddie, who was asleep in the room adjacent to that house, confessed that he never shot out of bed in such a hurry!

A group of fighter pilots were watching an air attack on Ta' Qali from the terrace of the officers mess, at Xara Palace, Mdina. A dog fight between some Messerschmitts and Spitfires was raging high above. Another pilot joined the group. He hardly had the time to look up and see what was happening, when he was hit by a stray bullet which fell from the sky and killed him instantly.

I could go on and on with a string of similar stories, but these would be beyond the scope of this account.

The third summer of the war was now approaching, after the gruelling experience of a winter and spring of continuous bombing. On 1st July, 1942, at about 4.00 am, there was an air raid warning. As it was now quite warm, it was not so hard to get up and go out, at that early hour. All I had to do was to put on a pair of shorts and an under-vest and my rope sandals. My group of friends did not go down into the shelter right away and we sat down on some steps opposite the shelter entrance, so that, if danger approached, we could swiftly take cover down there. There were some five men talking at the entrance, as usual and, every now and then, one of them went inside to have a smoke. It was still prohibited to smoke outside after dark, because of the "Black-out".

After some twenty minutes, the searchlights came on, probing the night sky over Luqa airfield. Gradually, the searchlight beams approached Sliema and we heard the drone of aircraft. The girls in our group ran for cover down the shelter. The men who were at the entrance followed suit and the last one turned to us and said: "Wouldn't it be better if you'd come down as well?" We were about to troop down into the shelter but Vince, his brother Joe and I lingered at the entrance. Soon enough, the guns opened fire although we could not see the aircraft. We edged in a bit further, as shrapnel had started raining from the sky. After about four minutes, we heard the screeching sound of a bomb coming down dangerously close — a sound with which we had become very familiar. We shot down the spiral staircase into the shelter, faster than the bombs were falling from the sky. We braced ourselves for the explosion but nothing happened. There was not even the usual tremor felt when bombs exploded under water. We came to the conclusion that the bombs must have fallen into the sea and failed to explode.

We left the shelter before the "raiders passed" signal was given and carried on with our chit-chat in the corner of St. Joseph Street. Some other people had also left the shelter and were about to return home. These were mostly the men who wanted to go to work early in the morning and the wives who had to prepare their lunch pack.

We heard a commotion and saw people running from the direction of St. Dominic Street. There was a great deal of knocking on front doors and doors slamming. At first, we could not understand what was happening as it was still quite dark. We walked down to the lower part of Prince of Wales Road, near St. Dominic Street, to find out exactly what was going on. No sooner had we got there, than a man ran up to us, breathless, and told us to turn back and warn everybody to take cover and remain in the shelter because there was an unexploded bomb. The news spread like wildfire and everybody returned to the shelter.

Later on, I got to know from my uncles, who lived in St. Lawrence Street that a certain Mr. Rossone, a rather old man, had returned to his house in St. Dominic Street, to rest in the comfort of his bed. On entering his dining room, he saw a cloud of dust and masonry strewn all over the place. He walked further in and, to his surprise, found that the roof had caved in and that, lying on the ground almost next to his leg, was an unexploded bomb. At first he was glued to the ground and even lost his voice. He could not even scream. Then he plucked up some courage and bolted out of the house shouting at the top of his voice, "Get out...! Get out....! There is an unexploded bomb!" banging on all the doors in the neighbourhood. The police and the special constables, who were doing the rounds outside, soon converged on this house and saw to it that everybody living in the vicinity quickly went back to the shelter.

Very soon there was not a soul left in the street. Everybody had gone underground and a policeman was stationed at every entrance, to stop people from leaving the shelter. Soon after 4.30 am, two explosions made the shelter tremble. Two delayed-action bombs had exploded underwater at The Strand, close by the ferry-boats jetty.

Sometime later, there was yet another explosion but this was quite distant. I later got to know that it had taken place in the junction between Castelletti Street and St. Rita Street. Then, soon after, another bomb went off, this time closer to our shelter. In fact it was not more than forty yards away further down Prince of Wales Road, near St. Dominic Street. Nobody was aware of this last bomb, because the owner had not yet returned to the house where it had landed.

A fifth explosion took place at about 5.00 am in St. Dominic Street and many buildings were demolished as a result. Had it not been for Mr. Rossone and his bomb, I am sure that there would have been many victims of this delayed-action bomb attack.

Unfortunately, Police Sergeant Peter Cordina was hit by a fragment of an iron beam which was dislodged and landed on his head. He was killed instantly. "Is-Surgent

Piet", as he was affectionately called was carrying out his duty, stopping people from leaving the shelter. Two other police officers, P.C. Fava and P.C. Searthal, were wounded. Although some other buildings had been blown up in Prince of Wales Road, no one else had been injured.

Chapter XIX

"OPERATION PEDESTAL"

Although by June 1942, after the fall of Tobruk, Operation Hercules had been shelved and postponed, Marshal Kesselring, on Field Marshal Goering's orders, continued to insist that, "Malta had to be wiped off the map!" General Rommel was still on the offensive in North Africa and was almost at the gates of Alexandria, on his way to Cairo. Malta was still a thorn in the side of the Axis and its aircraft and submarines were continuously harassing the movement of seaborne traffic between Italy and North Africa. Kesselring was determined to eliminate all such harassment to his convoys from Malta. He did not have to worry about other naval ships, because these had long since disappeared from Malta's harbours.

After the convoy MW10 of 25th March, 1942, made up of *Talabot, Pampas, Breconshire* and *Clan Campbell*, which had all been sunk with very little of the supplies they carried salvaged, the situation in Malta went from bad to worse. Two other attempts to send convoys to these

Islands ended in failure, as they were disrupted by the efforts of the Luftwaffe and the Regia Aeronautica as well as by E-Boats, destroyers, and submarines of the Italian Fleet and German U-boats.

Stocks of foodstuffs were almost exhausted and those that were left were being destroyed by bombs. Very little agricultural produce came from local farming as few farmers risked working in the open, either because of danger from marauding enemy aircraft, or because their fields were full of bomb craters. Precious agricultural land had been taken over by the fighting services for defence purposes. Goats were also being slaughtered to provide fresh meat and there was hardly any milk available. Parents with young children were reduced to a state of despair, when they saw their kids going hungry, days on end. I saw tears in my mother's eyes whenever she could not give us anything to eat. Like my mother, there must have been many parents who went hungry themselves, to give their part of the daily ration to their children.

The authorities responsible for the defence of the Island had worked it out that, unless another convoy reached our shores by the 7th August, there would only be supplies of food and fuel to last two weeks. Meanwhile a trickle of supplies was reaching Malta on the fast minelayers, *H.M.S. Manxman* and *H.M.S. Welshman*. Submarines also brought in some vital stores. But that was all.

With the Battle of the Atlantic in full swing, the war in the Pacific and the Russia-bound convoys, there were very few cargo ships, tankers and naval ships to form an armada to force the Malta blockade. In London, it was decided that, come what may, Malta needed immediate assistance, if it was not to fall in German and Italian hands. Sir Winston Churchill, the then British Prime Minister, laid great emphasis on this and plans for the now famous Operation Pedestal were drawn up.

On 10th August, 1942, a fleet of fifty-nine warships and fourteen cargo ships assembled off Gibraltar. Destination: Malta. The enemy's secret agents in Spain did not take long to notice these movements. The destination of the convoy was obvious. The Axis rapidly deployed their forces between Malta and Gibraltar. They could rely on twenty-one submarines, eighteen German and three Italian, twenty-three E-Boats and seven hundred and eighty-four aircraft, based in Sardinia and Sicily. These were all within range of the course which the convoy would have to steer to Malta. Reconnaissance aircraft kept a constant vigil over the waters between Malta and Sicily and reported their findings on radio to Kesselring's General Headquarters in Sicily.

The Pedestal Convoy sailed through the Straits of Gibraltar under the cover of darkness, during the night of the 10th - 11th August 1942, bound for Malta, under the command of Vice Admiral Syfret. The thirteen cargo ships, making up the convoy, were all fast ships, which could carry a considerable load. These were accompanied by a large American tanker from the Texas Oil Company, which was leased to the British Government and manned by an all-British crew. Even this tanker had been picked out because of its size of 14,150 tons and its high speed. It could carry a load of 11,500 tons of oil. The ship's name was *Ohio* and this was to be etched in gold in the annals of war. The warships included two battleships, *H.M. Ships Nelson and Rodney* and three aircraft carriers, *Eagle, Victorious* and *Indomitable*. These last two were the most modern carriers in the Royal Navy and, between them, could carry seventy-two aircraft. They were escorted by seven cruisers, thirty-three destroyers, a number of corvettes, tug boats and minesweepers. Later on, they were joined by the aircraft carrier *H.M.S. Furious*, which was ferrying thirty-eight Spitfires to Malta.

Tragedy soon struck! At midday on 11th August, a German U-Boat unexpectedly torpedoed the aircraft carrier *H.M.S. Eagle* and this sank in a few minutes, taking with her two hundred members of its crew of one thousand one hundred. At about 8.00 pm, thirty-six German and Italian aircraft, from their bases in Sardinia, made the first aerial attack on the convoy, luckily, without success.

The following morning, at about 9.00 am, there was another air-raid; this time by nineteen aircraft. They were intercepted by the aircraft from the carriers in the convoy. At noon, seventy other aircraft, with a heavy fighter escort, succeeded in sinking the cargo ship *Deucalion* and a large, armour-piercing bomb caused considerable damage to the flight deck of *H.M.S. Victorious*, forcing her aircraft to land on the other aircraft carriers in the convoy. During these first two days of the battle, the enemy lost two submarines, *Dagabur* and *Cobalto*.

At sunset, another air attack by one hundred aircraft found the convoy between Sardinia and Algeria. The destroyer *Foresight* was sunk. This time, the aircraft carrier *Indomitable* sustained damage to its flight deck and its aircraft had to land on *H.M.S. Victorious*, after the latter had had its flight deck patched up.

When the fleet approached "The Narrows", between Sicily and Cape Bon in Tunisia, as planned, the battleships *Nelson* and *Rodney* and the three surviving carriers turned back and Rear Admiral Burroughs took command of the convoy, flying his flag in the cruiser *H.M.S. Nigeria*. However, he soon had to transfer his flag to the destroyer *H.M.S. Ashanti*, as the *Nigeria* was hit and suffered considerable damage and had to turn back to Gibraltar.

The cruiser *Cairo* was also sunk and *Ohio* was hit by a torpedo and caught fire. This was extinguished soon after. Both the *Ohio* and the two cruisers had been hit by the Italian submarine *Axum*. Two other cargo ships, *Empire Hope* and *Clan Ferguson* were sunk by air attack. The cruiser *Kenya* was torpedoed and the cargo ship *Brisbane Star* was also hit, but both of them could carry on with their voyage to Malta.

During the night of the 12th - 13th August, what remained of the convoy had rounded Cape Bon and had now entered the most dangerous stretch of its journey, the narrow channel between Tunisia, Sicily and the Island of Pantelleria. The enemy was waiting for the convoy and lost no time in launching a fierce E-Boat attack from Pantelleria. These E-Boats went in as close as fifty yards to the ships of the convoy, before launching their torpedoes and raking the ships with machine-gun fire. Four other ships went down in this attack, the *Santa Elisa* and the *Almeria Lykes*, both American vessels, and the British ships *Wairangi* and *Glenorcky*. The cruiser *H.M.S. Manchester* sustained heavy damage and orders were given to scuttle her. Next morning, there was another air attack and this time it was *Waimarama*'s turn. *Ohio* was hit again and a Junkers 88 actually crashed on its bow while a Stuka also crashed on its stern. Soon after, the tanker's engines stopped and the ship went adrift.

The last attack took place at about noon of the 13ᵗʰ August, *Dorset* and another ship were sent to the bottom.

In Malta, we were unaware of this naval saga which was unfolding itself a few hundred miles from our beleaguered shores.

It was the Italian radio station that gave us the first inkling of what the convoy was going through. According to the Italians, they had sunk more vessels and warships then there were actually sailing with the convoy! The arrival of Pedestal was no longer a closely guarded secret and everybody was talking about it. We had almost given up hope of ever seeing a single cargo ship enter Grand Harbour.

On 13ᵗʰ August, in the afternoon, my friends and I were at Fond Għadir on the Sliema promenade, when we made out three cargo ships and some warships on the horizon, slowly approaching Grand Harbour. These were *Port Chalmers*, *Rochester Castle* and *Melbourne Star*. The incredulous watchers, who happened to be on the water-front, could not believe their eyes. Then, as the full meaning of this sight sank in, they gradually started clapping, cheering, waving their handkerchiefs and thanking God for the safe arrival of these vessels. The soldiers manning the harbour defences were now reassured that, at least, they would now have enough ammunition for their guns.

Some R.A.F. pilots, gathered in front of the Meadow Bank Hotel and the Crown Hotel, were cheering their heads off at the sight of the arrival of the ships. They were throwing their caps in the air and prancing around. Word soon spread like wildfire and many flocked to the Valletta bastions to welcome these war heroes. A military band on the Lower Barrakka played the ships in. All vessels bore the scars of war. As they entered Grand Harbour, they looked battered, charred, rusty, holed and appeared to be in imminent danger of sinking.

Detailed preparations had been made beforehand for the unloading of the cargo. Stevedores, lorries, barges and empty warehouses were all ready to receive the stock of supplies that had been so long in coming.

After sunset, there was an unusual glow above Valletta, Floriana, and Grand Harbour, the likes of which we had not seen since the onset of war. It was the glow from arc-lights that had been lit up to illuminate the vessels during the unloading operation, ensuring that work would continue uninterruptedly through the night. The following day, 14th August, *Brisbane Star* arrived with a cargo of petrol and ammunition at about noon. It had a gaping hole caused by a torpedo's explosion in its bows. But the most poignant scene was still to come!

Early in the morning of 15th August, the mid-summer feast of Santa Maria, a large tanker loomed on the horizon, very painfully edging its way towards Grand Harbour. It was down, low in the water and supported on either side by the destroyers, *Penn* and *Ledbury*. The minesweeper *H.M.S. Rye* was towing the tanker. It was *Ohio*, the hero of the convoy, laden with a cargo of kerosene, oil fuel and aviation fuel which were so badly needed.

That morning I had planned to go to swim with my friends on the shore near Sliema Point Battery, the present site of the Sliema Aquatic Sports Club. On seeing the *Ohio*, however, we quickly decided to go and watch it enter Grand Harbour. We rushed down to The Strand to board the Ferry and crossed over to Valletta. There, we hurried up the steps to the city and down to the Lower

Barrakka gardens. These were already crowded with people, anxious to see the tanker safely enter between the break-water's arms. A group of men, who appeared to have been sailors in their younger days, were debating whether the tanker would make it into port. One said that even if it made it up to the breakwater, it would not manage to get past the lanterns. Another gloomily predicted that, as soon as the destroyers cast off the lashing and towing cables, the tanker would go to the bottom. Yet another sea dog was of the opinion that it would be better if the tanker were not towed into harbour as there was probably nothing left inside its tanks, other than sea water.

Just after 9.00 am, *Ohio* was literally carried between the breakwater arms, which seemed to welcome and embrace it. The tanker was still being supported by the two destroyers and nursed into harbour by tug boats. It was charred from the fires that had erupted on it. Its iron works were twisted and it was holed in many places, presenting a terrible sight. The crowds on the bastions at first were silent. Then they exploded into an orgy of cheering, clapping, shouting and waving of Maltese flags and Union Jacks, to the accompaniment of the military band, playing from the Lower Barrakka bastion. Their hearts went out to the heroes of the *Ohio*, who had been close to death a hundred times and had only been egged on by the courage and determination shown by the skipper Captain Dudley Mason who was, in no small way, responsible for seeing this tanker arrive at its destination with its decks almost awash. Dudley Mason was awarded the George Cross for his unstinting efforts to sail the vital tanker to its beleaguered destination.

Vice admiral Neville Syfret, who commanded the

close escort force which enabled what was left of the convoy to reach Malta, wrote in his despatch:-

> *"The steadfast manner in which these ships pressed their way to Malta was a most inspiring sight. The memory of their conduct will remain an inspiration to all who were privileged to sail with them."*

Although the official name of this convoy was Operation Pedestal, the Maltese placed it on an even higher plane. To this very day, it is still affectionately referred to as the "Santa Maria Convoy"!

After the arrival of this convoy, things changed dramatically in Malta. R.A.F. aircraft flew more frequently, the gunners were now allowed to make full use of their prowess and had enough ammunition at their disposal, and, above all, the population could look to their future with some hope. Tension abated not because enough food had arrived, but because a breathing space of two months had been won. The worse was over. Operation Stonehenge, another convoy arrived in Malta, in November, with four ships carrying 35,000 tons of mixed cargo. Two other convoys arrived in December, 1942. One of them was Operation Portcullis, with five cargo ships, landing 55,000 tons, and the other Operation Quadrangle, with fourteen vessels, which unloaded 120,000 tons of supplies. With this last convoy, the supply situation eased considerably.

Balloon barrages were now being hoisted around and above the harbours to deter low flying enemy aircraft. These balloons were moored to the ground with steel cables and made life difficult for pilots of low-flying aircraft. One of these balloons had been hoisted behind the Sacro Cuor Church from a garden in Carmel Street on the present site of St. Benild's School. Another new type of defence gadget, which came into use at this time, was the smokescreen. This was released from green canisters, which were ignited whenever there was an air-raid warning. The thick smoke covered the harbours and made vessels invisible to the enemy. However, although this deterred the enemy from raiding the harbours, it also almost asphyxiated everybody else on land, because our houses were literally engulfed in smoke with a peculiar, sunflower smell. A detachment of the Basutos Pioneer Regiment was in charge of igniting these smoke-screen canisters.

On the night of the 23rd October, 1942, General Montgomery, at the head of the 8th Army, also popularly known as "The Desert Rats",* commenced his famous offensive at Alamein, in the Western Desert and after a week-long, slogging battle, the Afrika Korps began their long retreat. The German army, led by Field Marshal Erwin Rommel, nicknamed "The Desert Fox", was on the verge of defeat. The Luftwaffe had left us in peace for some time, because of this offensive in North Africa. Some of its squadrons in Sicily had been moved to the North African Front, to cover the long withdrawal of Rommel's troops, all the way from Egypt to Tunisia.

We still had air raids, of course, but nothing like the previous onslaught, in intensity and frequency. Some Ju88s, with a heavy Me109 escort, would fly over the Island occasionally and now and then, Italian Macchi and Reggiane fighters, Cant Z1007s and Savoia Marchetti SM79 bombers would also make an occasional appearance.

The number of Spitfires available for Malta's defence was now in the region of two hundred and there were also squadrons of Beaufighters which performed night-fighter duties, Beaufort torpedo-bombers, Mosquito fighter-bomber and reconnaissance aircraft, Baltimore bombers and Wellington medium bombers.

Whenever some enemy aircraft managed to dodge the fighter defence, but was unable to release its bombs on the harbours and airfields, it would jettison its bomb-load wherever it happened to be and quickly head back to base. Some bombs fell on Sliema, Gzira and St. Julian's, during the October Blitz. Those falling on Sliema were dropped on Prince of Wales Road and St. Alphonse Street and damaged some buildings without leaving any casualties. These bombs fell on the 27th October, 1942, at about 10.00 am, I happened to be in my father's room in the Protection Office, at the time.

The following day, as I was strolling by the Carmelite Church in Balluta Bay, an air raid warning sounded. I stopped near Balluta Buildings, where there were many airmen looking up at the sky. One of them exclaimed that he had spotted three Ju88s at a considerable height, approaching from the direction of St. Andrew's. They were in line with the Cable and Wireless aerial mast, the present site of the Maltacom offices at St. George's. The large calibre guns at Fort Spinola quickly opened fire, with a salvo of four rounds, which completely deafened us. The Ju88s flew straight at us and one of the airmen shouted that they were probably heading for the har-bour, where some warships were moored. Suddenly, they were jumped by three Spitfires, which opened up with their 20 mm cannon. One of the 88s started trailing a wisp of smoke. It dropped out of formation and re-leased a bomb, which appeared to be falling quite close to where we stood, right in the middle of Balluta Square, close by the statue and fountain. We rushed to the underground public toilets, but the bomb was faster than us. We had not even taken the first step, when we were smitten by an explosion and a strong blast. A large column of smoke and dust mushroomed up from Birkirkara Road. I ran to the site of the explosion and I found many demolished buildings but luckily, nobody had been hurt.

On that same day, at about 9.00 pm, I was leaving the cinema, after watching a film show with my friend William. An air raid was in progress. As soon as we emerged from the cinema, we heard the screech of falling bombs and this was followed by explosions coming from the direction of Gzira. It all happened so quickly, that we just froze at the cinema entrance. We heard nothing except the explosions and, as there were no flashes, we could not say where the bombs had fallen. Later, I learnt that they had fallen on Freres Street and Fleet Street in Gzira. One person was killed and others were injured.

* This evocative name properly referred to one of the most effective fighting units of the 8th Army, the famous 7th Armoured Division. It was later on attributed to the entire 8th Army.

Chapter XX

THE SWING OF THE PENDULUM

We turned over a new leaf in 1943 and gradually, we began to see many positive changes and interesting developments. Although life was still somewhat difficult, particularly with regards to the supply of food, danger was fast abating from our shores. We started sleeping in our homes instead of down in the damp shelters. We could sit down to a quiet meal and young people like me, returned to school. Men could go to work safely and the occasional bottle of beer or a packet of cigarettes was now available, even though it was still rationed.

Enemy aircraft came over in small groups of five or less and only when they managed to evade the intercepting Spitfires. In this case, they would release their bombs hurriedly and erratically, and these very often ended up on the odd house or in the countryside. I loved watching dogfights in the sky. They were worth watching, particularly when they took place at some distance and not directly overhead, as empty cartridges, stray bullets or

20 mm cannon shells and other debris from damaged aircraft would rain down from the sky. Canon shells often exploded on hitting the ground and could easily injure or even kill anyone close by. Once, while I was watching one of these dogfights from our roof-top, one of these cannon shells exploded on the retaining wall. Luckily, the tiny fragments from this exploding shell only hit me on the chin and face, and I was not hit in the eyes. I remember, for many months, tiny pieces of metal kept emerging from my skin.

One of the best dogfights or aerial battles, which I remember vividly, took place over St. Julian's Bay, while I was having a stroll with my friends on the promenade between Għar id-Dud and Balluta. The sirens came on when we were near The Exiles. Used to taking air-raid warning not too seriously, we walked on regardless. One of my friends noticed that the guns of Fort Spinola were pointing skywards. We stopped at Balluta Square to take cover in the underground public toilets, in case things got dangerous.

After a short while, we started hearing the sound of aircraft engines, high up in the sky, accompanied by the stutter of machine-gun fire. We strained our eyes and saw a battle between some ten Messerschmitt 109s and about twenty Spitfires, all milling around at about 10,000 feet. It was a clear winter's day, sunny and with a few clouds dotting the blue sky. The visibility was excellent. The guns of Fort Spinola, Ta' Giorni and other surrounding batteries remained silent and left the Royal Air Force to take care of the enemy.

At one point, I saw a black streak of smoke fading into the distance in the blue sky. It was a Me109, being chased by a Spitfire which was emitting beads of white smoke. Then came the sound of cannon fire. The Messerschmitt 109 nose-dived and the pilot seemed to bale out. A few seconds later, the parachute blossomed open and the pilot drifted down over the blue Mediterranean.

All those who had been watching this circus of death started applauding and jumping for joy. I could hear a lot of cheering coming from the terraces of Balluta Buildings, which were then occupied by the Royal Air Force as a Sergeant Pilots' Mess.

We heard a snarl from the engine of a Spitfire and it came down spinning towards the water as well. It looked as if it was going to ditch in the middle of the bay. When the Spitfire was about 2,000 feet high, the pilot leapt out of the aircraft but, unfortunately, his parachute streamed and he hurtled down towards the sea. Everyone held his breath and, in the dead silence that followed, I overheard a Carmelite monk, from the nearby church, who was standing nearby, quickly reciting the last rites. Then, suddenly the parachute blossomed open. The Spitfire crashed further away from Dragonara Point and the pilot was carried further out to sea, by the offshore wind.

Another enemy aircraft crashed in flames. The pilot could not be seen and no parachute was visible. We started cheering again until we were curtly interrupted by the same monk who chided us that we had better pray for the poor pilot's soul. When the aircraft hit the waves, the monk crossed himself and muttered: "Requiescat in pacem".

When this brief spectacle in the skies was over, the Air Sea Rescue launch sped out to rescue the pilots from the sea. It first picked up the Spitfire pilot who was close inshore and then it steered further out to sea and picked up the German pilot, who must have been floating about five miles offshore.

We left Balluta Bay and headed for The Strand to see the pilots being landed from the High Speed Launch (H.S.L.). The first to come ashore was the German, who was helped by two R.A.F. airmen. He looked injured and part of his flying suit was charred. I remember to this very day, the gentlemanly gesture of the English pilot, who turned to the German officer and, after offering him a cigarette, shook his hand. The German flyer, with a deep German accent, sadly mumbled: "Zhank you." On seeing this, the few onlookers started cheering and applauding. Usually, when a German or Italian pilot was brought ashore, he was often the subject of abuse. This was not the case on that occasion!

With the westward Allied advance in North Africa, the end of Rommel's Afrika Korps was becoming inevitable. On 23rd January, 1943, the 8th Army marched into the streets of Tripoli, led by the pipes and drums of the Highland Division. There was great rejoicing in Malta at this victory. In Sliema, particularly in The Strand, that evening soldiers and sailors made merry and danced away, beer bottles in hand. Soldiers were wearing sailors' hats and sailors donned soldiers' caps. Għar id-Dud and Fond Għadir presented a similar sight. R.A.F. airmen and civilians were singing and shaking each other's hands. Many of the pilots were merrily blowing their whistles. Red and green Verey-lights streamed upward, into the air. The merriment only came to an end very late that night.

With the fall of Tunis, on 8th May, the war in Africa was over and the curtain came down on Act One of the Second Great War in the Mediterranean theatre.

United States President, Franklin D. Roosevelt, and the British Prime Minister, Winston Churchill had earlier, met in conference, with the Allied leaders in Casablanca, Morocco, on 23rd January 1943. After much discussion and deliberation as to where the Allied invasion of Europe should take place, it was finally decided that the Allies should first attack Italy, after invading Sicily. The plans and discussions were not completed before the middle of June. The Allied generals had to tackle gigantic problems and see how best to land eight divisions on the enemy coast. This was to be the largest amphibious military operation, since the beginning of the war.

In Malta, we became aware of many military movements and the talk of invasion was on everybody's lips. Many new regiments started arriving and Sliema Creek was full of every type of warship. Military traffic on the roads had now reached its peak. I saw large tanks for the first time and there were other very strange vehicles, the likes of which I had never seen before. These were the DAWKS, or amphibious vehicles. Jeeps and lorries towing guns travelled in convoy, towards St. Andrew's and St. George's barracks.

Many new squadrons of aircraft, made up of Mosquitoes, Beaufighters, Baltimores and more Spitfires started landing on the airfields. For the first time, we also had United States Army Air Force aircraft like Mitchels, Lightnings, Bostons, Marauders, Kittyhawks and Mustangs. The airfields now housed no less than thirty-two R.A.F. Squadrons with five hundred twenty-seven aircraft and three United States Army Air Force Squadrons with seventy-five Spitfires, operating from Gozo. They flew round the clock. Cargo carrying Douglas DC 3's or

Dakotas which were also used for dropping paratroops, were often seen at Luqa.

A large number of assault craft and invasion barges entered Marsamxett Harbour and assembled at Sliema Creek. These included craft that carried troops: Landing Craft Infantry (L.C.I.), and those that carried guns, tanks and motor transport: Landing Craft Tanks (L.C.T.). They were berthed, side by side, all along the Sliema Strand to Gzira, and all along Lazzarrett Creek, round Ta' Xbiex, Msida and Pieta' Creeks. These assault craft were berthed with their gaping open bows facing inwards, on hards which were prepared in record time by gangs of Maltese workmen, from the Demolition and Clearance Department, (Mosta Squad), under the direction and supervision of architect and civil engineer George J. Galea. These men feverishly dumped fallen masonry and debris into the sea and levelled the reclaimed land with a 15-ton steam-roller, previously used to level filled-in craters on the runways. The larger L.C.T.s and troop ships were berthed in Grand Harbour. A repair yard for these invasion barges was built on the Sliema side of Manoel Island, on the present site of the Yacht Repair Yard.

The Sliema Government School was converted from an A.R.P. Centre to an emergency Military hospital. St. Patrick's Barracks followed suit.

There were so many troops that, both because many barracks had been destroyed by enemy action and because in any case there was not sufficient space to accommodate three extra divisions, many military tented camps sprouted up all over the Island.

There were soldiers from all over the British Empire; Australians, New Zealanders, Indians, Malaysians, Mauritians, Canadians and the famous Gurkhas. There were also Pioneer Regiments from Basutoland and these soldiers were nicknamed "Tal-Basuta". These ebony-skinned men from Basutoland once created quite a stir in Sliema, when they were seen swimming stark naked in Qui-Si-Sana. Because of this incident, for a short while, we dared not take our girlfriends on the promenade at Għar id-Dud.

New airfields had to be constructed. When Safi Strip was completed, No. 126 Squadron was transferred there from Luqa. Later two other squadrons No. 111 and No. 112 operated from there. Another airstrip was built at Qrendi. Construction started in 1942 and, before the runways were finished, it was used as a decoy airfield, to divert the enemy's attention from other airfields. On 23rd November, 1942, 249 Squadron was transferred to Qrendi airstrip and was later joined by No. 229 from Ta' Qali and No. 185 from Hal Far. Another airstrip had to be built in Xewkija, on the neighbouring island of Gozo. To every-body's amazement, this airfield was constructed in just fifteen days between the 8th and 23rd June 1943 by E Company of the 21st Engineer Aviation Regiment of the United States Army. For the first time, new construc-tion equipment like bulldozers and other earth-moving machines were used. Although it was a small airfield, the United States Army Air Force stationed there the 307th, 308th and the 309th Fighter Squadrons from the 31st Fighter Group, all equipped with Spitfires Mk.Vc. Kittyhawks and Mustangs also made use of this airstrip and Mitchels or Bostons occasionally landed with mail or urgent stores.

Malta's useful contribution in this operation is borne out by a message that General Dwight Eisenhower, Supreme Commander of the Allied Forces in Europe, sent to Air Vice Marshall Sir Keith Park, Air Officer Commanding Malta:

"It is clear to everyone in the Allied command that had it not been for the air cover provided from Malta, the attack on Sicily would not have been considered!"

Sir Keith Park himself wrote the following on Malta's leading role during the landings in Sicily:

"The fighter squadrons from Malta provided air cover to three thousand vessels and landing barges, which carried our armies to the southern coast of Sicily. I co-ordinated the activities of six hundred aircraft from Maltese air bases and I had an equal number of aircraft in reserve in North Africa."

One day, in February, 1943, father told me that the following day I was to accompany him to the Command Pay Office, where my brother Joe was employed when he was killed, as he wanted to speak to Major Howell. The office had by then been transferred to Ramel Buildings in Isouard Street, Sliema. The next day I donned my Sunday-best clothes, consisting of a green jacket belonging to my late brother. It had been recovered from beneath the debris of Villa Rosa and it was slightly oversize because my brother had been taller and slightly better built than I was. In those days, everything passed muster and nobody would smirk at you for wearing an oversized jacket. In fact, you were considered lucky to have one at all. I remember that once, a large consignment of clothes was sent from America, and these were distributed free of charge. Although the clothes were not brand new, they were in excellent condition. I had been allotted a pair of flannel trousers and a pair of shoes.

When I was led into Major Howell's office, he made me feel at home at once. He had been very fond of my late brother. After asking some questions about my educational background, the Major offered me a job. I did not turn it down as I had been hoping to start working for sometime. He then introduced me to an officer who was in charge of the Detachment Stores. The next day I was at work on my first job.

For a while, I was very happy at this job, particularly when I was sent to collect stores from the Royal Army Ordinance Corps (R.A.O.C.), who had their Depots at the present-day premises of St. Edward's College and at Villa Refalo, near San Anton Gardens, the site of today's Corinthia Palace Hotel. Thanks to these 'excursions', I could see for myself many of the military activities and preparations that were taking place.

But I was getting older and longing to be able to join the armed forces as a volunteer. But this to me, seemed to be ages away. Given a choice, I preferred to enlist in the Royal Air Force, as I had always been very fond of anything connected to flying. An opportunity to join up, even before I attained the required age, soon presented itself. One day in June 1943, my friend William told me he intended to join the Air Force and that I had better hurry and sign up, because recruitment was soon coming to an end. He was right and, in fact, very few managed to join after I did. Next morning, although still much younger then the minimum age required for signing up, I went to the Recruiting Office at No. 38, South Street, Valletta, and joined the queue of aspiring recruits. Surprisingly, nobody asked me to present any certificates. They just had a quick look at me and thought that I was tall enough to look seventeen. After filling in a form with a long list of questions, I was sent to the Sick Quarters at No. 1, Windmill Street, for a medical check-up. This was a somewhat embarrassing experience because I had to strip stark naked and wait in line for the medical exam, at the end of which, I was inoculated - an ordeal which left me practically paralysed for twenty-four hours.

The next day, I was taken to Scots Street (Mikelang Vassalli Street), where I was issued with the coveted summer, khaki R.A.F. uniform; a forage cap, two khaki shirts, a pair of shorts, a pair of khaki trousers, two sets of underwear two pairs of stockings, two towels, a pair of army boots, a kit bag, a gas mask and a steel helmet. Only these items were available from the clothing stores at that time. Then I proceeded to be sworn in. Henceforth, I was to be known as "Aircraftsman second class, Charles Grech ".

I was subsequently ordered to report to the physical training instructor, Sergeant Crawley, at the Air Headquarters gymnasium at Marsamxett. Sergeant Crawley instructed us in small arms drill and physical training. He was the R.A.F. Mediterranean boxing champion and was a perfect gentleman. We used to do some sparring in the gymnasium, where we had a boxing ring, and sometimes, we even took on Sgt. Crawley. Once, I was asked to do one round with him. After hitting out at him for about five minutes, during which time he never actually punched me, he finally let fly at me and I suddenly felt as if I had been thrust into space and saw all the stars in the universe. On recovering consciousness, I found that I was bleeding profusely from my nose and Sgt. Crawley and my new friends were standing around me laughing their sides out!

We numbered twenty-eight new recruits and got on very well. We never had the slightest incident throughout our recruitment course, although this could probably have been the result of the military discipline we had been subjected to. We were very excited when we were taken to do some work on one of the airfields, either carrying petrol from the dumps or from the stores at Tal-Balal in San Gwann or Misraħ il-Barrieri, at Santa Venera. Sometimes, we transported bombs and on other occasions, we also escorted Spitfires to Gasan's Garage where the Aircraft Repair Section was situated.

Between the 6th and the 8th July, there was uninterrupted activity in Sliema. Military transport crowded the streets at all times of day. The tyres of these vehicles had chains tied around them to enable them to move in mud, sand or snow and therefore, made a loud clanking noise. Others had exhaust pipes rising up above the vehicle, higher than the driver's cabin or the tank's gun turret, to prevent vehicles from stalling when they were submerged in water during landings or fording of streams. Jeeps and other small vehicles had an upright angle iron protruding in front, about six feet high, to cut any obstacle wire, which might be spanning the road. All vehicles carried coils of barbed wire.

It was now apparent that the final stages of the preparation for the invasion were under way. After the vehicles were loaded on the invasion barges, it was the turn of the tanks next and these made a great deal of noise, whenever they came clanking down Prince of Wales Road.

The final embarkation of the troops on the invasion barges berthed in Marsamxett Harbour took place between 8th and 9th July. Some of these troops were transported on lorries to the barges and others marched all the way from St. Andrew's or St. George's Barracks to The Strand, in Sliema, whistling or humming military tunes. By nightfall, on 8th July, everything seemed in place and the following morning, while I was on my way to Valletta, the invasion fleet was ready to set sail for Sicily. The ferry to Valletta took longer than usual to cross over because of these shipping movements.

I could not see what happened to the invasion fleet because as soon as I reported for duty, I was ordered to fall in, put onto a Dodge 15 cwt. truck and in a jiffy, transported to Luqa airfield. After leaping from the truck, a Flight Sergeant ordered us back to the lorries and we were taken to the Wellington bombers' dispersal, to help out with the loading of bombs. Luqa was packed with aircraft of all types that morning. Aircraft were taking off and landing without interruption.

We found this work rather tough as we were not used to it, with the scorching sun not helping. But in the Armed Forces, "Their's not to reason why. Their's but to do….." Do what you are ordered to do and complain afterwards! It was work which required team spirit, speed without panic and great concentration, because the slightest mistake could cause a fatal accident. I do not remember getting very tired, probably because of the day's excitement. We were often given tea from a warm container, nearby. You could leave the British soldier hungry for days on end but never without his "cuppa tea". Tea in the Services in those days hardly deserved this appellation, as it tasted more of dish-washing water.

That afternoon, the Flight Sergeant ordered me to return home and inform my family that I might not be able to go back home before the next eight days. He told me to report for duty in full kit the next day. I was not too pleased at this news having to spend a whole week away from home. But, orders were orders.

By the time I returned to Sliema that evening the harbour was completely empty. The invasion armada of landing ships had left and there was nothing to be seen after all that feverish activity. The only trace of the previous days' operations was some litter, left by the soldiers on the hards, being blown around by the strong north-easterly wind. Among the papers and empty "V" cigarette packets, I spotted and picked up a photo. It had probably been dropped by a soldier, in the confusion of the embarkation. It showed a young, pretty woman and two small children, a baby, a few months old and a two-year old boy. On looking at it closely, I asked myself: "Who knows whether these kids will be lucky enough to see their father again?"

I walked home and told my parents that they might not see me for the next eight days and that I was not aware where I was going to be stationed. Father was not too pleased with the idea and mother quickly burst into tears. Father gave me the usual lecture, to be careful and avoid getting hurt and not to do this and not to do that. It was as if I was going to the front!

At nightfall, from the Sliema promenade, I saw the last ships of the invasion fleet heading north for Sicily, and disappearing over the darkening horizon.

"OPERATION HUSKY"   had begun.

Chapter XXI

ITALY CAPITULATES

T hat night, we could hear what sounded like thunder in the distance and, from the Għar id-Dud promenade, we could actually see gun flashes in the direction of Sicily. The guns of the fleet were bombarding the coast, before the troops went ashore. This bombardment went on the whole night and I could hardly sleep. I could not forget the faces of those soldiers, whom I had seen the day before, waving at us from the invasion barges, as they were leaving harbour, revealing the tension of those who were about to face the enemy for the first time. Those among them who already had experienced battle in the North African campaign might have been more resigned and less tense. These and other thoughts flashed through my mind all through that long, sleepless night.

On reporting back for duty the next morning, we were taken to Luqa airfield to help out with the loading of bombs on a squadron of Mosquitoes. These were twin-engine aircraft, with a top speed of three hundred and eighty mph, armed with a Molin 37 mm cannon and four .303 inch machine guns. They could also carry two, five hundred pound bombs each. These aircraft were constructed entirely of wood, unlike most contemporary aircraft and carried a crew of two - a pilot and a navigator.

As the day wore on and whenever any of these aircraft returned to base, we eagerly asked the crew for any news about the landings. One of the crew of the Mosquito I was working on, confirmed that the invasion of Sicily had commenced and that all seemed to be going well. The Allied troops had landed, established beach-heads and were already advancing inland. The resistance they met appeared to be much softer and weaker than expected.

All operations were co-ordinated from Malta and were controlled from the underground headquarters at Lascaris in the deep ditch around Valletta. This underground labyrinth housed the Operations Headquarters, the Command Operations Room, the Naval Operations Room, the Fighter Operations, the Sector Operations and Filter Room. These War Rooms are now open to the general public.

By the end of July, the invasion forces were already well-established in Sicily and gaining ground.

Meanwhile, I was posted to Gozo, at the American airstrip in Xewkija, the practical use of which was already over, because this airfield had only been constructed to provide fighter cover for the initial landings in Sicily. We were ordered to dismantle the huts and equipment and transport everything back to Malta. I spent the entire period I served in Gozo, under canvas. I was not short of food as I used to eat with the Americans, who had very good rations. Compared to our own, it was luxury!

Even the Gozitans fared well as a result of this operation. Very often, we would share our rations with them and they would reciprocate by giving us tomatoes, eggs, fruit and Gozo cheeses. As we had more than enough to eat, we brought these items of food back to Malta, whenever we came back for a half-day's off duty spell. I flew back to Malta in style on a Mitchell Bomber, which crossed over to ferry stores.

Some Gozitans also helped themselves! It was not unusual to find camp beds, cans of petrol or even 40-gallon drums missing as all these stores were lying about, unguarded. Complete tents, which had never been unpacked or used, also vanished. But the episode that struck me most was when, on the last day, we had gone to load the last item, a Spitfire which had landed in Xewkija and could not be repaired in time to fly back to Malta. We had left this Spitfire on the quay at Mgarr the night before, ready to be loaded on a Landing Craft, first thing next morning. When we went to load it on the barge the next day, we found that its wheels, instruments, radio and anything else that could be dismantled, were missing.

Our task in Gozo being completed, I was again recalled to Malta. On 20th July, after I had been to the cinema in the evening, I had something to eat and was about to retire to bed. At about 9.30 pm, the air-raid warning siren sounded. It had been some time since we had heard the air-raid warning and we paid little attention to it. Father, however, insisted that it might be safer to go down to the shelter just in case. Mother took hold of my newly born baby brother Joe, named after my elder brother, who had died one year before. The baby had also been called Joe, as mother was very devoted to St.

Joseph. She and my other brother Victor left for the shelter, while father and I remained home to close the doors and windows and switch off all the lights. Father followed mother to the shelter and I, as usual, remained at the entrance to the shelter with my friends. We felt we need not bother to go down to the shelter again, thinking that the Germans had other things to worry about and that the air-raid warning signal had probably been given because one of our aircraft had not identified itself.

We chatted for about twenty minutes, mostly about the progress of the war in Sicily, and cracking the odd joke, now and again. The joke quickly turned on me, and my pals started teasing me, saying that we were surely going to win the war now that I had joined the Royal Air Force. They asked me mockingly how many aircraft I had "downed" since I had joined up. I could only grin back. What could I say? Sometimes one has to be at the receiving end. Next time round it would be some other friend's turn.

I had my back to the shop window of an electrician's shop, next to the shelter's entrance, and was proudly wearing my steel helmet, according to regulations. I heard the droning of an aircraft in the distance, while one of the bystanders said: "It's one of ours, and I am going home to have a snooze." Two others followed him and walked off in the direction of St. Joseph Street.

The drone of the aircraft gradually passed over us and faded into the distance. When it could not be heard any longer, one of my friends exclaimed: "You see; it must have been one of ours." Shortly afterwards, however, the noise of an approaching aircraft was again heard and this was quickly followed by the usual orders being barked out to the gunners in Fort Manoel. I strained my ears to pick out whether the noise of the aircraft was that of a German or of a friendly aircraft. The droning was now right above us. It was pitch-dark until the searchlights came on and started probing the sky. Then, suddenly, we heard the aircraft diving down and the shout of: "Take Cover", coming across the water, from Fort Manoel. In that silence, the shout appeared to be coming from close by. Those of us who were at the entrance to the shelter stampeded down the steps. When no other noise followed, to show off my expertise, I quickly told them: "It's all right. Everything is over." I had barely uttered these words, when we heard the noise of bombs screaming down nearby, followed by a big explosion, which almost burst my eardrums. The hot blast hit me in the face. The shutter of the shop window, that I had been leaning against, was blown off its hinges with the blast and ended up right on top of me.

As I lay there, underneath this shutter, I heard cat-calls from the steps leading down to the shelter: "Congratulations clever Dick! You really know what you are talking about, don't you?" I started calling for help, hoping that somebody would come up and remove the heavy shutter from on top of me. But they could hardly come out of the shelter to my assistance because part of the shop's show-window had collapsed and was blocking the entrance. Meanwhile, the men who had earlier on, left to go home, returned and promptly removed the shutter and helped me get up, making sure I had not been injured. I only suffered a painful bruise on my shoulder, where I had been hit by the flying shutter, as well as some contusions on my side and on my knee from my being violently thrown on the ground.

The men, who had come back from St. Joseph Street,

appeared quite agitated and jittery. They informed us that the bomb had fallen somewhere up that street. We could hardly see each other in the darkness and the billowing smoke. Someone suggested that we should go to the bombed site to help those in need. When we had gone half way up the street, I suddenly remembered what had happened to the young man, in St. Rita Street, who, after having escaped death from a bomb explosion, had been electrocuted on stepping on some live electricity wires. I warned everyone to stop in their tracks and not to proceed, insisting that it would be safer if we all waited further down, until the rescue workers arrived with their lights. They wisely followed my advice and we slowly backed down the street again.

One of my friends later told me: "It was a good thing you thought of going back in time because, a few feet up from where we had come to a stop, there were live electricity cables on the ground. At least, you have recovered some credibility, after almost burying us all with you under that shutter!"

The A.R.P. rescue workers and the police soon arrived on the scene and started digging for survivors under the debris. They asked people if any members of their family were missing and if any neighbours had remained at home. They soon discovered that there were four missing persons and the search for them quickly got under way, with the aid of kerosene lanterns and torch lights. Bystanders were asked to make way but as I was in uniform and wearing my steel helmet, I was allowed to remain on the spot. I asked an A.R.P. officer whether I could be of any help. He declined after thanking me politely. He was right because it was better to leave it to the experts. I moved over to one side to watch the proceedings, without being of hindrance to the rescuers. Women were crying in the darkness and confusion reigned. Some were asking where this German aircraft could have come from, once the Allies had overrun all the enemy bases in Sicily. A neighbour surmised that it was probably one of our own aircraft, returning damaged back to base, which had released part of its bomb load on top of us. This was not the case however, because other bombs had been dropped on Zabbar during the same air raid. These were the last bombs to be dropped on Malta!

After sadly observing the rescue operation for about half an hour and seeing that I could not be of any help, I returned home to snatch some sleep, as I was on duty, early in the morning. As you can imagine, when I finally got home I was greeted by further mocking remarks from my parents about the shutter incident.

Next morning, before reporting for duty, I went back to have a quick look at the damage caused the previous night. The bomb had fallen in St. Trophimus Street, close to St. Joseph Street. Many buildings had been demolished and the street was completely blocked with fallen masonry and rubble. One of the entrances to a shelter had also been blocked but had by then been cleared of debris. A friend of father's informed me that the four victims included Joseph Vella and his eleven year old son Lino. I knew both of them very well as they had relatives living close to our house. The boy attended religious instruction classes at the M.U.S.E.U.M. with me and also served as an altar boy at the Sacro Cuor Church. The other two victims were Ramiro Floridia and Joseph Galea.

During the two weeks I had spent in Gozo, I had eaten quite well. However, I soon had to pay for it dearly when I was subsequently stationed at Qrendi Airstrip. There I tasted real military discipline for the first time.

This airfield had been planned since 1940 but had only been inaugurated on the 10th November, 1942, by Air Vice Marshal, Sir Keith Park, who "beat up" the airfield in his personal Hurricane, coded OK2. After landing, he inspected a Guard of Honour.

A detachment from the King's Own Malta Regiment, under a young Maltese officer, Lieutenant (later Major) Joseph Bartolo Parnis, was stationed on the airfield. It was their duty to help R.A.F. ground crews refuel Spitfires and load ammunition belts for the machine guns and cannons of these aircraft. Because of the scarcity of petrol, these soldiers had to march all the way from their billets, which were quite a long way from the aerodrome, at dawn. Their officer had subsequently been decorated with an MBE (Military Division) for the exemplary courage and determination he had shown, while bombs were raining down on Qrendi Airstrip.

The entrance to the airfield was by the road flanking San Niklaw Reservoir. The Main Gate was flanked by a sentry post on the left and a concrete pill-box on the right. Further in, was the main guard room and next to it, was another structure, which served as the N.A.A.F.I. canteen, by which were a few small buildings, serving as ablutions and latrines. The sergeants' mess stood near the cross-roads, facing San Niklaw Church. This became a recreation room. There was a huge farmhouse to the right of the church which was used as the station stores.

The sick quarters lay further down along the road, housed in a high building, which looked like a tower. Close by were the billets for the sergeants stationed on the airfield. A large building, which housed the main cookhouse and the airmen's mess stood at the far end of the road that leads to Tal-Providenza Church. The officers' mess stood in the present-day site of Dar Tal-Providenza, Villa Monsignor Gonzi and Villa Mons. Dandria. The motor transport section was on the site of the present-day Villa Papa Giovanni.

Qrendi Airstrip had two runways, one lying in an east/west direction, 27/09, measuring 1,000 meters long and 46 meters wide and another in a north-west/south-east direction, 13/31, measuring 1080 meters long and 46 meters wide. Although these runways were not very long, they were long enough for the Spitfires of the three squadrons stationed there to operate from.

No. 249 Squadron, had its dispersal on the side of the present-day panoramic road that stretches between Wied iż-Żurrieq and Għar Lapsi. This was a very famous Squadron and could boast at having the highest score of enemy aircraft shot down over Malta. Air aces, like George "Screwball" Beurling, Ray Hesselyn, Paul Brennan and P.B. "Laddie" Lucas, had flown with it during the worst times of the air Battle of Malta.

No. 229 Squadron's dispersal was near the road leading from Siġġiewi to Dar Tal-Providenza. This was another Squadron which had done very well for itself during the siege.

I was attached for a short spell to the third Squadron, No. 185 which also played a very important role in the air defence of Malta as it was one of the first squadrons to be formed on the Island. It had been originally equipped with Hurricanes Mk I and later with Mk IIs. Other famous pilots like Jack "Slim" Yarra, Tony Boyd, Bob Sim and Ronnie West had flown with this Squadron.

No. 185 Squadron had been first formed in East

Fortune, in England, on 21st October, 1918, as a torpedo-bomber squadron, equipped with Sopwith Cuckoo aircraft, under the command of Major A.N. Gallehawk. It did not see any action during the First World War and was disbanded on 14th November, 1919.

On 1st March, 1938, it was reformed at Abingdon, under the command of Flight Lieutenant Addenbrook, with Hawker Hind bombers and later with Fairy Battles. In September, 1938, it was stationed at Grantham, under the command of Squadron Leader A.E. Louks, and, on 13th October, it flew to Thornaby. In June, 1939 it was equipped with Handley Page Hampden, twin-engine bombers.

On 24th August, 1939, it moved to its wartime station of Cottesmore, where it conducted navigational training. The Squadron was again disbanded on the 5th April 1940 and absorbed into No.14 Operational Training Unit.

No. 185 Squadron was then reformed at Hal Far on the 12th May, 1941, from "C" Flight of No. 261 Squadron, under the command of Squadron Leader P.W. Mould D.F.C. On that same day, it conducted the first operational sortie, when four of its aircraft engaged a group of Messerschmitt Me109s, ten times larger in number and shot down one of them. No. 185 Sqn. Hurricanes were few and indeed, very precious. The history of the Squadron is closely linked to the wartime history of Malta of those days.

In June, 1941, when the Luftwaffe had left Sicily, the Malta Squadrons had gone on the offensive. Aircraft from No. 185 Squadron which had, by then, converted from Hurricane Mk Is to the more powerful Hurricane Mk IIs, armed with four 20 mm cannon, started making sweeps over Sicily and Pantelleria. A substantial number of Italian aircraft were destroyed in these sorties. They also attacked and destroyed a seaplane base in Syracuse. This latter raid was led by Sqn. Ldr. Mould and it is said that he broke the world low-flying record by cruising at wave-top height all the way there and back. 185 Squadron started operating as a Fighter Bomber Unit in September, 1941.

It attacked the airfield at Comiso, which was quite heavily defended. The Hurricanes dropped their bombs and returned to base without any opposition from Italian fighters. An important incident in the history of the squadron is tied to the E-Boat attack on Grand Harbour, already described in a previous chapter.

Sqn. Ldr. Mould was killed when his Hurricane was shot down by a Macchi 202 of the 9th Gruppo piloted by Capitano Pluda, on the 1st October, 1941. Sqn. Ldr. McGregor then took command of the Squadron.

In the latter half of 1941, there had been little air activity over Malta, that is, until the Luftwaffe returned to Sicily. The following months became notorious for the pitched air battles over Maltese skies. In March, 1942, Sqn. Ldr. Rose took command of 185 Sqn. and in May, it received its first Spitfires Mk.Vc. In August, 1942, it provided the air cover over the famous Santa Maria convoy and during the same month, No. 185 Squadron Spitfires attacked military installations in Sicily. It could only stop to catch its breath when the 8th Army started its advance in North Africa, though whenever German and Italian aircraft flew over to Malta, they were regularly engaged by No. 185 Squadron fighters.

The Squadron was very active during the invasion of Sicily and even launched attacks as far as the north of that Island. Once, No. 185 Squadron Spitfires surprised a group of Cant seaplanes, just off the Island of Capri. The last victory for No. 185 Squadron, before leaving Malta, was on 22nd July, 1944, when its fighters downed a Junkers 88. In the three years since its reforming at Hal Far airfield, its score sheet showed:-

Enemy aircraft destroyed	137
Enemy aircraft damaged	165
Enemy aircraft probably destroyed	66
Submarines sunk	1
Motor torpedo boats sunk	4
Trains destroyed	7

No. 185 Squadron left Malta under the command of Squadron Leader T.W. Willmott D.F.C., for Grottaglie in Italy, to join No. 244 Wing in Perugia. Among the decorations awarded to 185 Sqn. pilots, were fifteen Distinguished Flying Crosses and eight Distinguished Flying Medals.

No. 185 Squadron's Crest is unique in that it carried a motto in Maltese. It consisted of a Griffin, a mythical animal, half lion and half eagle, signifying the co-operation between the aircrew and the ground crew, superimposed on a Maltese cross, with the motto in Maltese: "ARA FEJN HU " (Look, there it is). The Squadron was disbanded at Campo Formio, in Italy, on 14th August, 1945.

After the war on 15th September, 1951, No. 185 Squadron was again reformed at Hal Far, with the new jet fighter-bomber Vampire F.B. 5. It moved to Luqa on 23rd July, 1952 and on 14th August, 1952, the Squadron left for Idris Airfield, now Tripoli Airport in Libya. It was the first Squadron to introduce jet-propelled air-craft to Malta.

Some years ago, while on a television news assignment, I met Flight Lieutenant Billing, an ex-pilot of 185 Sqn. who had served here at the height of the battle of Malta, in 1942. From what he told me, I gathered that he happened to be the same pilot I had seen drifting down by parachute at Għar id-Dud many years before.

When I was posted to Qrendi Airfield, I was billeted in a Nissen hut, without any proper doors or windows. This building was previously used as No. 185 Squadron dispersal, until it moved to the ground floor of a large farmhouse nearby, flanking runway 13/31. The roof was used as a temporary control tower and the first floor for wireless communications. Another control tower was built on the side of runway 09/27 and the latter also housed the Station Operations Room, telephone exchange and the station power generator, underground.

The first impression one got on entering this Nissen hut, was that of a small hospital ward as there were eighteen stretchers lying on the floor, in two rows. These were to be our beds, as there were no proper ones available. Stores were still very short of stocks. In fact, we were not issued with full kit and up to November, I still did not have a winter uniform which was an army battle dress to be worn on a light blue shirt and a black tie. The R.A.F. blue service uniforms were only issued late in 1944.

Our duties lasted from 7.00 am till sunset, as no flying operations were conducted at night time. Normally, I had also to do four hours patrol on the airfield, during the night. For the first fifteen days, I was attached to the R.A.F. Regiment, for field training. This consisted of small-arms training, hand-grenade throwing, shooting practice with Sten guns, pistols, and various types of rifles like the Lee Enfield No.4 Mk.2, the American P14 rifle, and the Canadian Ross rifle. This last type had a very long barrel and the recoil was very strong. It would bruise your shoulder if you were only wearing light summer clothing when you fired it. The weapon I enjoyed firing most was the German Schmeiser, MP40, machine-pistol. It was of the same calibre as the 9.5 mm Sten gun, but had a higher rate of fire.

Besides learning how to fire and use these weapons, we were also trained to dismantle them and reassemble them again blindfolded, in case we would have to do this at night time. We were also getting intensive training in drill and long route marches. Our instructor, Sgt. Long, was a man of strict discipline but he was kind hearted. He was a member of the Royal Air Force Regiment, one of the elite units of the British Armed Forces.

During daytime, our Spitfires were constantly airborne. Initially they were operating in support of the troops in Sicily, escorting bombers and transport aircraft and also carrying out bombing sorties. These Spitfires were equipped with bomb racks on the wings to carry two, two hundred and fifty pound bombs. They also carried out photo reconnaissance sorties. On landing, their exposed film would be swiftly carried off to the central photographic section, which was located at St. John's Cavalier, in Valletta.

I went home once a week and my day off was Friday, when I then had a 24 hour pass.

Once, at about six in the evening, I had just finished eating supper and was returning to the Nissen hut, where I was billeted, when I heard Verey-pistol shots being fired from the roof of the control tower, at No. 185 Squadron dispersal. At first, I thought that it was a scramble for our Spitfires and, in fact, I saw men running towards the pens and other station buildings and pilots rush out of the dispersal buildings. Coloured Verey-lights were soon shooting up from all directions. Jeeps, lorries and other vehicles started milling around the airfield, hooting their horns. On seeing this pandemo-nium, I ran to the control tower to find out what was going on and, on asking the flight sergeant on duty what had happened, he shouted ecstatically: "Italy has capitu-lated!"

I hurried down from the tower and ran to our Nissen hut to break the news to my friends. From there, we went to the canteen, where we found the hall already packed. All those present, without distinction of rank, bottles of beer in their hands, were celebrating in a big way, cheering, singing, and shaking hands. Near the ser-geants' mess, I was met with the same sight and I was dragged inside by my flight sergeant. We carried on merrymaking very late that night. The date was 8th September, 1943. In Malta, this day is dedicated to Our Lady of Victories!

To cap it all, in the middle of all that celebration, the siren sounded the air raid warning. Everybody took it as a joke, until the searchlights came on. Our sergeant ordered us to man the twin Hispano 20mm cannon, which were deployed around the airfield. Although I had done some training on this type of weapon, I had never had any experience of action on it. We were stood down after about half an hour and were later informed that the intruder had been a Ju88 and that it had been shot down over the sea by a Beaufighter.

All the regulations in the book, particularly those relating to canteen opening times, the messes, the driving of vehicles and, most of all, the firing of Verey-lights had been thrown overboard. It was a good job that none of these Verey-lights fell near any of the Spitfires, which were all parked in their pens, as the merry-making would soon have been over and some of us would have ended up in the lock-up, at the Corradino Military Prisons.

This was the last noteworthy episode I was involved in, at Qrendi Airstrip. Three days later, I was taken ill and spent three weeks in the 45th General Hospital, at St. Patrick's, suffering from dysentery. When I was discharged from hospital and returned to the station, I found that all three Squadrons had left Qrendi airstrip and that the airfield had closed down for flying operations, on 30th September, 1943. The airfield now housed No. 5051 Squadron, which was not an operational flying squadron but an airfield construction squadron, then engaged in the construction of Safi airstrip and which had also taken part in the construction of the Gozo airstrip. I remember that the men of this squadron were the dirtiest bunch I had ever seen in the Royal Air Force. Their uniforms were covered in tar and oil and so was their Motor Transport. They spent about two months at Qrendi and subsequently left for the Middle East. Qrendi airstrip was then relegated to the function of a petrol and ammunition dump, known as No. 143 Maintenance Unit which previously was stationed at Fort St. Lucian.

On the day following the 8th September rejoicing, I was off duty. I again witnessed the same spectacular festive scenes in Sliema. I had never seen so many drunken sailors, soldiers and airmen, jumping into the sea at The Strand. The bars, all along the waterfront, were packed with service personnel drinking and singing. They formed a conga and started dancing around in bigger and bigger circles. Maltese bystanders, of both sexes, also found themselves dragged in and were soon in the thick of it, kissing and embracing the British. Many of the wounded military personnel, who had been brought back from Sicily after the invasion and were housed in the primary school, also made it down to The Strand to join in the merriment. They were easily distinguishable as they wore a blue uniform, a white shirt, a red tie and their particular service head-dress.

They had started arriving in large numbers, soon after the invasion got under way. I remember a long line of ambulances commuting between the hospitals at Mtarfa, St. Patrick's, Bighi and the Sliema Government School. Once they recovered, they were either sent back to their country of origin or else, if they were not seriously wounded, they were sent to carry on with their service tour. Often they presented a sorry sight. Those with amputated lower limbs had to rely on crutches. Others had empty sleeves hanging down, or bandaged faces with just two holes for the eyes and another opening for the mouth, to enable them to eat. Legless soldiers were pushed around on wheelchairs while the blind had to be led by their friends. Many of these wounded soldiers were invited in private homes and entertained to tea or coffee. It was a repetition of what had happened in Sliema during the First World War, when Sliema boys were often teased by their schoolmates from other towns: "Mummy, get me a wounded soldier!"

On 10th September, the first Italian warships, the battleships *Dulio* and *Doria* and the cruiser *Pompeo Magno*

The main entrance to Qrendi Airstrip, showing the former guard room, the canteen and San Niklaw Chapel, in the background.

An aerial view of Qrendi Strip, where the author was stationed.

229 Squadron's Spitfires Mk Vc on Qrendi's runway 31/13. The building in the background was used as No. 185 Squadron's dispersal and Control Tower.

A low-flying Spitfire Mk.Vc, buzzing Qrendi airstrip.

The author near a Mosquito aircraft at Luqa Airfield.

The author on the control tower at Qrendi Airstrip, in 1943.

RAF Observers at No. 501 AMES, Fort Tas-Silg, November 1944. The author (left) with LAC A. Aquilina and Cpl. C. Caruana.

Plotting instrument at Fort Tas-Silg.

Maltese telephone operators at the Operations Room in Lascaris.

Maltese plotters receiving incoming information at Lascaris Operations Room.

A happy group of off-duty plotters of No. 8 SOR.

German prisoners-of-war resting while building the RAF Lido at Delimara.

The prisoner-of-war camp at St. Andrew's.

Anthony Grech, the author's father, shakes hands with the Governor, Lord Gort, when the band clubs of Malta presented the Sword of Honour to Lord Gort at Zebbug.

The Sliema War Victims Memorial.

under the command of Admiral Dzara, arrived in Malta. The flagship *Roma* was sunk en route by a German PC 1400 FX radio-controlled bomb, with the loss of many men including the Commander in Chief, Ammiraglio d'Armata Carlo Bergamini. Admiral Dzara landed at Customs House Steps at Valletta and was met by a guard of honour. Then he was driven up to Naval Head Quarters in Lascaris, where he signed the formal documents for the surrender of the Italian Fleet. Admiral Sir John Cunningham received the documents on behalf of the Allies. Although they could have easily walked up a few steps right into Lascaris from the Customs House, Admiral Cunningham took Admiral Dzara on a short tour, so that the Italian Admiral could see for himself some of the devastation caused by Italian and German bombing in Floriana and Valletta. By 20th September, seventy-six Italian Naval vessels were anchored in Malta's harbours, including five Battleships, six Cruisers, six Destroyers, twelve Escorts, six Corvettes, twenty-three Submarines, nine Anti-Submarine Launches, six Motor Torpedo Boats and three Auxiliary Vessels.

Admiral Cunningham proudly signalled to the Admirality:

"PLEASED TO INFORM YOUR LORDSHIPS
THAT THE ITALIAN FLEET LIES ANCHORED
UNDER THE GUNS OF FORTRESS MALTA."

Chapter XXII

THE END IN SIGHT

Our hopes that the war in the Mediterranean theatre would quickly be over were soon dashed. On Italy's capitulation, the Germans swiftly occupied the rest of the country. The Italian fascists remained loyal to their Nazi allies and this prolonged the war in Italy till the bitter end, in April, 1945. Although the sirens did not sound anymore in Malta and we started to hear the soothing peal of church bells again, food was still scarce. The situation improved gradually, and at least, the bread available was of a better quality.

Service personnel started getting bigger rations and they also saw an improvement in the quality of food. Cigarette rations were also increased and the quality of tobacco got better. I still wonder what the tobacco of the "V" cigarettes, of which fifty a week were issued to servicemen, was actually made of. Some said it was mixed with straw. British servicemen used to call it "dried horse shit". Whatever it was, everybody still smoked it and non-smokers would barter their rations for foodstuffs or beer.

When I ended my tour of duty at Qrendi airstrip, I was posted to Air Headquarters and to No. 8, Sector Operations Room. This lay in the underground labyrinth beneath hundreds of feet of solid rock below the Upper Barrakka gardens, in Valletta. This operations room was accessible through a tunnel from Lascaris Ditch. Besides the filter room, there was the fighter operations room, the command operations room, the naval operations room, and a host of other rooms, crammed with tele-printers and wireless telegraphy equipment all tucked in the rock-hewn spaces.

Some of these rooms were quite large and sizeable. The only Maltese civilians who worked in there were young women. They worked as plotters, clerks and decoders. The latter used to decipher coded messages, received by wireless into plain language. The plotters worked around a large table about eighteen feet by twelve feet. This carried a large scale map of the Islands of Malta and part of Southern Sicily showing the main enemy airfields. The map was marked off into lettered squares, and each square was sub-divided into numbered grids with co-ordinates. The plotters marked the position of aircraft, ships and convoys flying or passing through the area, with 'counters', marked red for enemy, black for friendly aircraft. Numerals showed the estimated height and strength of a raid and arrows indicated direction and the reference number of sorties. Ships and other sea craft were marked with special markers in different colours. A special clock, marked to give five minute segments or divisions of an arc, in different colours and triangles of blue, red and yellow were used to mark each raid. The girls moved the counters with long sticks, like billiard cues, to grid positions on the table. The plotters were in direct contact with the Filter Room which relayed to them information regarding aircraft approaching or leaving the Island.

One could follow a running commentary of what was going on during an air battle or air raid through loudspeakers. Some of the girls often took a deep personal interest, while plotting the positions of these aircraft, particularly if one of the pilots involved happened to be an acquaintance or, perhaps, sometimes even a lover. It was not uncommon for heart breaking scenes to take place on the plotting floor, whenever some bad news was relayed on the loudspeaker or whenever a friendly pilot's voice went suddenly silent and one of his fellow pilots reported that his friend had been shot down. Those, who had been working there for some time, told me that such moving scenes were very frequent especially at the height of the Battle of Malta.

In 1941-42, the control of air operations was in the able hands of Group Captain "Woody" Woodhall, who was reputed to have enjoyed the absolute trust of the fighter pilots in the skies over Malta. His control of some of the major air battles had been masterly. It was in this control room that a fictitious Pilot Officer Humguffery was created. He was supposed to be flying a Spitfire and was given dummy orders from the controller of fighter operations control, to deceive the enemy, when no friendly aircraft was airborne. Humguffery was credited with two Messerschmitt 109s, when they shot each other, mistaking one another for Humguffery.

In one of the sections of this underground complex in Lascaris, there was a closely guarded unit, in which no one could enter, without special authorisation. This was known as the S.L.U. (Special Liaison Unit) and was one of the only two units based outside Britain. The other one was in Cairo, Egypt. The unit in Malta was even larger than that at Bletchley Park, in England, from where top-secret information used to be sent to the units in the Mediterranean and Egypt.

The Unit received its information in cipher on an Enigma machine, a top-secret German invention which, very early in the war, had been stolen by a Polish citizen and taken to England. The capture of the German U-Boat 110, commanded by Fritz Julius Kemp, about three hundred miles south of Iceland on May 9th, 1941, by *H.M.S. Bulldog* under the command of Commander J.B. Cresswell, provided British intelligence with an Enigma machine complete with books on the setting procedures which enabled the British to read the German ciphered messages. My friend Anthony Buhagiar, at that time, was a Leading Steward serving on *H.M.S. Bulldog*. He was detailed to prevent the machine and the code books which were printed on rice-paper and which could be dissolved quickly in water, from falling into enemy hands. The British then developed another machine, called Ultra, which enabled them to break the German code. The machine in Malta was even more modern then the original code breaking gadget and was known as "R.A.F. Type X". It had been developed with great care and precision after the breaking of the German codes. These Type X machines were installed in a very restricted number at Main Head Quarters and the intelligence gleaned from them was placed at the disposal of all the Services.

The staff who worked in this section, belonged to the "Y" Service and were all carefully screened and hand-picked. At the time nobody, apart from them, knew what was going on in this part of Lascaris underground Head

Quarters. They worked very long hours - six hours a watch, grouped up in small, stuffy rooms. There was no air-conditioning down there in those days.

The operations room, as it had now come to be called, once fighter interception operations were no longer necessary, was a centre which controlled friendly aircraft flights all over Southern Europe, the Mediterranean, North Africa and part of the Middle East. Information was received from abroad by wireless and relayed to the centre by tele-printer from underground wireless stations situated at Kalafrana and Ta' Kandja, then through a wireless room, adjacent to the operations room. Other information came in from the six R.A.F. radar stations which, by this time of the war had been installed in Malta and Gozo. Radar was then still in its infancy and had a limited range of sixty miles. Radar stations were fitted to receive a special coding device - "I.F.F.", (Identification Friend or Foe), which was transmitted by friendly aircraft. If an aircraft failed to show "I.F.F.", it was automatically assumed to be hostile and classified as a raider.

Radar was regarded as one of Malta's main assets which contributed to the enemy's defeat. Initially known as R.D.F. (radio direction finding), it was first brought to Malta in March 1939. This was the first Radar Station to be installed outside the United Kingdom.

By July 1941, the number of radar stations was increased by three, No. 501 at Tas-Silġ, 502 at Madliena and 504 on top of Dingli Cliffs. These three were COL (Chain Overseas Low) and plotted low flying aircraft, while No. 242 A.M.E.S. was COH (Chain Overseas High) capable of plotting high flying aircraft. Radar was so successful that eventually four other stations were set up at Għar Lapsi, Qawra, Wardija and Gozo.

At one stage in 1942, the benefit of this early warning system was almost lost due to jamming by powerful German transmitters installed in Sicily. The local stations, on instruction from the Air Ministry, continued scanning to give the impression that the jamming was not successful.

After a few weeks the Germans gave up and dismantled the jamming stations

Useful information also reached the centre from outlying visual observation posts, through direct telephone links. Few people knew about the importance of this service during the Battle of Malta. These posts were manned by the Royal Air Force Observer Corps, mainly staffed by Maltese airmen. There were five Stations in Malta and one in Gozo, manned by Gozitan airmen. The Malta Stations were at Torri l-Ahmar, Għargħur, Valletta on top of St. John's Cavalier, Dingli and at the old Victorian Fort at Tas-Silġ, close to Delimara. The Station in Gozo was on the Citadel, in Victoria.

After spending some months stationed in the main operations room, I was posted to Tas-Silġ station as a ground observer. Although it was a tough job, particularly in winter, due to the cold and rain, it was very interesting work and I very often felt like staying on after duty hours. Our work consisted in relaying reports to the main operations room on what we observed in the sky, on the sea and on the ground. We worked in two 24-hour shifts. Each shift was composed of six airmen in two watches of three airmen each. A corporal was in charge.

The R.A.F. Observer Corps (Malta) was set up early in 1942 and was made up of one hundred men, ninety of whom were Maltese. The function of this Corps was to supplement radar with visual information. The men on duty came into the picture as soon as we reported something to the operations room or whenever the latter received some information from anyone of our other posts or from radar stations. At this point, the six observation posts would be called to come to readiness on the phone and would be placed in contact with each other. A girl in the operations room would pass on all the information she had and instruct us what we had to keep a look out for. For example, when aircraft were spotted approaching Malta, the message would normally take this form: "Aircraft incoming, plot 4836, angels 28", which meant that aircraft were approaching on grid-position 4836 at a height of 28,000 feet. This was followed by the identification of the aircraft and the number of planes. One of us would then set the instrument to the appropriate height and the others would scan the skies with binoculars in the given direction. As soon as an aircraft was sighted, we would then align the plotting instrument with it and pass on all the information about the number of aircraft, type, height and position to the operations room. We referred to co-ordinates on a map on which the instrument was set and which divided the area into squares, each representing areas of twenty square miles each. These squares were then sub-divided into smaller quadrants representing two square miles. We would follow the aircraft in, until it landed on one of the airfields.

The same exercise took place whenever an aircraft took off and we tracked it until we could see it no longer. If something went amiss, such as if we noticed smoke leaving an aircraft, we immediately reported this and fixed its position. If the aircraft happened to crash, we had to file a full report, particularly, as to how many parachutes we had seen open and where they had landed. We also had to pass on information on any vessel sighted at sea and on any smoke over the Island. We also relayed information on weather conditions, visibility, amount of cloud and temperature. Our area covered a radius of thirty miles, visibility permitting, between Hal Far and Zonqor Point. The information was then passed to the filter room, where, as the name implies, it was sifted and a decision was taken by the controller as to what action was to be taken. The controller sat in an elevated position above the plotting table together with his assistant, "Ops B.", and the Gunnery Liaison Officer, an army officer who kept the military authorities informed of "the plot". Looking at the display on the table, the controller would, at a glance, be able to tell what the situation was and make his decisions accordingly. It was he who gave the order for the air-raid warning to be sounded all over Malta and for the fighters to scramble.

The old Victorian fortress at Tas-Silġ also housed one of the three larger radar stations as well as a Royal Navy signals station. Our plotting instrument was mounted on the roof of a tower, which is no longer in existence. This station was known as No. 501 A.M.E.S. (Air Ministry Experimental Station) and was commanded by a Canadian officer, who was a radar expert. There was very little military discipline and everybody behaved in a happy go lucky way. There were no formalities regarding messes and everybody, including the commanding officer, shared the same Mess.

I remember that later, in the closing days of the war, on 22nd March, 1945, the R.A.F. Observer Corps (Malta) held a parade at R.A.F. Station, Hal Far and the members of the Corps were inspected by the Air Officer Commanding Malta, Air Vice Marshal K.B. Lloyd CBE, AFC. In a short address, he was full of praise for our work and our great efficiency and dedication. He also praised the accuracy of information we had passed on aircraft identification and our precise assessment of height and distance of approaching aircraft, despite the difficulties of bad visibility and low cloud. This information had been of great help to our fighters in tracking and intercepting the enemy. The A.O.C. had concluded his speech by stressing the important contribution the Corps had given to the defence of these Islands, during the Air Battle of Malta.

The pressures of war had now eased and life in camp became more leisurely and relaxed. Once a month, a dance was organised. We, observers, used to invite some of the girls who worked in the operations room. We could pick and choose from the bevy of girls working there who would not demur at being asked out to a party. The British airmen, who worked on the radar, looked after the organisation and the decoration of the dance hall. They also obtained gramophone records of contemporary big bands, famous to this very day, like Glen Miller, Benny Goodman, Harry James, Victor Sylvester, Joe Loss, the bands of the brothers Jimmy and Tommy Dorsey and Xavier Cougart and his South American music. We also danced to the rhythms of fox-trot, quickstep, jitterbug and other more formal types of ballroom dancing, like waltzes.

The Flight Sergeant, who looked after the bar, was not too keen on dancing, as he was getting on in years. He looked forward to organising these dances to see us enjoy ourselves. Profits from the bar went to cover any expenses involved. Once a week, the Army Kinema Corporation (A.K.C.), would screen a film show at the

Fort. Occasionally, a small stage was set up in the main hall and the Entertainment National Service Association (E.N.S.A.), would put on a live show by top artistes, some of whom had even performed in the London West End. As ours was a relatively small station, we often invited personnel from other A.M.E.S. to these shows.

E.N.S.A. had been set up in Britain to entertain military personnel on active service overseas; much the same way as the Americans had their U.S.O. These performers visited the fronts to raise servicemen's morale and make them forget the stress of war. Sometimes, these performers took great risks and paid for it by the loss of their own lives. A case in point was the loss of Glen Miller. He was lost over the English Channel, while flying in a Norseman 64 on 15th December, 1944. He was on his way from Bedford, in England, to France, where he and his band were scheduled to give concerts and shows. To this very day, nobody knows exactly what happened to him.

In Malta, E.N.S.A. was based at the old Sacred Infirmary of the Knights, then the Command Hall and now the Mediterranean Conference Centre. All sorts of entertainment took place there. The entrance fee was only three pence and for this pittance, we were treated to the best shows by singers, comedians and stars of cinema and stage fame. The best films were also screened there and some of these never appeared in public cinemas. We were allowed one guest, male or female, for these shows.

Another section of the Command Hall housed games, billiards rooms, table tennis, darts and a .22 shooting gallery. Those who preferred some intellectual relaxation could spend time at the library. For just three Shillings, (15 cents), one could have supper, a bottle of beer and see a film show.

By that time, the Allies had advanced far up to Central Italy and had entered Rome on 4th June, 1944. When the news reached us, we again had the usual scenes of joy at The Strand, in Sliema. The waterfront was again crammed with sailors, soldiers and airmen dancing around and singing until late into the night. Two days later, early in the morning, the B.B.C. announced that Operation Overlord, the invasion of Normandy, in France, had begun.

I happened to be in the recreation room at Fort Tas-Silġ, when the news broke and bottles of beer were immediately opened for a celebration. The British had even greater reason to be happy because now they could put their minds at rest about the safety of their families in Britain. At least, they would no longer have to be subjected to the heavy aerial bombardment and, particularly, to the devastating "V1" and "V2" German rockets, launched from France.

It was indeed a good thing that the Germans had not succeeded in developing these weapons earlier, as history might have taken a different turn. When we first heard about the pilot-less aircraft, aeroplanes without propellers and bombs delivered by rockets from one country to another, we thought that this was the limit of technological progress. Little did we know what more sophisticated weapons we were to come across in future years!

It was while I was serving at Fort Tas-Silġ, that I first came in personal contact with the enemy. At Fort Welsely, a short distance from our Station and Fort Delimara, there was a camp for an Italian pioneer regiment, which had been brought to Malta, to perform some military works. These Italians were not prisoners in the real sense of the word, because they could leave camp and walk down freely to Marsaxlokk and move around within a certain distance, although, they could not frequent towns and villages. They could speak to anybody they wanted to and their camp was not guarded. This was because, in 1943, the Italians had switched their allegiance from their Fascist Government and the Nazis to the Allies. Nevertheless, as our Station was classified top secret, we could not invite them to any of the shows we organised there.

They were quite happy to see us whenever we visited their camp and they made us feel very welcome. Because of the language difficulties, our British friends hardly ever came to the Italian camp, unless we dragged them there with us. When we visited our Italian friends, we took cigarettes and chocolate bars from our canteen and, sometimes, even a few bottles of beer. We also took some wine which had been recently imported from Sicily. Maltese grapes had as yet not been pressed because of the war. To reciprocate, the Italians would ask us over for a "Spaghetti alla Bolognese" treat which we relished, eating to the accompaniment of a small guitar and mandolin group, singing Neapolitan songs.

On Sundays, after Mass and breakfast, football matches were played in the football ground constructed by Italian sailors who had been interned there before them, when three warships of the Italian Navy were anchored in Marsaxlokk Bay under Fort Delimara. The Italians either played against each other or against teams from the British services. Whenever one of these latter games was played, the tension was as high-pitched as in any international cup match!

Later on, German prisoners were also brought to Malta to work on construction sites, excavation sites and in the erection of water and electrical installations. Others were employed in clearance works. As the war with Germany was still on, they were treated as prisoners of war and did not enjoy the freedom enjoyed by the Italians. They were guarded by armed soldiers. All in all, there were some 2,500 prisoners of war in Malta and they were kept at the P.O.W. Camp at St. Andrew's and at a newly erected camp at Safi Strip, close to Kirkop Cemetery.

A small group of these German prisoners had been detailed to construct a Lido for R.A.F. personnel at Kalanka t-Tawwalija, at Delimara. We also gave cigarettes and chocolate bars to these P.O.W.'s. They often asked us for bits and pieces of aluminium from which they managed to make cigarette lighters. They also made cigarette cases, photo-frames and table cigarette boxes out of pieces of perspex from crashed aircraft. They had a knack of carving interesting designs on these items and invariably included the Maltese Cross in their designs. Some also carved very original ornaments out of Malta stone.

The prisoners of war, who were kept in Malta, were very lucky and surely received better treatment than their fellow prisoners, held in prisoner-of-war camps elsewhere.

Later, when even Germany was out of the war, German prisoners were allowed to leave their camp and visit towns and villages. I remember them all dressed in olive green, denim battle dress with round, blue patches on the front and on their trousers. They still wore the cap of their respective arm of service that is of the Kreigsmarine, the Wehrmacht or the Luftwaffe. Sliema was full of German P.O.W.'s, strolling about on the promenade, between St. Julian's and Għar id-Dud. Some of them even befriended Maltese civilians. Up to a few months before, this would have been unheard of but man remains human, in spite of everything. There were even some Maltese who invited these German prisoners home for a cup of tea or coffee. Later on, these Germans even plied some small trade, selling the hand-made items they produced and using the money for their daily needs or perhaps to be able to afford seeing a film show, every now and then.

These Germans were also paid a small allowance by the British services. During the day, they were fully occupied on military projects, like the construction of the R.A.F. new Site Barracks, (now the Armed Forces of Malta Barracks and Headquarters and Air Malta Head Offices, close to Malta International Airport) and other sites. It is rumoured that they even offered to reconstruct the Opera House in Valletta, which had been destroyed by a German aerial mine, on the 7th April, 1942 and that the British Authorities had turned down this offer, at the instigation of Maltese trade unionists. These German prisoners of war had to return to camp at 8.00 pm in winter and 9.00 pm in the summer months. As far as I am aware, there was only one attempt at escape. In fact, two prisoners had tried to leave the Island on a small boat, which they had stolen but they were soon intercepted and brought back ashore after putting out to sea.

Football games between these German prisoners and Sliema Wanderers F.C. were also played at St. Andrew's Barracks' football pitch. These matches would draw large crowds, as local association football had not yet resumed. It was during these matches, that I heard for the first time the crowd, egging on the goalkeeper, taking a goal kick while running to the ball, with the shout "EEEEEEEEYUUUUUPP." It is probably the only legacy which these German P.O.W.'s left us to this very day.

The Americans, British and French continued with their slogging advance through Europe and the Russians advanced from the East, closing the circle around Nazi Germany.

The same thing was happening in the Far East with the Allied victories over the Japanese.

On 8th February, 1945, the British Army, under Field Marshall Montgomery, crossed over into German territory for the first time and, in March, the Allied forces crossed the Rhine, the biggest obstacle they had to face so far.

Mussolini was captured by Italian partisans and shot on 28th April 1945 by Walter Audisio and the partisans hung his mutilated body by the ankles, from the girders of the roof of a half-built garage, in Piazzale Loreto, in Milan.

By late April 1945, the Red Army was at the gates of Berlin. On 30th April, the German dictator, Adolf Hitler, committed suicide and he was cremated in a bomb crater outside the Bunker of the Reich Chancellery.

On 2nd May, the Commander of the German troops in Italy capitulated and surrendered unconditionally in Caserta. The fighting in Italy had now come to an end.

The German Armed Forces, in Germany itself, ceased fire on 4th May, and Germany surrendered unconditionally on 7th May. This brought the curtain down on the European theatre of war. This long-awaited event was marred by the gruesome discovery of the atrocities committed in the concentration camps, where over six million people had been exterminated by the most sadistic of means. I could not believe my eyes when I saw scenes of these concentration camps in the press and in newsreels, on the cinema screens. Could such things really happen in twentieth century Europe?

In Malta, the lights had come on again, just as in the pre-war years. There were celebrations all over the Island and, I remember, the two Sliema Bands had even played and marched together. Flags were hoisted on roofs and balconies were lit up, just like on *festa* days.

Naval vessels, berthed in Sliema Creek, were dressed overall and had their masts festooned with lights at night. They also sounded their fog-horns and sirens. I could barely walk through with the huge crowds thronging The Strand, as tipsy soldiers and sailors danced and sang in the middle of the road. Groups of drunken sailors pranced around on the quay and quite a few of them ended up in the water. More and more men joined them in the warm waters of Sliema Creek.

That evening, my friend William and I were enjoying this happy spectacle outside Tony's Bar, when a group of sailors dragged us in and made us drink as much beer as we could gulp down. Luckily, the sailors started arguing among themselves about who was going to pay for the next round of beer and William and I managed to slip away. Had we remained there longer, we would surely have had to be carried out, stone drunk! I can only imagine what happened in Valletta and other towns and villages, on that glorious day.

On 6th August at 8.15 am, a United States Army Air Force Boeing B29, Super Fortress, named Enola Gay, piloted by Colonel Paul Tibbets, dropped the first Atomic Bomb on the city of Hiroshima from a height of 32,000 feet. Within seconds of the explosion, a ball of fire, 1,800 feet in diameter and a flash, as dazzling as the sun, spread through the sky. It generated a temperature of 100 million degrees in its centre and had the explosive force equivalent to 20,000 tons of T.N.T. Hardly anything remained standing within a radius of five miles from the zero area of the explosion. 70,000 people were killed and an equal number injured in Hiroshima, according to a report by the Atomic Energy Commission of the United States of America.

A few days later, a second Atomic Bomb was dropped over the city of Nagasaki killing 36,000 and injuring another 40,000. Reports, issued in 1968 by the Japanese Broadcasting Corporation, give much higher figures and state that between 240,000 and 270,000 actually perished as a result of these explosions within five years, mainly as a result of illnesses and wounds, caused by radiation. These Atom Bombs had changed the whole perspective of war and we were positively terrified, when the detailed reports of the conflagration began to reach us. We became very apprehensive, particularly about the long-term consequences of such explosions.

The final act of the Second World War came on 2nd September, 1945, almost six years to the day from the start of hostilities on the Polish frontier on that fateful 1st September, 1939. Japan formally capitulated in a ceremony held on board the American battleship, *U.S.S. Missouri*, anchored in Tokyo Bay. Service personnel again indulged in the usual wild celebrations and the destroyers and frigates in Sliema Creek were once again dressed overall with flags, from bow to stern. At night, they were illuminated with light bulbs hanging from the masts. Church bells once again pealed in joy and thanksgiving processions were held in the streets of many

Maltese towns and villages. Balconies were illuminated with fairy lights and few were the rooftops that did not sport a festive flag or banner.

●●●●●●●●

It was now definitely over! The war, that had initially intrigued me as a curious schoolboy, had completely overshadowed my youth and had only come to an end when I was on the threshold of manhood.

But the scars of war were to remain with us for many years to come. Thousands of buildings had been demolished and in my home town, in particular, there were hardly any streets which had not been hit by bombs. The three Sliema parish churches of Stella Maris, the Nazarene and our own church, that of Our Lady of the Sacred Heart had all been severely damaged by air raids.

Many would still suffer from the harsh effects of this conflict. Those, who had lost their dear ones, the homeless, the disabled, and those who had succumbed to serious illness, from lack of proper nutrition, the night-long vigils in the damp, rock underground shelters, fear or exhaustion, would not forget that easily!

They had all paid the cruel price of war!

APPENDIX A
Malta War Statistics

Number of Maltese civilians killed 1,468
Number of Maltese civilians injured 3,720
Demolished buildings 40,000
Enemy aircraft sorties 26,000
Bombs dropped over Malta .... tons 16,000
Enemy aircraft destroyed by the RAF 888
Enemy aircraft destroyed by A/A Guns 363
Enemy aircraft probably destroyed 383
Enemy aircraft damaged 1,050
R.A.F. aircraft destroyed 547
R.A.F. aircraft destroyed on the ground 160
Number of flying hours logged by the R.A.F. ... 112,250

APPENDIX B

Air Raids over Malta Statistics

Month	1940	1941	1942	1943	1944
January	—	57	263	25	2
February	—	107	236	5	—
March	—	105	275	7	1
April	—	92	282	7	1
May	—	98	246	30	—
June	53	68	169	30	—
July	51	73	184	10	1
August	22	30	101	9	3
September	25	31	57	4	—
October	10	57	153	—	—
November	32	76	30	—	—
December	18	169	35	—	—
Total	211	963	2031	127	8

There were 3,340 air raids, spread over a period of 2,357 hours and 6 minutes.

The first air raid took place on 11th June, 1940 at 6.55 am.

The last air raid warning was given on 28th August, 1944 at 8.43 pm; the final all clear signal being sounded at 9.00 pm of the same day.

The longest air raid took place on 7th February, 1942 and lasted 13 hours and 40 minutes.

Between 8th and 9th March, 1942, air raid warning signals covered a total of 21 hours and 30 minutes out of 24 hours, with 16 alerts throughout the day.

APPENDIX C
Sliema War Statistics

Killed 119
Seriously injured 263
Slightly injured 572
Totally demolished buildings 294
Heavily damaged buildings 505
Buildings damaged by blast 1,193

APPENDIX D
Statistics of damage and casualties from enemy action
in Sliema and its environs.
(Compiled from Malta Police records.)

Date	Time	Street or Area	Damage
1940			
11th. June	19.45	St. Mary Street.	Modern Imperial Hotel damaged.
	-	Ponsomby Street, Gzira.	Demolished buildings, 7 killed and others injured
14th. June	-	Sliema and Gzira.	Demolished buildings, and people injured
1941			
27th. February	16.00	Off St. Julian's tower.	Gozo Boat hit a mine; 2 killed, and 9 injured.
6th. March	20.00	Prince of Wales Rd, near Balluta.	Damaged Buildings.
11th. March	21.45	St. Rita Street and St. Publius Street.	30 demolished buildings, 25 killed, 30 injured.
19th. April	-	Ghar id-Dud Street, Howard Street.	Demolished Buildings.
11th. May	21.00	High Street and Lapsi Street, St. Julian's.	Demolished Buildings.
31st May	21.15	St. Elizabeth School. Villa Portelli (Savoy).	Demolished Buildings Mine. Unexploded Mine.
7th. July	-	Paceville and Dragonara.	Houses Demolished.
9th. July	20.00	Naxxar Road, Msierah (San Gwann).	4 houses demolished.
27th. July	23.30	Swieqi.	Farmhouse demolished.
3rd. August	04.00	St. John the Baptist Str.	Houses demolished.
		Victoria Avenue.	Houses demolished
		Church Street.	Sacristy of Sacro Cuor Church.
2nd. September	10.00	High Street.	Capua Palace damaged.
10th. October	11.00	Tower Road, The Strand, St. Anne's Square and Victoria Avenue.	Incendiary bombs.
1st. November	05.00	Fort Manoel.	5 British soldiers killed, Barracks demolished.
10th. November	01.00	De La Salle Avenue, Gzira.	3 houses demolished, others damaged, 2 injured.
14th. December	18.45	Dingli Street and Howard Street.	3 houses demolished and others damaged, 3 people killed
16th. December	10.00	High Street, St. Julian's.	Buildings damaged.
17th. December	01.00	Cameron Street, Gzira.	
		Reid Street, Gzira.	Houses demolished Nos. 11 - 14

			Nos. 127 - 129
21st. December	23.30	Tigne' Barracks.	Barracks Demolished.
29th. December	16.00	Off Dragonara Point.	Gozo Boat "Marie Georgette" sunk, Paul Azzopardi (52) from Gharb, Gozo, killed.

1942

1st January	23.45	Stuart Street, Gzira.	27 houses demolished, 20 killed, 17 injured.
5th January	04.45	B'Kara Road, Msierah.	House No. 50 demolished.
15th January	15.30	Pembroke Barracks.	Soldiers killed and wounded.
21st January	23.30	Tigne Barracks.	Demolished buildings.
28th January	03.00	Blue Sisters Hospital.	Incendiary Bombs.
31st January	22.45	Fabri Lane St. Julian's	Houses demolished.
		Nos. 14 - 20 Reid Street, Gzira.	Houses demolished, 6 persons wounded, Parish church damaged.
5th February	10.20	St. George's Road, St. Julian's	In the Bay, Houses Nos. 55 -57 demolished.
7th February	11.00	St. Paul, St. Peter and High Streets and Tower Road.	15 houses, a Bank, and The Gaiety Cinema demolished 3 killed and 16 wounded.
1st March	17.00	Old College Street, Stella Maris Church, The Strand, Sliema. Grenfell and High Streets, St. Julian's.	Persons wounded. Woman killed, Ferry -Boat sunk. Persons wounded.
6th March	11.45	Prince of Wales Road, Prince Albert, Bugeja Buildings and Prince of Wales Junction.	Many buildings demolished. 4 people killed including 6 month old baby.
10th March	03.00	Mensija Street, St. Julian's.	Houses demolished, 2 people killed.
18th March	08.00	Annunciation Street	Houses demolished.
17th March	08.00	Prince of Wales Road.	Police Station demolished, 20 people killed and 22 wounded.
19th March	14.30	Ta' Giorni R.A. Battery, Gzira Road and Garden Street, Gzira.	A number of soldiers killed and wounded. Houses demolished, 4 people killed and others wounded.
20th March	08.00	Forrest Street, St. Julian's Spinola Bay.	Houses demolished. Houses demolished and Police Station damaged, people killed and wounded.
24th March	12.15	Luqa Briffa Street, Gzira.	Houses demolished.
25th March	14.30	Stuart Street, Gzira.	20 houses demolished and 2 people killed.
29th March	14.15	Msida Road, Gzira(Near the Garden).	3 soldiers killed and 10 wounded.
31st March	15.00	Msida Road, Gzira(near the stadium).	Houses demolished.

316

1st April	14.30	Church Street.	Sacro Cuor Church, The Friary and houses demolished and damaged, 28 killed, 23 wounded,
2nd April	10.30	Army Pay Office, Villa Rosa, St George's Bay.	Partly demolished, 5 soldiers killed, 3 civilians killed and many wounded.
2nd April	17.30	St. George's Barracks.	One soldier and his wife killed,
6th April	18.00	Hughes Hallet Street and Thornton Street, Tigne.	Houses demolished,
7th April	18.30	St. Agatha Street, Victoria Terrace, Rue d'Argens, Nazju Ellul, Luqa Briffa Streets and Sliema Road, Gzira.	Houses demolished, 3 people killed,
18th April	14.00	Dragut Street. Msida Road, Gzira.	Houses demolished 4 people killed.
19th April	09.30	Annunciation Street.	Houses demolished, People wounded.
19th April	13.30	Prince Albert Street, Stella Maris Street, Gzira. Victoria Avenue, Sliema.	Houses demolished, People wounded.
25th April	19.30 20.45	St. George's Barracks. High, Carmel, St. Mary and St. Trophimus Streets.	5 soldiers killed others wounded. Houses demolished.
26th April	18.00	St. Anthony and Pace Streets, Tigne	Nazzarene Church, Houses demolished.
8th May	02.00 07.15	Muscat's Garage, Gzira. Muscat's Garage, Gzira.	Partly demolished. Time bomb explodes, killing 13 and wounding others.
14th May		Annunciation Square	Houses demolished, 7 people killed
1st July	04.45	Castelletti Street, St. Dominic Street, The Strand and Prince of Wales Road.	Time bombs killing P.S.P. Cordina and wounding two Police constables.
10th August	21.15	St. Mary Street. St. Trophimus Street.	Buildings damaged. Sliema Band Club garden damaged.
27th October	10.00	Prince of Wales Road, St. Alphonsus Street.	Houses demolished.
28th October	09.15	Fleet and Freres Streets.	Houses demolished, one person killed, others wounded.
28th October	10.00	B'Kara Road, St.Julian's.	Houses demolished.
1943			
20th July	20.00	St, Trophimus Street.	Houses demolished, 4 people killed and others wounded.

A large number of bombs were dropped in the waters of Marsamxett Harbour, in the sea off Tigne' Point and off St. Julian's. Others fell in the surrounding countryside. No records of these bombs are available.

APPENDIX E

SLIEMA RESIDENTS' ROLL OF HONOUR

Abela Melita (26)
Agius Francis (20)
Agius John (20)
Alvarez Mary (88)
Amadio Joseph (24)
Attard Anthony (17)
Attard John (25)
Attard Joseph (42)
Azzopardi Carmel (40)
Azzopardi Edwin (21)
Azzopardi John (15)
Azzopardi Joseph
Bajona Edgar
Balzan Carmel (71)
Bartolo Edgar (22)
Bartolo Edward (38)
Bartolo John (28)
Bartolo Joseph (38)
Bates Carmen (6)
Bates George (9 months)
Bates Imelda (5)
Block John (45)
Bonello Alfred (45)
Bonello George (22)
Bonello Saviour
Borg Annunziata (60)
Borg Dolores (66)
Borg Emanuel (16)
Borg Georgina (22)
Borg Giovanni (24)
Borg Giuseppe (12)
Borg Joseph
Borg Maria Assunta (48)
Borg Michael (64)
Borg Saviour (20)
Briffa Joseph (45)
Brincat Gianni (32)
Brownrigg Joseph (18)

Bugeja Liberata (75)
Busuttil Rosina (35)
Buttigieg Carmel (23)
Buttigieg Emanuel (40)
Buttigieg Tonina (30)
Cachia Joseph (36)
Cafiero Edwin (27)
Calapai Alfred (54)
Calascione Maria (40)
Calascione Rose (70)
Caligari Anthony (19)
Calleja Carmel (50)
Calleja Dolores (17)
Callus Silvio (22)
Camenzuli Carmel (17)
Cannataci Polly (26)
Carbone Agustino (42)
Caruana Galizia
Ant. MD. (46)
Cassar George (27)
Cassar Giuseppe (74)
Cassar Joseph (31)
Cassar Vincenza (20)
Castagna Laura (74)
Cauchi Censa (80)
Churchill Dorothy (4)
Churchill George (6 weeks)
Churchill James H. (50)
Clarke Hilda (34)
Clarke Ivy (5)
Clarke Joseph (2)
Coppola Carmelo (50)
Coppola Doris (17)
Cordina Peter P.S (57)
Cuschieri Carmel
Cuschieri Dominic
Dandria Carmel (27)
Debono George (7)

Degiovanni Andrea (43)
Deguara Giuseppa (20)
Ellul Joseph
Falzon Angelo (73)
Falzon Anthony (22)
Falzon Iro (37)
Falzon Sarah (67)
Farrugia Annie (67)
Farrugia Joseph
Farrugia Gay John (18)
Fava Albert (1)
Fava Antonio (20)
Felice Grace (12)
Felice Mary Rose (8)
Fiteni Anthony
Ferro Alfred M.D. (27)
Floridia Ramiro (66)
Formosa Aristide
Formosa Paul (50)
Frendo Eric (15)
Galdes Diego Fr. O.F.M. (52)
Galea Joseph (60)
Gatt Alfred (50)
Gatt Giulia (46)
Gatt Philip (44)
Gatt Rose Marie (4)
Gauci Salvatore
German Victor (17)
Giorgio Albert (11)
Giorgio John (9)
Gollcher Frank (43)
Glover Frank (36)
Grech Alex (15)
Grech Annie (11)
Grech Anthony (41)
Grech Francis (17)
Grech Joseph (17)
Grech Mary (16)

RAIDERS PASSED

Grech Teresa (3)
Incorvaja Adelaide (6)
Inguanez Joseph (26)
Laferla Alberto A&C.E.(45)
Laferla John M., M.D.(31)
Landolina Salvatore
Lanzon Charles (36)
Letard Giuseppa (65)
Lewis Thomas (54)
Magro Pauline (18)
Mallia Emanuel (37)
Mallia John (20)
Mamo Attilio (45)
Mercieca Emanuel (41)
Micallef Alfred (16)
Micallef Espedito
Micallef Giuseppa (54)
Micallef John (30)
Micallef Joseph (11)
Micallef Lonza (50)
Micallef Roger (33)
Miceli John (21)
Mifsud Albert (14)
Mifsud Carmelo (55)
Mifsud Herman (42)
Mifsud Joseph (66)
Mizzi Emanuel (24
Montebello George (23)
Montford Alfred (75)

Montford Perinia (88)
Muscat Carmelo
Muscat Joseph (35)
Naudi James (45)
Orr Douglas
Pace Antonia (77)
Pace Bonello Edward (51)
Padovani Ginies Sam (18)
Parnis Carmel (23)
Pisani Anthony (38)
Pisani Joseph (36)
Pitre' Annie (28)
Pitre' Rennie (2)
Riviera Michael P.S. (45)
Rogers Carmela (81)
Saliba Angelo (16)
Sammut Bardon Louis (48)
Scicluna Beatrice (14)
Scicluna Benedict (17)
Scicluna George (38)
Scicluna John (28)
Scicluna Kenneth (6 months)
Scicluna Nazzareno (%0)
Scicluna Vincent
Sghendo Carmela (15)
Sillato Saviour (19)
Simler Joseph (29)
Smith Winnie (56)
Spiteri Alfred (22)

Spiteri Emanuel (2)
Spiteri Frances (14)
Spiteri Joseph (29)
Spiteri Paul (41)
Squibbs Robert (31
Sultana Vincent (21)
Tabone Antonia (7)
Tabone Giusa (14)
Vassallo Carmelo (43)
Vassallo Ettore LL.D. (41)
Vassallo William (37)
Vella Anthony (23)
Vella Alfred P.C. (45)
Vella John
Vella Joseph (53)
Vella Lino (11)
Vincenti John (45)
Vincenti Edwidge (37)
Xuereb John Baptist (21)
Yabsley Caroline (72)
Zahra Dolores (60)
Zammit Alfred (4)
Zammit Alfred (34)
Zammit Carmelo
Zammit J.
Zammit John (51)
Zammit Marianna (45)
Zammit Salvatore

APPENDIX F
MALTA OPERATIONS ROOM SET UP
1940 -1945

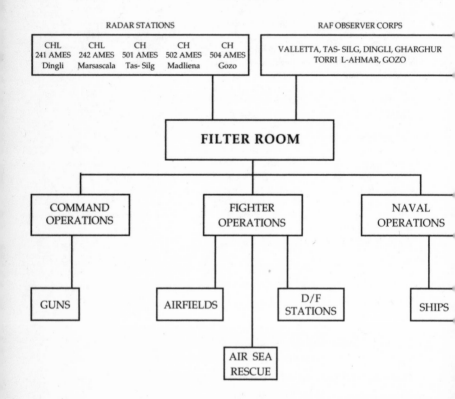

RADAR STATIONS

RAF OBSERVER CORPS

CHL 241 AMES Dingli	CHL 242 AMES Marsascala	CH 501 AMES Tas- Silg	CH 502 AMES Madliena	CH 504 AMES Gozo

VALLETTA, TAS- SILG, DINGLI, GHARGHUR
TORRI L-AHMAR, GOZO

FILTER ROOM

COMMAND OPERATIONS

FIGHTER OPERATIONS

NAVAL OPERATIONS

GUNS

AIRFIELDS

D/F STATIONS

SHIPS

AIR SEA RESCUE

APPENDIX G
MALTA ANTI-AIRCRAFT AND
COASTAL DEFENCE GUNS

(1)   10th Heavy anti-aircraft Brigade (3.7" and 4.5"):
2nd Heavy anti-aircraft Regiment Royal Malta Artillery
11th Heavy anti-aircraft Regiment Royal Malta Artillery
(Territorial)
4th Heavy anti-aircraft Regiment Royal Artillery
7th Heavy anti-aircraft Regiment Royal Artillery
10th Heavy anti-aircraft Regiment Royal Artillery

(2)   7th Light Anti-aircraft Brigade (Bofors 40mm)
3rd Light anti-aircraft Regiment Royal Malta Artillery
(10th, 15th, 22nd and 30th Batteries)
4th Searchlight Regiment R.A./R.E.(including 8th Searchlight Battery R.M.A.)
32nd Light anti-aircraft Regiment Royal Artillery
65th Light anti-aircraft Regiment Royal Artillery
74th Light anti-aircraft Regiment Royal Artillery

The normal strength in guns of a Heavy Anti-Aircraft
Regiment was twenty-four guns spread out in three
batteries of two troops each with four guns per troop.
The range of a 4.5" H.A.A. gun was 42,000 feet, and that
of a 3.7" Mk 2C was 32,000 feet.

Normally, a Bofors Regiment had three batteries
with three troops of six guns each. The maximum effective range of Bofors guns was 1,500 yards, and the
maximum rate of fire was 120 rounds per minute.

The Heavy anti-aircraft gun positions consisted of a troop of four guns facing their primary arcs of fire. Each troop had its Predictor, to control the guns during action procedures. The gun crews lived and slept in on the gun sites in stone and concrete bunkers

The war-time H.A.A. sites formed roughly three concentric rings of fire, enclosing the principal vulnerable areas with Valletta and the Grand Harbour in the centre. This area comprised the following locations; the dockyard, power station, fuel oil depots, stores, ship anchorages, quays and, last but not least, the administrative centres.

The next important areas were the airfields of Luqa, Hal Far, Ta' Qali and, later, Qrendi airstrip which was completed in November 1942. The heavy anti-aircraft gun sites were sited at Tigne (3.7"), Manoel Island (3.7"), Ta' Cejlu (Jesuit Hill Marsa) (3.7"), Ta' Giorni (3.7"), Tal-Qroqq (3.7"), Fleur-de-Lys (3.7"), Hompesch (3.7"), St. Peter (3,7"), Fort St. Leonardo (3.7"), Zonqor (near St. Nicholas Church) (3.7"), Marnisi, Xrobb l-Ghagin (3.7"), San Nikola (near Zejtun) (3.7"), Delimara (3.7"), Ta' Karax (near Hagar Qim) (3.7"), Guarena (3,7"), San Blas (near Hal Muxi, Zebbug) (3.7"), Bizbizija (near Targa Gap) (3.7"), Għargħur (Ta' Stronka) (3.7"), Salina (3.7") and Wardija (3.7").

Fort Spinola, where Portomaso stands today and Fort San Giacomo above the Addolorata Cemetery, were equipped with 4.5 inch naval guns.

Low Level Defence (Bofors) gun positions also consisted of a number of inner and outer rings with the innermost proximity to vulnerable points to tackle dive-bombing attacks. Most of these guns were located round the Grand Harbour area, especially the dockyard. This latter locality was mainly defended by the 30th Battery, 3rd L.A.A. R.M.A., also known initially as the Dockyard Defence Battery. Its personnel were drawn from among dockyard workers. The next priority was the airfields and many were the Axis aircraft which failed to return to their bases due to the action of these 40mm guns. Incidentally, they are just as effective today, in a modernised version of course, against low-flying aircraft.

Some of the individual Bofors gun-sites were located at: Upper and Lower Barrakka, St. James Cavalier and Counterguard, Marsamxett, and St. Elmo in Valletta; Sheer Bastion and Senglea Point; St. Rocco, Capuchin Cemetery (near the Red House), Xghajra Salt Pans, Kalkara Gardens, and Porte Des Bombes, Floriana; Ricasoli, Tigne' (Near Bonavia Press), Qui-Si-Sana (in front of Hughes Hallet Street), Sliema; Gzira (Near Viani Street), Msida, at the top of Princess Margaret Street, now part of the Ta' Xbiex Housing Estate and Fort Manoel Ravelin facing Sliema.

Fixed Coast Defence
Royal Malta Artillery; 1st Coast Regiment and 5th Coast Regiment.
Royal Artillery; 4th Coast Regiment.
Coastal Forts:
Fort Campbell (near Selmun) 2 x 6 inch guns,
Tigne 3 x 6 inch, (Naval guns)
San Rocco 3 x 6 inch (Naval guns),
Fort Manoel 2 x 6 inch (Naval guns),
Fort Delimara 2 x 6 inch Mk 7,
Fort Madliena 2 x 9.2 inch.
Fort Bingemma 2 x 9.2 inch;
Fort St. Leonard 2 x 9.2 inch,

Fort Benghajsa 2 X 9.2 inch
Fort St. Elmo 4 x 6 pounder Twin Rapid-Firing Guns
Fort Ricasoli 3 x 6 pounder, Twin Rapid-Firing Guns.

APPENDIX H

Infantry Regiments based in Malta 1939 - 1945

1st, 2nd, 3rd and 10th The King's Own Malta Regiment
2nd Battalion The Cheshire Regiment
1st Battalion The Durham Light Infantry
1st Battalion The Hampshire Regiment
8th Battalion The King's Own Regiment
2nd Battalion The Dovonshire Regiment
11th Battalion XX The Lancashire Fusiliers
8th Battalion The Manchester Regiment (Ardwick)
4th Battalion The Buffs (Royal East Kent Regiment)
2nd Battalion The Royal Irish Fusiliers (Princess Victoria's)
2nd Battalion The Queen's Own Royal West Kent Regiment

APPENDIX I

Ancillary Corps

Royal Corps of Signals
Royal Army Service Corps
Royal Army Medical Corps
Royal Engineers
Royal Army Ordinance Corps
Royal Electrical and Mechanical Engineers
Royal Army Pay Corps
Corps of Military Police (226 Provost Company)
Royal Army Chaplain's Department
16th Fortress Company, Royal Engineers
Royal Marines
Army Dental Corps
Army Catering Corps
Intelligence Corps
Maritime Royal Artillery
1st Royal Tank Regiment
R.A.F. Observer Corps (Malta)
Queen Alexandra's Imperial Nursing Service
Malta Auxiliary Corps
Malta Pioneer Group

In support of the infantry there were two further mobile artillery units. These were: H.Q. Royal Artillery, 12th Field Regiment Royal Artillery and 26th Defence Regiment, Royal Artillery.

Besides the Maltese men serving with the regiments

of the Royal Malta Artillery and the King's Own Malta Regiment, there were members of the Home Guard, Malta Police Force and the Air Raid Precaution and Demolition Squads, numbering some 4,000 men. Other Maltese serving in the Royal Navy, 16 Fortress Squadron and the Royal Air Force, numbered about 3,500, bringing a grand total of 14,650 Maltese Officers and men who served during the Second World War.

APPENDIX J

RADAR IN MALTA

At the outbreak of World War Two the Royal Air Force possessed a radar air defence system that was invented by Watson Watt. This system was called RDF. Radar made a major contribution to the Battle of Britain.

Before the invention of radar, sound locators appeared to be the only means of having an early warning system. In 1938, a chain of giant concrete 'mirrors' was planned for Malta. Only two of these 'mirrors' however were built, one in England and the other in Malta, at Maghtab. The one in Malta is the best preserved and is situated at the present site of the Maltacom Satellite Station. The place is still known as "Il-Widna", the ear. The range of these 'mirrors' was between 15 – 20 miles. Due to the development of radar, the project was abandoned.

Malta's first RDF unit arrived in March 1939, consisting of two Crossley trucks one for the type MD1 transmitter and the other containing an RF1 receiver. The aerials were fixed on a pair of seventy foot telescopic masts and were set up on Dingli Cliffs, near the present site of the Civil Aviation radar station. This was known as No. 242 AMES (Air Ministry Experimental Station). This was the first Radar Station to be installed outside the United Kingdom and it was later joined by No. 241 AMES. It was then deployed to Għar Lapsi, where the Reverse Osmosis Plant now stands.

By May 1940, 242 AMES, with new seventy foot wooden lattice masts, could detect an aircraft flying at 10,000 feet at a distance of seventy miles but the range fell to about 30 miles when an aircraft was flying at 2,000 feet or below. 242 AMES was Type ACO (Advanced Chain Overseas).

In May 1941, 501 AMES was set up in the old, Victorian Fort Tas-Silg. 502 AMES was installed at Fort Madliena. A month later, 504 AMES was set up at Dingli. The three COL (Chain Overseas Low) Stations gave an all round low cover to supplement Dingli.

Radar was so successful that by September 1941, three more AMES's were set up, 256 at Fawwara, 341 at Qawra Point and another 521 AMES at il-Giordan, Gozo, next to the Light House.

On the night of the 25th July 1941, the Madliena COL Station detected the approach of the Italian E-Boat flotilla, which made the ill-fated attack on Grand Harbour. Our coastal Guns were alerted and despite the gallantry of the Italians, the attack was completely repulsed.

Another type of ground radar was introduced in March 1942. This was the GCI (Ground Controlled Interception) to cope with night bombers. For daylight attacks the COH's and the COL's with the control organisation developed with them were adequate but these were not accurate enough for night operations, where it was necessary to bring a Beaufighter to within either visual range of its target or within range of its airborne radar. GCI was operated by 841 AMES, first at Valletta, then at Ta' Qali. During daytime it was used against high altitude reconnaissance aircraft. The GCI was one of the most versatile radars available. It enabled our night fighters to make the most effective use of their airborne radar.

At one stage in 1942 the benefit of the early warning system was almost lost due to jamming by powerful, German transmitting jammers installed in Sicily, which neutralised the Radar Stations in Malta. The local stations continued scanning to give the impression that the jamming was not successful. After a few days the Germans switched off the jammers.

After the end of Malta's Siege and the defeat of the Axis forces in Africa, Malta temporarily hosted several radar units before they took part in the invasion of Sicily. These included 4 MRUs (Maritime Radar Units), four COLs, two GCIs, two Type 277s (10cm Naval coast watching stations), 1 CHL Type 11 (50cm) and the only permanent installation AMES Type 16 Fighter Control System. This was an extension of the GCI designed to control offensive fighter sweeps. It was hoped that it would prove helpful in the attack on Sicily but unfortunately the 50 cm waveband used, was seriously affected by echoes from Mount Etna.

Radar was regarded as one of the main contributors to Malta's defeat of the enemy.

APPENDIX K

CHANGE OF STREET NAMES

Former name

Present name

Former name	Present name
Prince of Wales Road, Sliema.	*Manwel Dimech Street*
Prince of Wales Junction, Sliema.	*Guze Ellul Mercer Street*
Prince Albert Street, Sliema.	*Freres Street*
Victoria Avenue, Sliema.	*George Borg Olivier Street*
Marina Street, Sliema.	*Sacro Cuor Street*
Parallel Street, Sliema.	*Sir Luigi Camilleri Street*
Grenfell Street, St. Julian's	*George Borg Olivier Street*
Kingsway, Valletta	*Republic Street*
Queen's Square, Valletta	*Republic Square*

INDEX

R.A.O.C., 271
R.D.F., 298
R.E.M.E., 208
Rabagliati, Squadron Leader A.C. 63
Rabat, 19, 102, 136, 137, 139, 140, 142,
    143, 145, 146, 160, 172, 177, 200,
    217, 218, 231, 233, 239
Radar, 18, 93, 119, 120, 172, 221, 222,
    298, 299, 301, 302, 328, 329, 330
Raiders passed, 11, 21, 23, 30, 76, 85,
    184, 226, 248
Ramcke, General Bernhard 212
Ramel Buildings, 270
Ras id-Dawwara, 210
Ratcliffe, Christina, 221, 222, 224
Ration book, 136
Recruiting Office, 271
Red Army, 308
Red Caps, 16
Rediffusion, 9, 10, 12, 17, 39, 178, 202
Regency House, 159
Regent Cinema, 158
Regent Theatre, 156, 158, 160
Regia Aeronautica, 39, 40, 216, 221,
    252
Republic Square, 156, 331
Republic Street, 156, 159, 331
Rhine, 308
Ricasoli Point, 91
Rinella Street, 241
Riviera, Michael 185
Rochester Castle, 256
Rockyvale, 150
Rodney, 253, 255
Rolls Royce, 208
Roma, 293
Roman Villa, 172
Rome Radio, 161
Rommel, Field Marshal 71, 215, 238,
    251, 260, 266
Roosevelt, Franklin D. 267
Rossone, Mr. 248, 249
Rovers, 10
Royal Air Force, 37, 63, 95, 130, 140,
    152, 154, 180, 208, 219, 221, 264,
    265, 271, 279, 289, 291, 299, 327,

328
Royal Army Ordinance Corps, 271,
    326
Royal Army Pay Corps, 194, 326
Royal Artillery, 56, 147, 321, 323, 326
Royal Engineers, 56, 326
Royal Malta Artillery, 24, 56, 62, 91,
    95, 321, 323, 327
Royal Navy, 47, 59, 63, 184, 244, 254,
    301, 327
Royal Oak, 196
Royal Opera House, 20, 152
Royal Ordinance Corps, 56
Royal West Kent, 56, 325
Rudolphe Street, 18, 85, 164, 196
Rue D'Argens, 102
Russians, 308
Rustenburg, 214
Rye, 257

S.C., 10, 19, 179
S.L.C., 92, 93
S.L.U., 296
Sa Maison, 128
Sacred Heart, 80, 83, 86, 87, 116, 125,
    187, 226, 311, 332
Sacred Infirmary, 303
Sacro Cuor, 22, 54, 78, 80, 130, 162,
    184, 196, 197, 199, 226, 260, 282,
    315, 317, 331
Sacro Cuor Church, 22, 78, 80, 162,
    184, 197, 226, 260, 282, 317
Sacro Cuor Friary, 54
Safi, 242, 269, 291, 306
Sajjan Street, 166
Salesian Boys Brigade, 60
Salesians Oratory, 44, 244
Saliba, Michael Angelo 24
Sammut, Dr. Giovanni 102
Sander, Sur 27, 28, 33
San Anton Gardens, 271
San Gwann, 273, 315
San Niklaw Church, 283
San Niklaw Reservoir, 283
Santa Elisa, 255
Santa Maria, 189, 200, 257, 259, 286

St. Mary Street, 23, 30, 31, 49, 108, 110, 112, 132, 182, 183, 185, 206, 227, 315, 317
St. Nicholas Street, 227
St. Patrick's Barracks, 268
St. Patrick's, 127, 194, 201, 268, 291, 292
St. Patrick's 45th General Hospital, 201
St. Patrick's Institute, 127
St. Patrick's Military Hospital, 194
St. Paul Street, 71, 204, 227
St. Paul's Bay, 91, 174, 204, 218, 235, 238
St. Publius church, 180
St. Rita Street, 76, 77, 79, 80, 89, 105, 249, 281, 315
St. Roque, 40
St. Thomas Bay, 214
St. Trophimus Street, 136, 163, 164, 182, 185, 196, 282, 317
St. Vincent de Paule Hospital, 35
St. Vincent Street, 127, 227
Stella Maris Band Club, 228
Stella Maris Church, 125, 227, 316
Stella Maris College, 162
Sten gun, 289
Strand, 15, 17, 22, 53, 76, 79, 89, 104, 119, 122, 125, 127, 129, 130, 137, 159, 194, 228, 229, 249, 257, 266, 268, 274, 291, 304, 309, 315, 316, 317
Streets, E.E. 231
Stuart Street, 123, 316
Student, General Kurt 209, 212, 214, 215
Submarine, 189, 293
Sunset, 189
Superga, 212
Swetu, Special Constable, 65, 85
Syfret, Vice admiral Neville 253, 258
Sylvester, Victor 302
Syracuse, 286

T.N.T., 310
Ta' Ġiorni, 146, 148, 149, 150, 167, 192
Ta' Ġiorni Battery, 148, 149, 150
Ta' Ġiorni College, 148
Ta' Ġiorni Ridge, 146
Ta' Xbiex, 91, 122, 268
Ta' Ċejlu, 178
Ta' Qali, 29, 37, 39, 63, 137, 139, 140, 141, 142, 143, 144, 145, 146, 148, 149, 171, 172, 173, 174, 176, 203, 205, 206, 207, 213, 217, 218, 219, 222, 224, 229, 231, 233, 235, 237, 246, 269, 322, 329
Ta' Xbiex, 15, 74, 323
Tabone, Giusa 187
Talabot, 177, 179, 180, 251
Tal-Balal, 273
Tal-Fatati, 126
Tal-Providenza Church, 284
Tal-Qroqq, 149, 167, 192, 322
Tal-Qroqq Batteries, 149
Tal-Qroqq Battery, 167
Tal-Virtu, 39
Taranto, 238
Tarxien, 25
Tas-Salvatur Fort, 102
Tas-Silġ, 223, 298, 299, 301, 304
Tessei, Maggiore Teseo 92, 94
Texas Oil Company, 253
The Desert Fox, 260
The Desert Rats, 260
The Glorious Tenth Of May, 221
The Malta Chronicle, 9
The Narrows, 254
The Times of Malta, 9, 39, 59
Thornaby, 285
Three Cities, 28
Tibbets, Paul 309
Tigne Garrison Boy Scouts, 126
Tigne', 74, 82, 91, 127, 128, 130, 213
Tigne' Barracks, 128, 130
Tobruk, 73, 215, 251
Tokyo Bay, 310
Tony's Grocery, 29
Tony's Bar, 309
Torri l-Ahmar, 223, 299
Tower Road, 89, 122, 127, 242, 315, 316

ACKNOWLEDGEMENTS

The ex-Commissioner of Police, Mr. Enoch Tonna.
The ex-Assistant Commissioner of Police,
Mr. Anthony Mifsud Tommasi L.P.
The Sliema Franciscan Community of the
Parish of Our Lady of the Sacred Heart.
Chev. E.S. Tonna, M.B.E. O.S.J.
Wickman Maritime Collection
Charles Abela Mizzi
Lawrence Mizzi
Guzè Cardona B.A. (Oxon.), M.A.
Mark and Aileen Grech.
Sqn Ldr P.J. Odling
The Principle, St. Dorothy's School
Sr. Doreen Cuschieri
Sr. Marie Depiro
Fiona Galea Debono B.A., Dip. Journalism,
(Univ. of Urbino)

BIBLIOGRAPHY

Malta Police Records
Ministry of Defence Historical Branch (R.A.F.)
The Second Great Siege (Ch. Boffa)
The Luftwaffe War Diaries (Cajus Bekker)
Red Duster White Ensign (Ian Cameron)
History of The Second World War (Purnell)

PHOTOGRAPHS

Times of Malta War Album
W. Jones
Charles B. Grech
National War Museum